This book belongs to:

Norma J. Krcmaric

INCENTIVE PUBLICATIONS, INC.
2400 CRESTMOOR DRIVE
NASHVILLE, TENNESSEE 37205

I CAN MAKE A RAINBOW

Things to CREATE and DO...For Children
and Their Grown Up Friends

by Marjorie Frank

illustrated by Gayle Seaberg

ISBN Number 0-913916-19-6

Library of Congress Catalog Card Number 76-506

Let me tell you about tall, green grasses
        that hide proud prowling tigers
            and purple ponies
            and yellow daisies that lie tickly in chains around your neck.

Hold my hand, and I'll introduce you
        to bean bag clowns with mop-string heads and paper-cup noses
                                                with spaghetti smiles

        and menageries of gauze butterflies
        and tin-can cobras
        and feather-tailed fireflies.

Come away with me on straw-whistle winds
        to the lands of goozles and whiffle whomps
            and astronaut princes and soap-bubble pies
        and I'll let you touch bright yellow drops of sun and pale washes of moon
        and stir your hand in mad rivers of purple elixir
            with whirlpools of winged witches and striped crocodiles.

Come, climb stars with me
        and help me build great pirate ships
        and paint golden sky castles in sand
        and spin fairy tails of pink silk thread

        . . . . and I'll make you a rainbow!

To Joy. . .

who never misses a rainbow

TABLE OF CONTENTS

CHAPTER 3 - THINGS TO PRINT & PAINT...77

CHAPTER 4 - THINGS TO DO WITH CLOTH, YARN, & STRING.......................................109

CHAPTER 7 - SOME SPECIAL THINGS TO MAKE.................................189

So you can make a rainbow.... How ??

Getting Started

Dear Rainbowmaker,

This book is for you. It is for learning, for making and doing, and for having fun. Most importantly, it is for getting you started at creating your own ideas for making and doing exciting, artistic things.

You _are_ an artist. There is no one quite like you. That's why the things you create will not be exactly like anyone else's. In art, there is not just one right way. The _best_ way is the way that makes you most happy and satisfied with your work.

You probably won't like every idea in this book. But I hope you'll like lots of them. Remember that each activity is just a "jumping-off place" for you to get started at creating your own things -- SO change anything you like and add your own great ideas. If you're disappointed with the way something turns out, don't be discouraged. That's life! Sometimes you'll feel proud of your creations and enjoy showing them off. Other times you'll want to say "YUK!" But don't throw those "YUKKERS" away right away. Keep them for awhile. They may look better next week -- or you may think of something new to do with them.

14

Here are some important things for you to remember if you (and the people you live with) are going to enjoy your artistic efforts:

1) Choose a good time to work -- preferably not just in time for lunch or recess or nearly bedtime.

2) Find a good place to work -- one where you have plenty of room and are not in anyone's way. Also, be sure to choose a place where there is no danger of ruining things like furniture, carpet, etc. (A screaming mother can spoil the fun and thrill of creating a great masterpiece.)

   An old plastic table cloth or shower curtain or a layer of newspapers spread carefully can keep Mom's stuff clean and you out of a lot of trouble!

3) Gather all the materials you will need before you begin working. (It's hard to hold a nail in place while you go off to look for the hammer!)

4) Start with clean hands and your clothes covered with an old shirt, smock, or apron. Work near a sink if possible.

5) CLEAN UP TIME!

   Always wash brushes well. (Clean oil with turpentine.)
   Clean and put away tools and materials so they will be ready to use again.
   Clean your working space with sponge, brush or broom.
   Clean yourself -- face, hands, fingernails...Reserve the "clown look" for body painting!
   Look at the floor around your work area -- WELL, don't just look at it -- Clean it up!

CAUTION: Always ask for help whenever you work with anything hot....like candles, irons, stoves, ovens, etc.

Supper!

Marge Frank

15

Especially for GrownUps

In our children lies the greatest potential the world can know.
I trust this is a firm belief of the grownup friends of the young people
who will use this book.

Kids possess such great creative potential. They are naturally curious.
They learn best by experience (don't we all?), and they benefit most when
given the opportunity to experiment, discover, dream, imagine, and express
their original ideas in a free and open environment where the individual
and his personal contributions are highly cherished.

In the world of creative expression, teachers
and parents ought never to play the role of critic. Rather, we are
the child's promoters -- his cheerleaders.

Our task is to help children become highly sensitive to the
world about them....Give them freedom....Let them try....Let them fail
....Let them succeed....Encourage them....Rejoice with them!!

This collection of ideas is not intended to serve as a project book. It has been created as a catalyst -- a book of beginnings.

Here kids are provided with many ideas for using artistic media and are given, not <u>the</u> way, but hundreds of possible ways to express a single, creative idea.

Create for them the opportunity. Then only be prepared to be amazed at the results!!

Marge Frank

On each page where this spritely little creature appears, you will find a practical suggestion for adapting the art activity for special classroom use or relating the artistic experience to a curriculum area.

TOOLS

crayons
colored pencils
soft lead pencils
marking pens
drawing pens
charcoal
cray-pas
china markers
colored chalk
watercolor paints
tempera or poster paints
acrylic or oil paints
fingerpaint
India ink
block printing ink
food coloring
brushes
scissors
craft knife
stapler and staples
compass
paper punch
erasers
rulers
hammer and nails
brayer
tape
white glue
rubber cement
plaster
wallpaper paste
clay
wire
sponges
cookie cutters
table knife
iron
easel
hot plate
saucepan
smock

Rainbowmakers' Tools and Supplies

construction paper
typing paper
tracing paper
drawing paper
tissue paper
crepe paper
waxed paper
contact paper
newspaper
wrapping paper
butcher paper
mural paper
shelf paper
wallpaper
newsprint
cellophane

PAPER STUFF

paper bags
paper cups
paper plates
tagboard
posterboard
cardboard
boxes
egg cartons
tin foil
magazines
old greeting cards
cardboard tubes

MORE TOOLS

turpentine
polymer
shellac
plastic dishpan
muffin tins
pie tins
bottles
tin cans
baby food jars
plastic containers
styrofoam meat trays
plastic fruit baskets
plastic spoons
fabric
old window shades
old shower curtains
wooden dowels
wood scraps and sticks
yarn and string
ribbon and trims
old socks and nylons
rags
straws
coat hangers
buttons and beads
corks
toothpicks and Q-tips
clothespins
rubberbands
keys
spools
tongue depressors
popsicle sticks
pipe cleaners
keys
sand
rocks

COOKING SUPPLIES

mixing bowls
saucepans
muffin tin
baking pan
cookie sheet
large spoon
pancake turner
egg beater
cookie cutters
sharp knife
rubber spatula
measuring spoons
potato peeler
rolling pin
timer
hot pads
hot plate
oven
candy thermometer

Being Organized

Keeping your supplies organized saves time and removes headaches from your creating and doing activities. Decide on a way to store your materials in one place. That way,

everything's easy to find
convenient to use
and speedy to put away.

In the classroom, organize your supplies in containers:

Keep crayons, pencils, pens, rulers, chalk, charcoal, scissors, compasses in small pails or large juice cans.

Collect fabric scraps and scrap paper in large plastic bags or 3-gallon ice cream tubs.

Fill a plastic pail with pieces of yarn, string, ribbon, lace and other trims.

Store paper in a long, flat suit box.

A tomato crate makes a great carrier for glue bottles!

Keep paint jars together in a large plastic dish pan.

Plastic fruit baskets (pint-sized) are good holders of buttons and beads and pebbles and rings and spools and corks and such.

At home, make yourself a craft kit. Gather tools and supplies that you use most often, and pack them into a basket or a plastic mop pail.

Include: pencils, pens
crayons, watercolors
brushes
a ruler and compass
scissors
clay
string and yarn
paper bags
assortment of paper

20

Chapter 1

Things to do with pencil, pen, crayon & chalk

WHAT'S the WORD?

Try to picture words that <u>look</u> like what they mean
....or like the things they name.

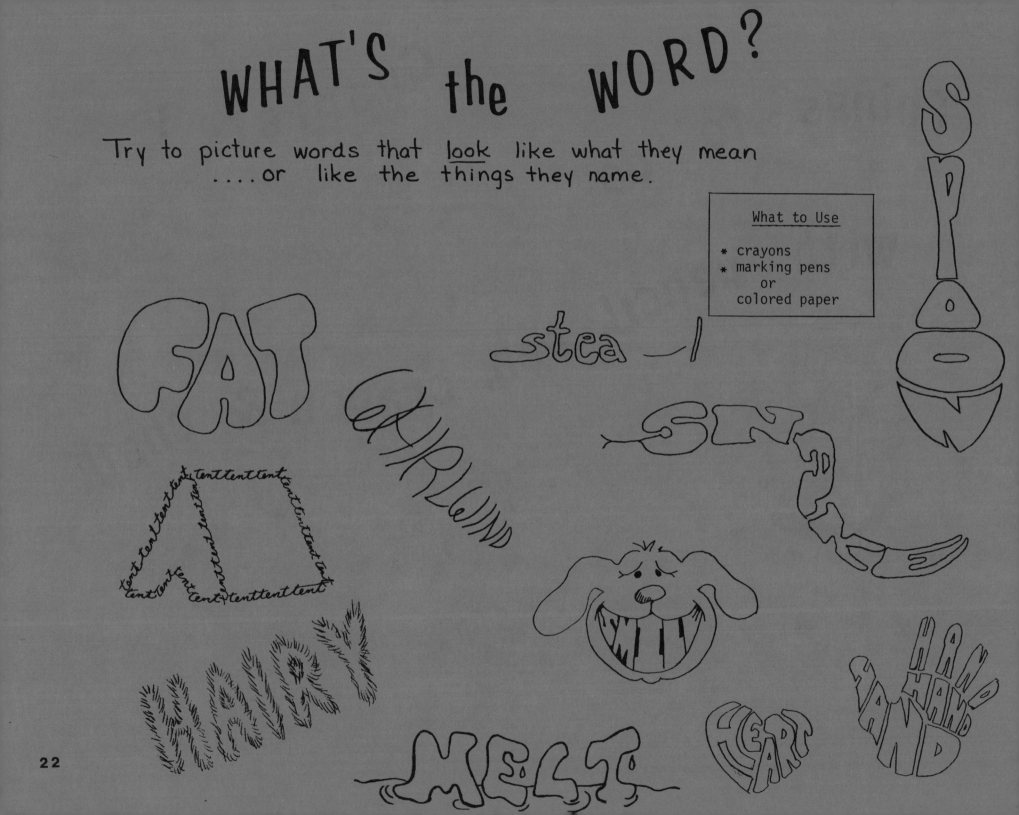

FAT

stea—l

SPIDER

tent tent tent tent tent tent tent tent tent tent tent tent tent

(K)(I)(R)(L)(N)

SNAKE

HAIRY

SMILE

MELT

HEART

HAND HAND HAND

22

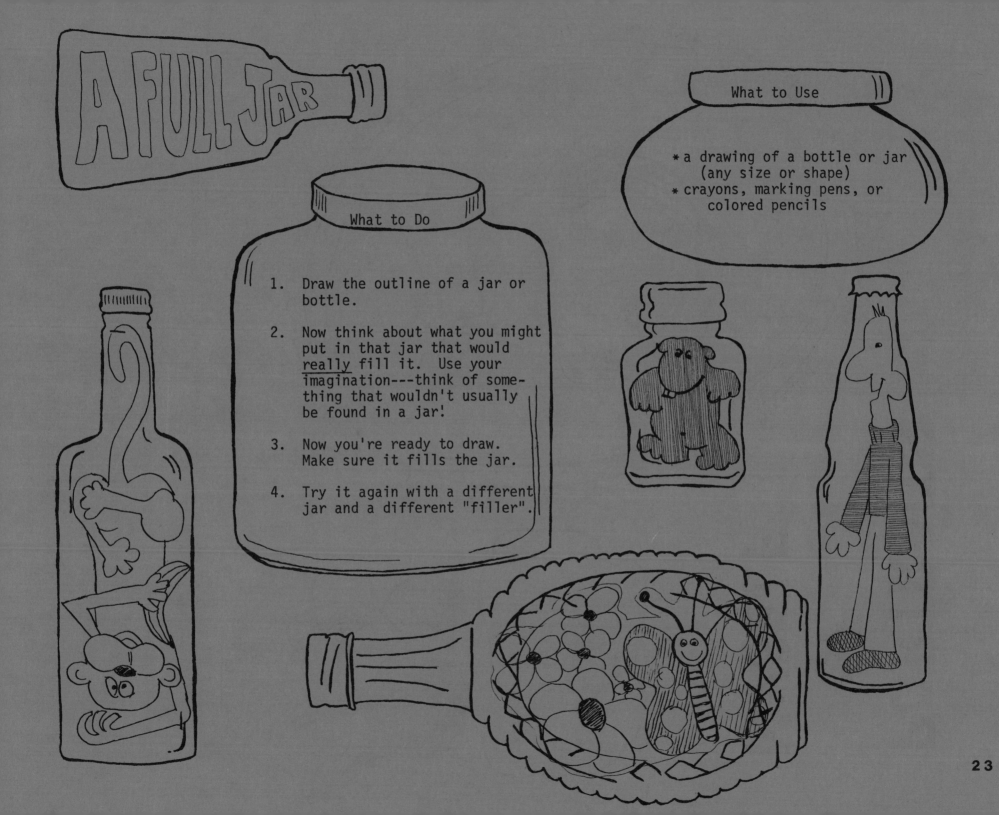

A FULL JAR

What to Use

* a drawing of a bottle or jar (any size or shape)
* crayons, marking pens, or colored pencils

What to Do

1. Draw the outline of a jar or bottle.

2. Now think about what you might put in that jar that would really fill it. Use your imagination---think of something that wouldn't usually be found in a jar!

3. Now you're ready to draw. Make sure it fills the jar.

4. Try it again with a different jar and a different "filler".

23

PORTRAITS OF MYSELF

There's nobody in the world exactly like me! This is the way I looked in 1976 in sixth grade. This is the portrait of a very special person! Here I am!

What to Use

* a hand mirror
* an oval or rectangular piece of drawing paper
* crayons or colored chalk

What to Do

1. Cut a piece of drawing paper in a shape that will be a good frame for showing off yourself.

2. Look at your face in the mirror.

3. Carefully draw and color what you see in the mirror.

4. Draw or paste a frame around your portrait.

5. Write something about yourself on the frame.

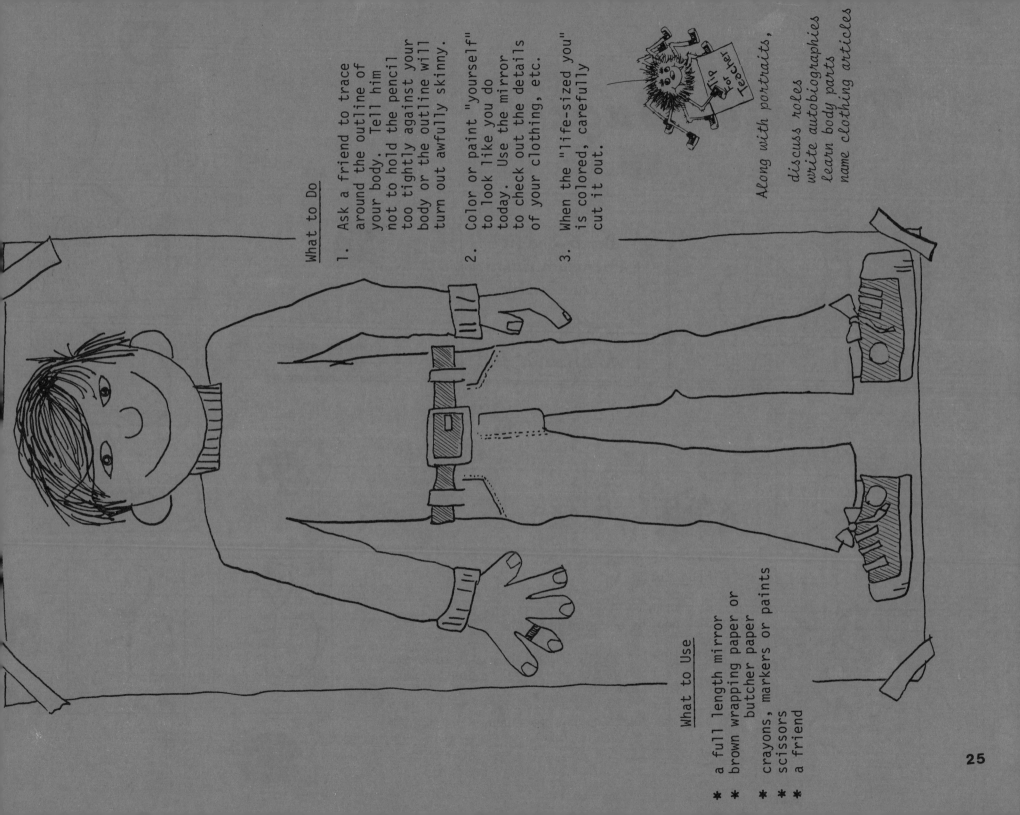

What to Do

1. Ask a friend to trace around the outline of your body. Tell him not to hold the pencil too tightly against your body or the outline will turn out awfully skinny.

2. Color or paint "yourself" to look like you do today. Use the mirror to check out the details of your clothing, etc.

3. When the "life-sized you" is colored, carefully cut it out.

Tip for Teacher

Along with portraits,

   discuss roles
   write autobiographies
   learn body parts
   name clothing articles

What to Use

* a full length mirror
* brown wrapping paper or butcher paper
* crayons, markers or paints
* scissors
* a friend

Doodle Bugs

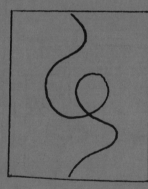

Do a doodle!
Then turn it into
a non-doodle!

Trade doodles
with friends, too!

What to Use

* drawing paper
* crayons
* black marker

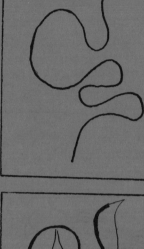

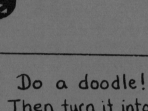

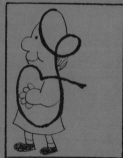

What to Do

1. With a black marker, draw a simple doodle on your paper.

2. Turn it every direction, and look at it hard until you "see" a possibility for a picture.

3. Use your crayons to change the doodle into a drawing!

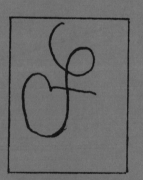

26

Line — Tales

This is the story of Little Red Riding Hood!

Each line shows the part of a different character.
    The first line is Red Riding Hood.
    The second line is the Wolf.
    The third line is Grandmother.
    The fourth line is the Woodcutter.

Can you follow the story?   Try to tell your own tale with lines.

What to Use *long paper
        *a different color crayon, pencil, or marker for each character

---

What to Do

1. Choose a color to represent each character in the story.

2. Draw each line to show the character's actions and feelings from beginning to end.

3. Your line story doesn't have to look like this one. You might want to use the lines in a different way.

4. Share your story with someone. . . . Tell why you chose the colors you did and explain how you used the lines.

YOUR NAME

What to Use

*large sheets of paper:
  newsprint
  butcher paper
  construction paper
*some of these:
  pens and ink
  crayons
  markers
  colored chalk
  paints and brush
  paper, scissors and
    glue
  wrapping paper

Here are some ideas......
but don't be afraid to try
Something really different!

Start with your own name.
Add lots of imagination.
You'll end up with some exciting name-art.

What to Do

Use a dark crayon or marker to
fill the paper with the letters
of your name. Color or paint in
the spaces formed to make an
interesting design.

.. OR

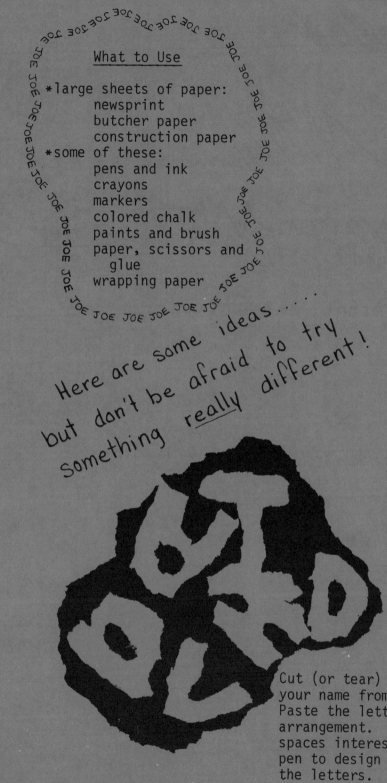

Cut (or tear) your initials or
your name from colorful paper.
Paste the letters in a pleasing
arrangement. Try to make the
spaces interesting too. Use a
pen to design the areas around
the letters.

ÍS a WORK of art!

. . . . OR

Make a chalk design using your initials. You might print or write your initials once or many times.

. . . OR

Repeat your name several times in a design or use it to make a picture that tells something about yourself.

Art with names contributes to the development of a positive self-concept, and is a project that usually provides great feelings of pride and success for all the artists.

It's a nice beginning-of-the-year activity; helps students get to know one another; and "shows off" well at a Parents' Open House!

Tip for Teacher

Alphabet Art

Try this with numerals, too!

CRAYON RESIST

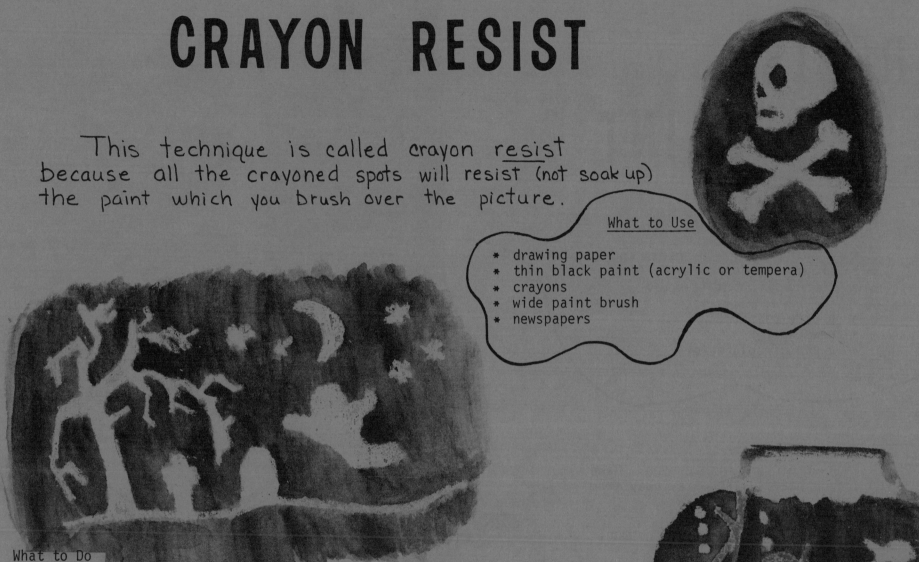

This technique is called crayon <u>resist</u> because all the crayoned spots will resist (not soak up) the paint which you brush over the picture.

What to Use

* drawing paper
* thin black paint (acrylic or tempera)
* crayons
* wide paint brush
* newspapers

What to Do

1. Prepare a thin mix of black paint.

2. Draw a design or picture with crayon. It is important that your crayoned areas be covered with a thick layer of crayon. Dark crayons won't show up well. If you want an area to remain white, you'll need to color it with a white crayon.

3. Put your drawing on newspaper. Lightly brush one coat of paint over the whole picture.

RESIST & PRINT

↑
crayon resist

↑
print

What to Use

* drawing paper - 2 sheets
* crayons
* thin dark paint (tempera or acrylic)
* a wide paintbrush
* newspaper
* a pan of cold water

What to Do

1. Draw a design or picture with crayon. Make sure you crayon heavily, and stay away from dark colored crayons!

2. Crumple up the paper that you've drawn on.

3. Dip it in cold water. Squeeze out the water so that it isn't dripping.

4. Spread the drawing out on newspaper.

5. Paint over the picture with dark paint (one quick coat).

6. Place the other sheet of drawing paper on top and press evenly with your hand. The second piece of paper will soak up the extra paint <u>and</u> will give you a print of the crayoned picture.

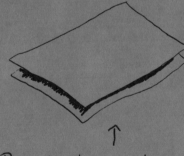

↑
Press the two sheets together to get a print.

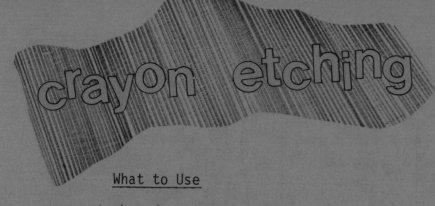

crayon etching

What to Use

* paper, tagboard, or paper plates
      (any shape)
* crayons
* nail or un-bent paper clip

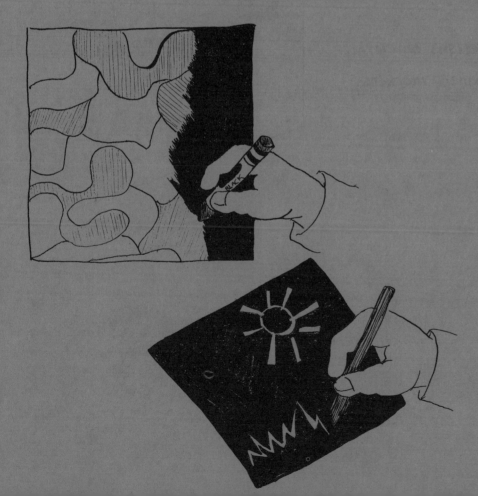

What to Do

1. Fill the paper with <u>heavy</u> blotches
   of crayon or a crayon design.

2. Color heavily over the whole paper
   with black crayon.

3. Plan a picture or design. You
   might sketch it on scrap paper
   first.

4. Use a sharp object to scratch the
   design on the black crayon. The
   black will come off and the colors
   will show through wherever you
   scratch. Try scratching sharp lines
   and larger areas too.

5. Gently polish the picture to finish
   it. Use another piece of paper, a
   kleenex or a paper towel for
   polishing.

Wallhangings

What to Use

* crayons or markers
* pencil
* cotton fabric
* newspapers ✳
* paper
* iron
* adult help

HAPPY MOTHERS DAY

Shadows
twisting, looming
wrapping around trees
lurking around corners
blanketing the town
hiding secrets

the TIGERS

You can make beautiful designs on cloth.....
with crayons or permanent markers.

What to Do

1. Plan your design first. Sketch it on paper, then draw it lightly on the cloth.

2. Use the crayon or marker and draw right on the fabric. If you're drawing with crayon, press hard.

3. If you've used crayon, iron on the back of the cloth between two sheets of paper to set the crayon into the cloth. Use lots of newspaper on your ironing board.

*Stitch small squares together into a group hanging or a class banner.

*These make nice gifts and are also a special way to show off original poetry.

Tip For Teacher

POINTILISM

with crayon

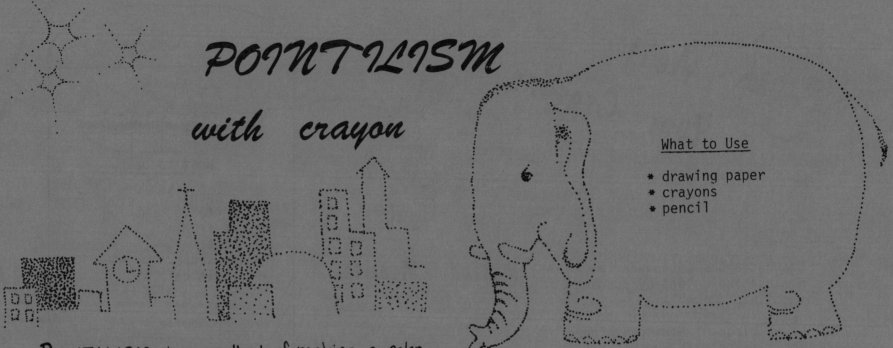

<u>What to Use</u>

* drawing paper
* crayons
* pencil

POINTILISM is a method of making a color
by combining tiny bits of other colors.
To make an area appear blue, you would fill it with points
or dots of green and yellow.
Experiment with pointilism! Don't draw lines, just points!

<u>What to Do</u>

1. Plan a design or picture. Sketch it on drawing paper.

2. "Color" each area by making dots of color. Use the
    point of your crayon, and place the dots close together.

3. Remember to mix dots of 2 colors to form the color you
    want.

4. Stand away from the finished picture, and you will
    see that the dots blend together.

35

Melt Your Crayons

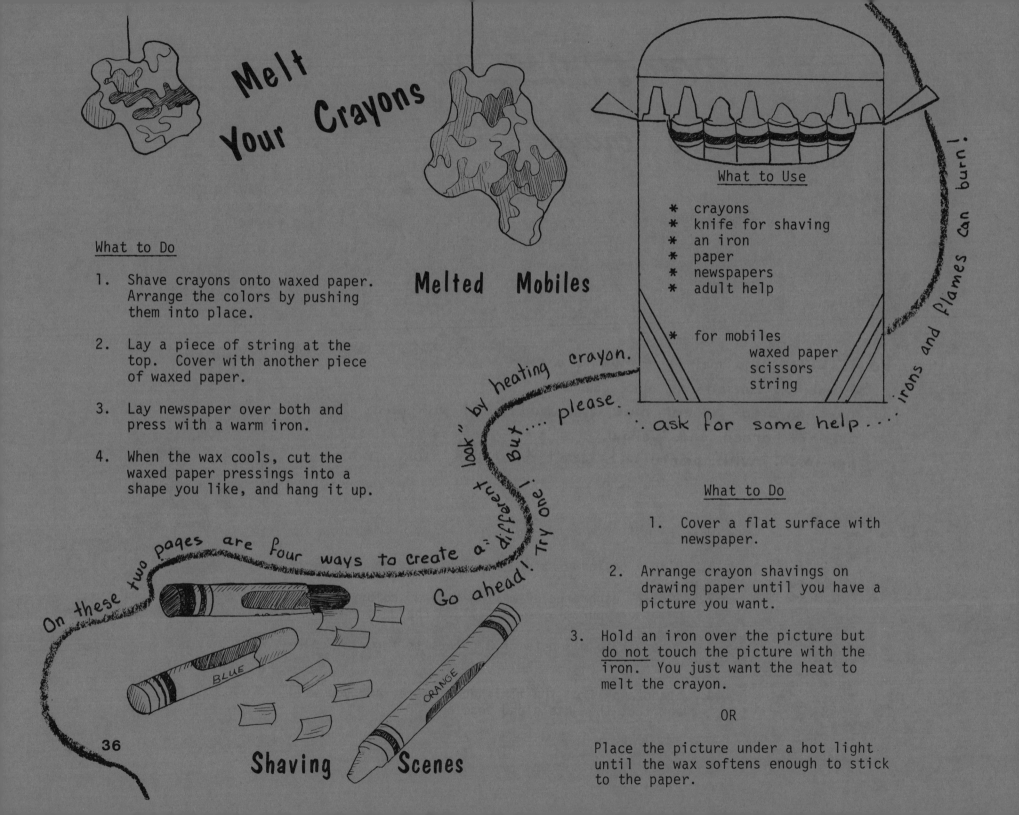

Melted Mobiles

What to Do

1. Shave crayons onto waxed paper. Arrange the colors by pushing them into place.

2. Lay a piece of string at the top. Cover with another piece of waxed paper.

3. Lay newspaper over both and press with a warm iron.

4. When the wax cools, cut the waxed paper pressings into a shape you like, and hang it up.

What to Use

* crayons
* knife for shaving
* an iron
* paper
* newspapers
* adult help

* for mobiles
  waxed paper
  scissors
  string

... ask for some help ...

irons and flames can burn!

look" by heating crayon. But..... please...

On these two pages are four ways to create a different. Go ahead! Try one!

Shaving Scenes

What to Do

1. Cover a flat surface with newspaper.

2. Arrange crayon shavings on drawing paper until you have a picture you want.

3. Hold an iron over the picture but do not touch the picture with the iron. You just want the heat to melt the crayon.

OR

Place the picture under a hot light until the wax softens enough to stick to the paper.

BLUE

ORANGE

Candle Crayoning

What to Use

* drawing paper
* crayons
* candle
* newspapers
* adult help

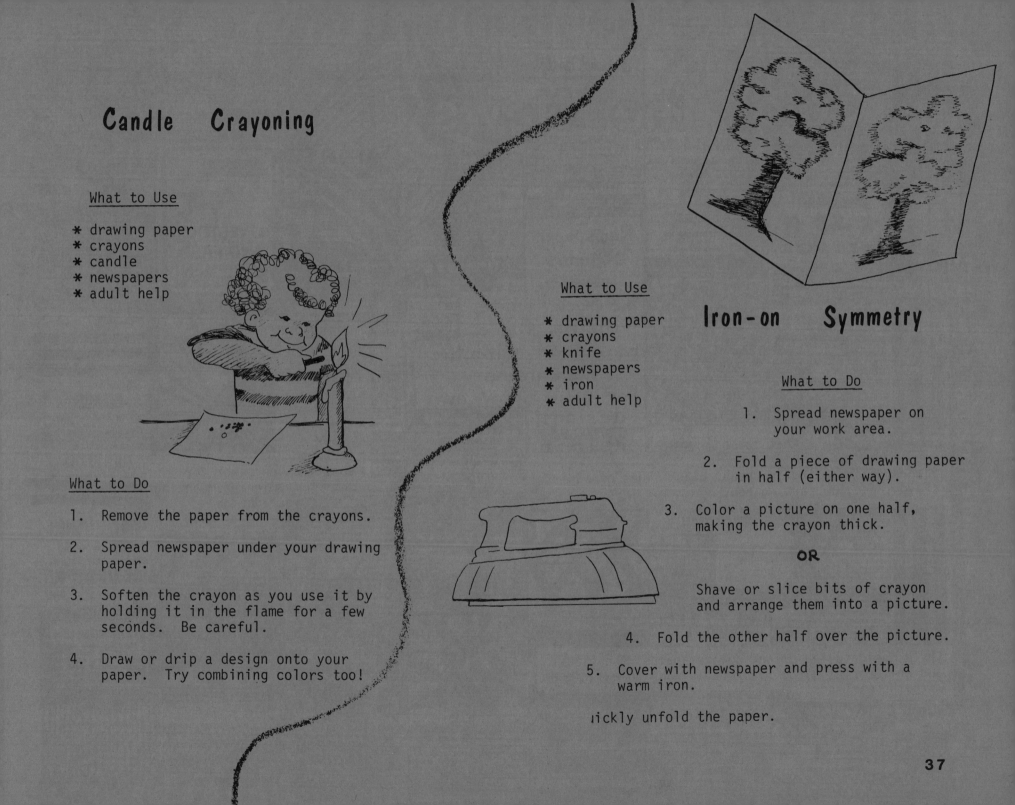

What to Do

1. Remove the paper from the crayons.

2. Spread newspaper under your drawing paper.

3. Soften the crayon as you use it by holding it in the flame for a few seconds. Be careful.

4. Draw or drip a design onto your paper. Try combining colors too!

What to Use

* drawing paper
* crayons
* knife
* newspapers
* iron
* adult help

Iron-on   Symmetry

What to Do

1. Spread newspaper on your work area.

2. Fold a piece of drawing paper in half (either way).

3. Color a picture on one half, making the crayon thick.

OR

Shave or slice bits of crayon and arrange them into a picture.

4. Fold the other half over the picture.

5. Cover with newspaper and press with a warm iron.

ickly unfold the paper.

Color the News

Newspaper Columns plus the black & white patterns there make an attractive background for your very own designs!

What to Use

* newspaper
* crayons
  or
* India Ink
  or
* markers
* construction paper for framing or mounting your design

What to Do

Plan a design using the heavy black lines of a dark crayon, pen, or marking pen.

OR

Try a design using bright colors against the black and white print. You'll probably want to experiment with the want ads.

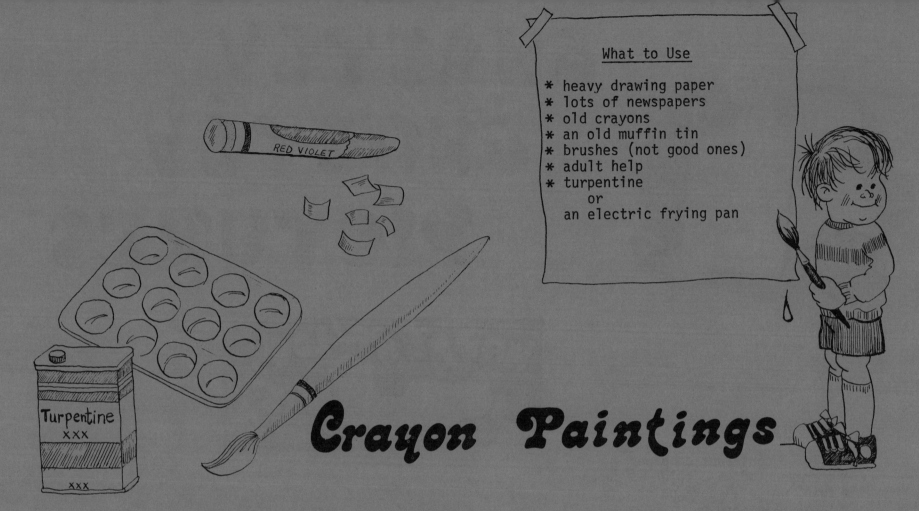

What to Use

* heavy drawing paper
* lots of newspapers
* old crayons
* an old muffin tin
* brushes (not good ones)
* adult help
* turpentine
     or
  an electric frying pan

RED VIOLET

Turpentine
xxx

xxx

Crayon Paintings

What to Do

1. Prepare crayon paint in one of two ways: Shave crayons into the muffin tin, keeping each color separate.

2. Then: Pour some turpentine in each section and let the crayons dissolve for about two weeks.   **OR**   Carefully set the muffin tin into an electric frying pan that is half full of water. Heat on low until the crayons melt.

3. Paint your design on paper. . . or you can try painting on wood or cardboard.

GHASTLY, GHOSTLY PICTURES

What to Use

* colored construction paper
* a crayon the same color as paper
* thin, white tempera paint
* large paint brush
* newspapers

What to Do

1. Choose paper and crayon of the same color (black crayon on black paper, gray on gray, blue on blue).

2. Draw a picture, making sure that you crayon heavily.

3. Paint over the crayoned part of your picture with one coat of thin white paint.

The paint won't stick to the part you crayoned!

COLOR ME JOYFUL !

What color is anger ?

What to Do

1. Choose an emotion or feeling that you have had or that any human being might experience.

2. Think about what color (or colors) that feeling is - or what colors might represent it.

3. Choose 1, 2, or 3 colors.

4. Use the whole paper to create a design which shows that emotion. Experiment with your chalk. You can use it to make sharp bold lines, wide lines, or pale shaded areas.

5. Make a frame for your design or mount it on a larger piece of colored construction paper. Label it with the word that names the feeling.

6. Would you like to try a different emotion?

This is a good beginning for a discussion of human emotions and a creative writing starter, as well.
Ask students to tell or write about a time they experienced the emotion they've pictured, or to describe an incident in which a person displayed that feeling.

What to Use

* white drawing paper
* 2 or 3 colors of chalk

What color is joy?

Loneliness

Jealousy

What color is fear?

Anxiety

41

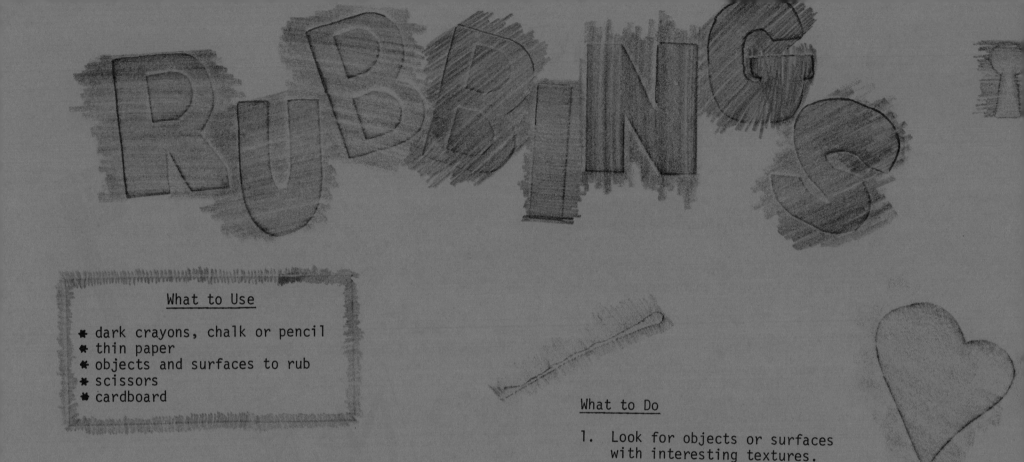

RUBBINGS

What to Use

* dark crayons, chalk or pencil
* thin paper
* objects and surfaces to rub
* scissors
* cardboard

What to Do

1. Look for objects or surfaces with interesting textures.

2. Put paper over the surface and rub hard with the side of the pen, pencil or chalk. Hold the object in one place while you rub.

3. Try rubbing lots of places and things! Don't forget to look outside!

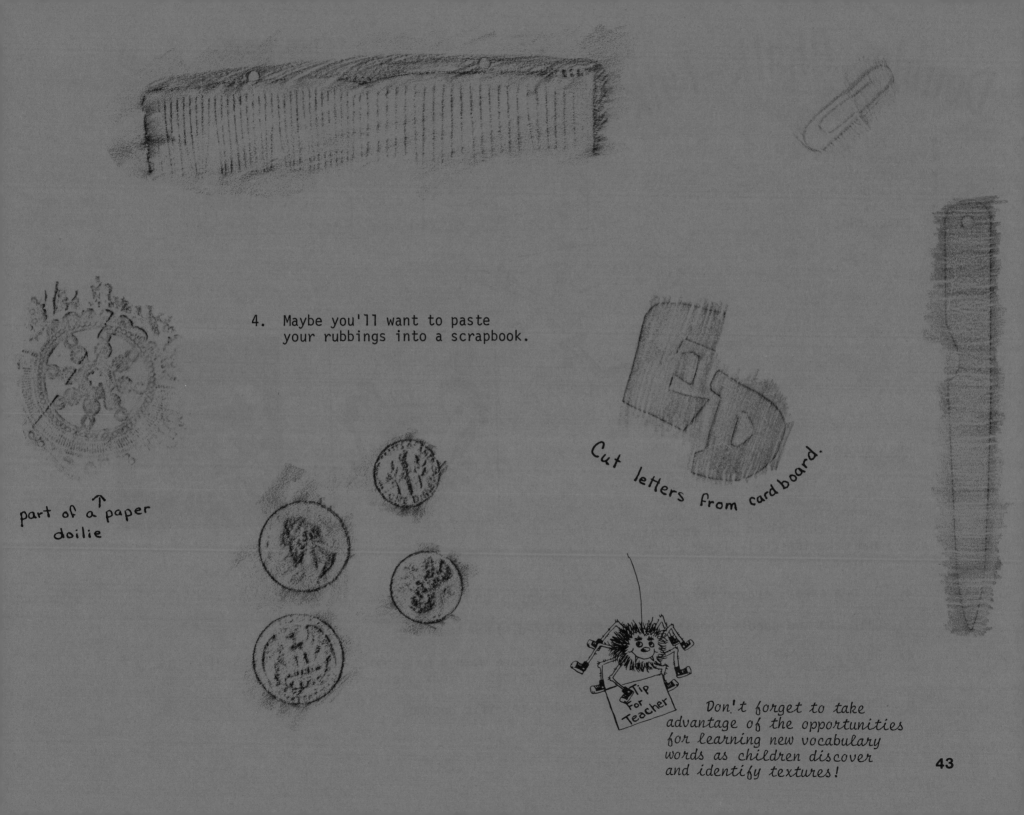

part of a ↑ paper
doilie

4. Maybe you'll want to paste
   your rubbings into a scrapbook.

Cut letters from cardboard.

Tip For Teacher

Don't forget to take
advantage of the opportunities
for learning new vocabulary
words as children discover
and identify textures!

43

Double Chalk-Talk

What to Use

* 2 pieces of drawing paper
* colored chalk
* a dark crayon
* a ball point pen (not too fine)
* a pencil
* 2 paper clips

What to Do

1. Use the chalk to cover both pieces of paper with stripes or sections of color. Choose colors that blend well together and make the chalk layer quite thick.

2. On one sheet, crayon very heavily over the _whole_ surface with the dark crayon.

3. Clip the two sheets together (with the colored sides touching).

4. On the back of the crayoned sheet, draw a picture with a ball point pen. Press hard! Use the flat side of the pencil lead to shade sections of your picture.

5. Un-clip the papers, and you'll find a doubly terrific design!

MORE
CHALK TRICKS

OR.... dip your finger in liquid starch and "paint" over the lines of the design.

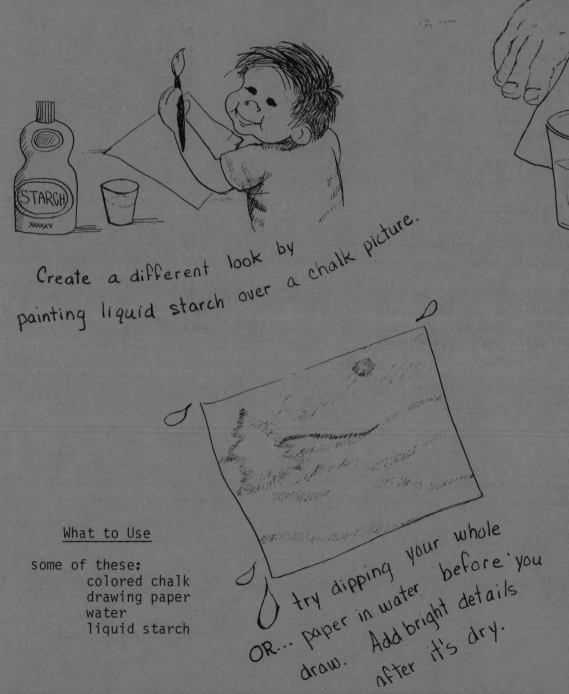

Create a different look by painting liquid starch over a chalk picture.

OR... try dipping your whole paper in water before you draw. Add bright details after it's dry.

OR... just wet the chalk before you draw each stroke.

What to Use

some of these:
  colored chalk
  drawing paper
  water
  liquid starch

STENCILS

What to Do

1. Draw a simple design on tagboard.

2. Cut it out carefully. Tape together any cuts you made.

3. You now have 2 stencils.

4. Crayon or chalk heavily around the edge of either stencil.

5. Place the stencil on drawing paper and rub the color onto the paper. You can use your finger or a paper towel to do the rubbing.

6. Use either stencil, or both, to make a design or picture.

What to Use

* tagboard
* scissors
* pencil
* tape
* crayons or
* colored chalk
* drawing paper
* paper towels

Use stencil A to make a design with lines going toward the center.

Use stencil B to make a design with lines going away from the center.

A.

46

B.

BLOW & DRAW

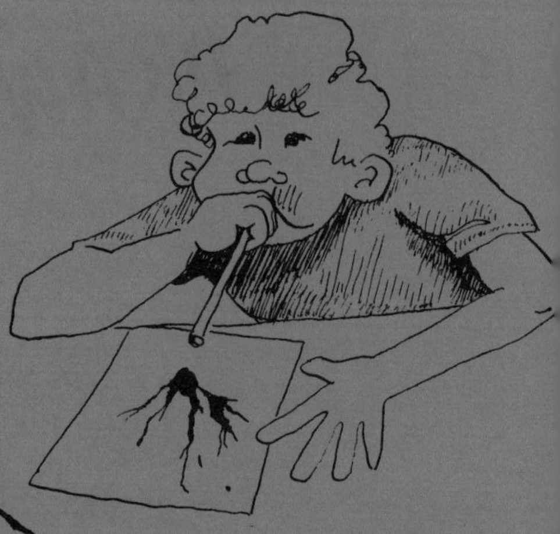

What to Use

* drawing paper
* black India Ink
* straws
* newspapers
* tissue paper
* marking pens or water colors
* black construction paper
* glue

Do this with just a few at a time, and a demonstration of gentle blowing! Believe-it-or-not, even little kids can do this without too much mess!

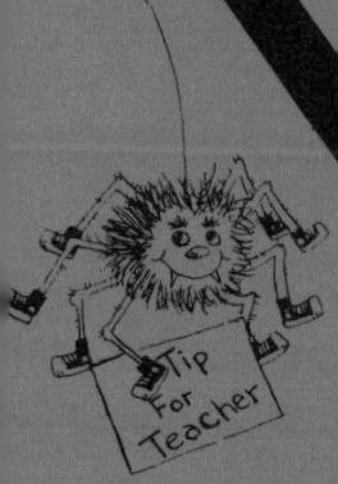

What to Do

1. Spread newspapers over your work area. Lay a piece of drawing paper (any shape) on the newspaper.

2. Drip a blob of ink on the drawing paper.

3. Quickly, use the straw to blow on the ink, spreading it in different directions to create spider-like designs. Blow gently.

4. Let the ink dry. Then add details and color to your design by using watercolor paints, marking pens, or bits of colored tissue paper.

5. Frame your design with black construction paper.

DRAW IT AGAIN... and again... and again....

What to Use

* India Ink and pen
   or crayons
* drawing paper

What to Do

1. Draw a basic shape or
   free form outline.

2. Repeat the outline inside
   the first line.

3. Continue repeating the
   shape until the paper is filled.

4. You might want to try making some of the lines thicker than the others.

What to Use

* 2 pieces of paper with a hard surface
* India Ink
* newspaper
* fine point black marking pen

What do you see.

When you look at this?

Turn it all around....
Look it over....

What could it be?

Watch the Blob!

What to Do

1. Drop a blotch of ink on the paper.

2. Press another piece of paper on top of it. Rub gently out from the center to spread the ink blob.

3. Remove the blotting paper.

4. Use a fine-point marking pen to create something from the "blob."

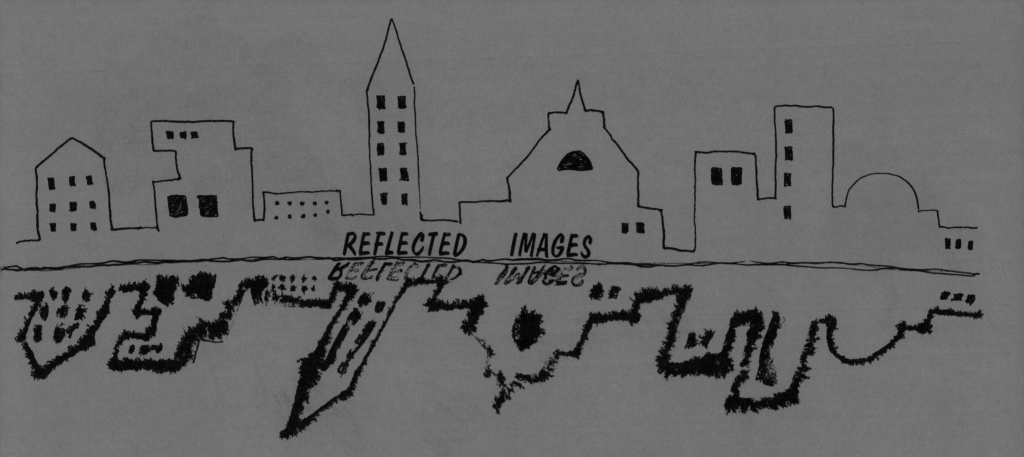

REFLECTED IMAGES

What to Use

* drawing paper
* a sink or pan of water
* India Ink
* drawing pens
* water colors and brush
* newspapers
* glue

What to Do

1. Spread newspapers over your work area.

2. Cut a piece of drawing paper in half lengthwise.

3. On the top half, draw a scene with India Ink. Think of a scene that would be on the edge of a river or lake.

4. Dip the bottom half of the paper in water. Lay it on newspaper. Lay your first drawing directly above it.

5. Use India Ink to draw a reflection of your first scene. Notice that the scene often reflects at an angle. The lines will grow fuzzy as you draw on this bottom half because the ink will soak into the wet paper.

6. When the picture is dry, glue the halves together. Then add touches of color with watercolors, and add fine-lined details with a pen or marker.

SNOW SCENES

What to Use

* gray or dark blue
  construction
  paper
* white chalk
* black ink or chalk

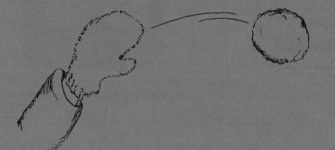

What to Do

Draw a scene as it would look during or after a heavy snow fall.

Use black ink or black chalk to outline objects and shapes.

Use white chalk to show how the snow would coat buildings, hang on trees, cover hills, etc.

See-Through Drawings

They're transparent!

They look great in a window!

Try some!

What to Do

1. Outline a design with black ink or marker on drawing paper.

2. Color in the spaces with crayons. You can leave some of the space white, if you wish.

3. Turn the drawing over. Lay it on newspaper.

4. Rub oil over the back of the picture. The oil makes your picture transparent!

What to Use

* drawing paper
* permanent marker or ink (black)
* bright colored crayons
* baby oil or cooking oil
* a rag
* newspapers

Chapter 2
Things to do with paper

MULTI·COLOR MOSAICS

A mosaic is made by using tiny pieces of colored material fitted together to make a design. This one is made with small bits of cut paper.

Keep a straight pin handy. It helps you pick up those pieces too little for handling with fingers.

A good mosaic takes time... so be patient!

What to Use

* colored construction paper
  or
  colored magazine pictures
* scissors
* white glue
* pencil
* drawing paper
* straight pins
* small milk cartons or other containers

What to Do

1. Plan a design or picture and sketch it with a pencil on drawing paper.

2. Choose the colors you want to use, and cut or tear colored construction paper into small pieces. You might want to use a milk carton or small container to keep each color separate.

3. Spread glue thoroughly over the surface of a small area. Use a <u>thin</u> layer of glue.

4. Pick up the pieces one at a time, with a pin, and set them in place on the glue.

5. Continue doing this until your design is finished.

Tip for Teacher

This is a good use for all those scraps you'd never let them throw away! A huge box or drawer of scraps works better than new sheets of paper - and is a lot less wasteful.

Cardboard Strip Creations

What to Do

1. Plan a simple picture or design.

2. Sketch it lightly with pencil on a piece of tagboard.

3. Cut a strip of cardboard (2 centimeters or 1 inch wide), the length of each line in your sketch.

4. Squeeze a line of glue along a line of the design. Stand the cardboard strip, on its edge, along the glue. Hold it in place for about 1 minute.

5. Glue the other strips in the same way.

6. When the glue is dry, paint or color the areas inside the "lines" (if you want to).

What to Use   * tagboard   or lightweight cardboard   or construction paper,   * paint and paint brush or markers,

* scissors,   * white glue,   * pencil

STRING-ALONG-FIGURES

What to Use

* construction paper
* scissors
* glue
* ruler
* pencil
* paint and brush (optional)

What to Do

1.

Fold a piece of paper (12 inches or longer) in 4 or more equal sections. You might need your ruler to measure equal sections.

2.

On the top section draw a design that touches the folds on both sides in at least one place! Cut out the design but be careful not to cut away the fold at those places where it touches the edges.

3.

Glue your string-along design onto another color of paper. Add finishing accents with paint if you'd like to.

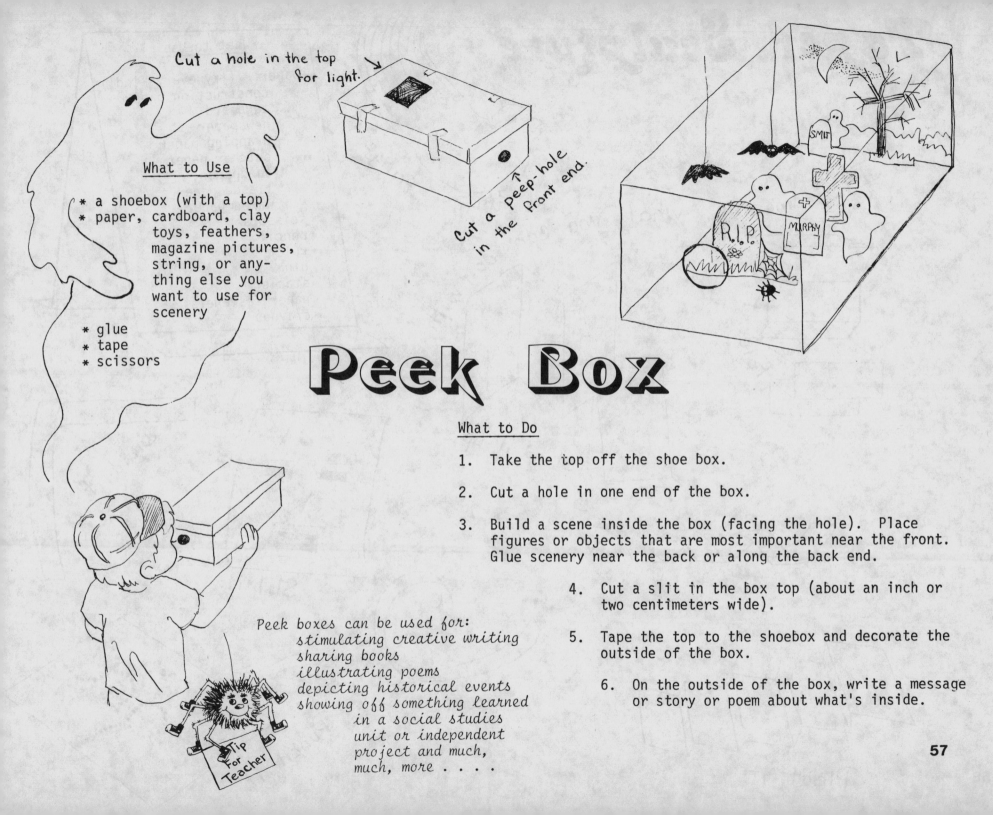

Cut a hole in the top for light.

Cut a peep-hole in the front end.

What to Use

* a shoebox (with a top)
* paper, cardboard, clay
  toys, feathers,
  magazine pictures,
  string, or any-
  thing else you
  want to use for
  scenery

* glue
* tape
* scissors

Peek Box

What to Do

1. Take the top off the shoe box.

2. Cut a hole in one end of the box.

3. Build a scene inside the box (facing the hole). Place
    figures or objects that are most important near the front.
    Glue scenery near the back or along the back end.

4. Cut a slit in the box top (about an inch or
    two centimeters wide).

5. Tape the top to the shoebox and decorate the
    outside of the box.

6. On the outside of the box, write a message
    or story or poem about what's inside.

Peek boxes can be used for:
stimulating creative writing
sharing books
illustrating poems
depicting historical events
showing off something learned
in a social studies
unit or independent
project and much,
much, more . . . . .

Tip For Teacher

Paper Sculpture

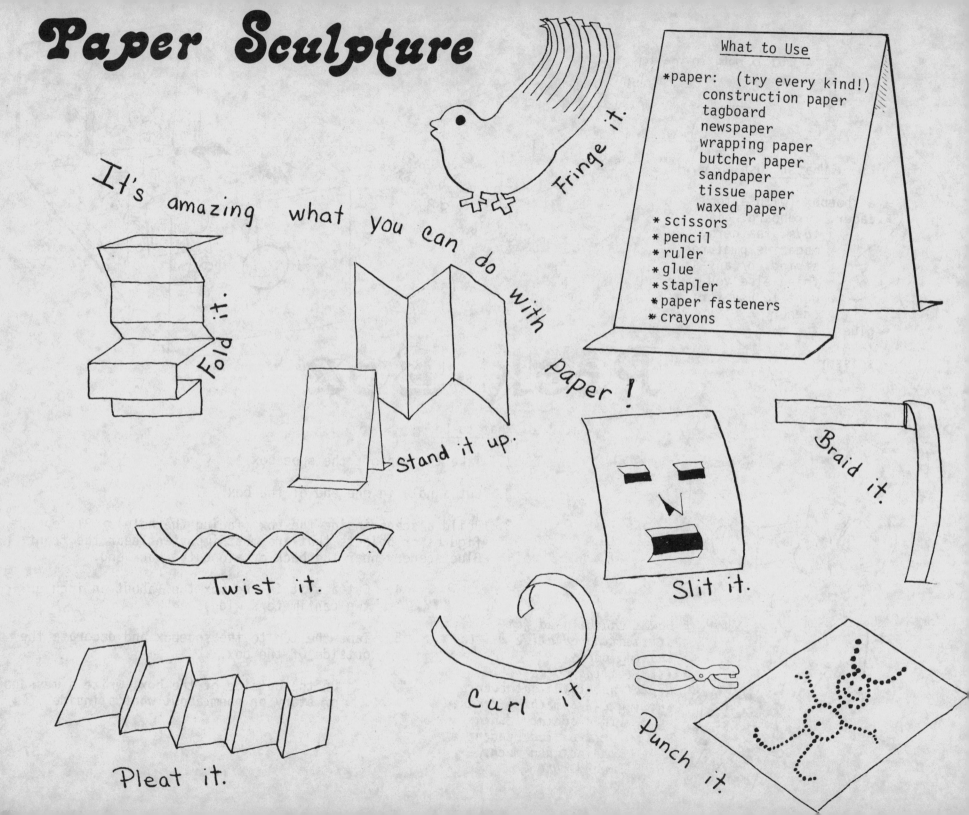

Fringe it.

It's amazing what you can do with paper!

What to Use

*paper: (try every kind!)
    construction paper
    tagboard
    newspaper
    wrapping paper
    butcher paper
    sandpaper
    tissue paper
    waxed paper
* scissors
* pencil
* ruler
* glue
* stapler
* paper fasteners
* crayons

Fold it.

Stand it up.

Braid it.

Twist it.

Slit it.

Curl it.

Pleat it.

Punch it.

58

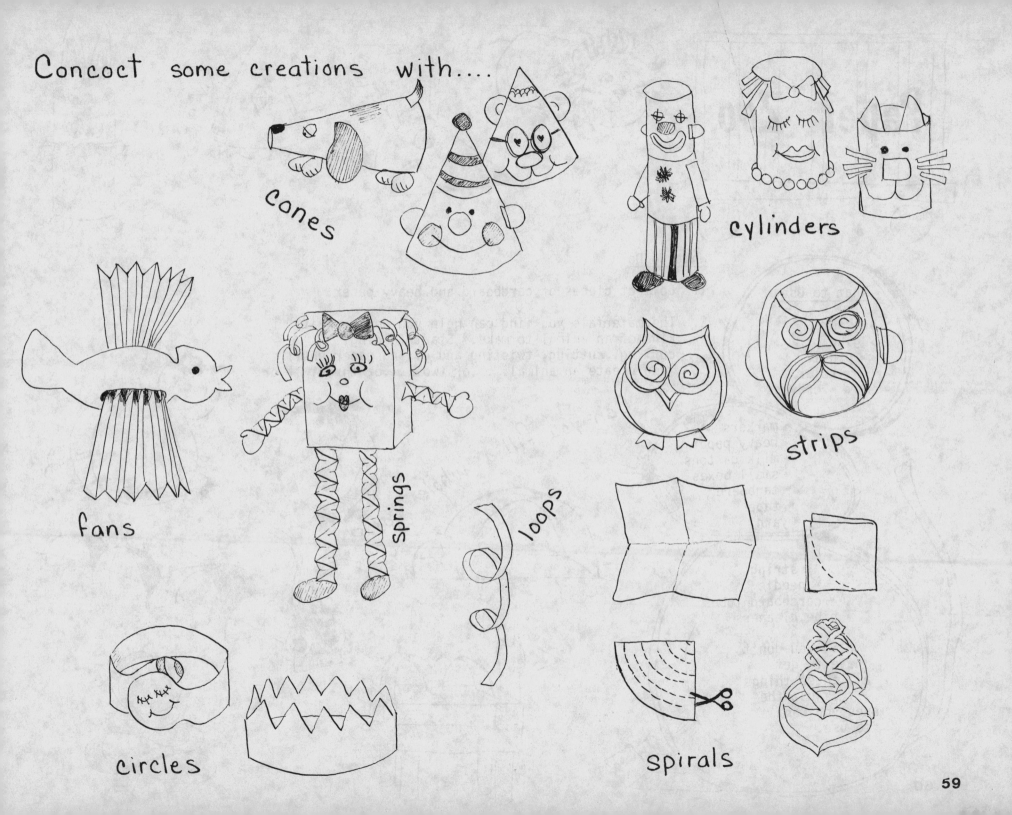

Concoct some creations with....

cones

cylinders

fans

springs

loops

strips

circles

spirals

59

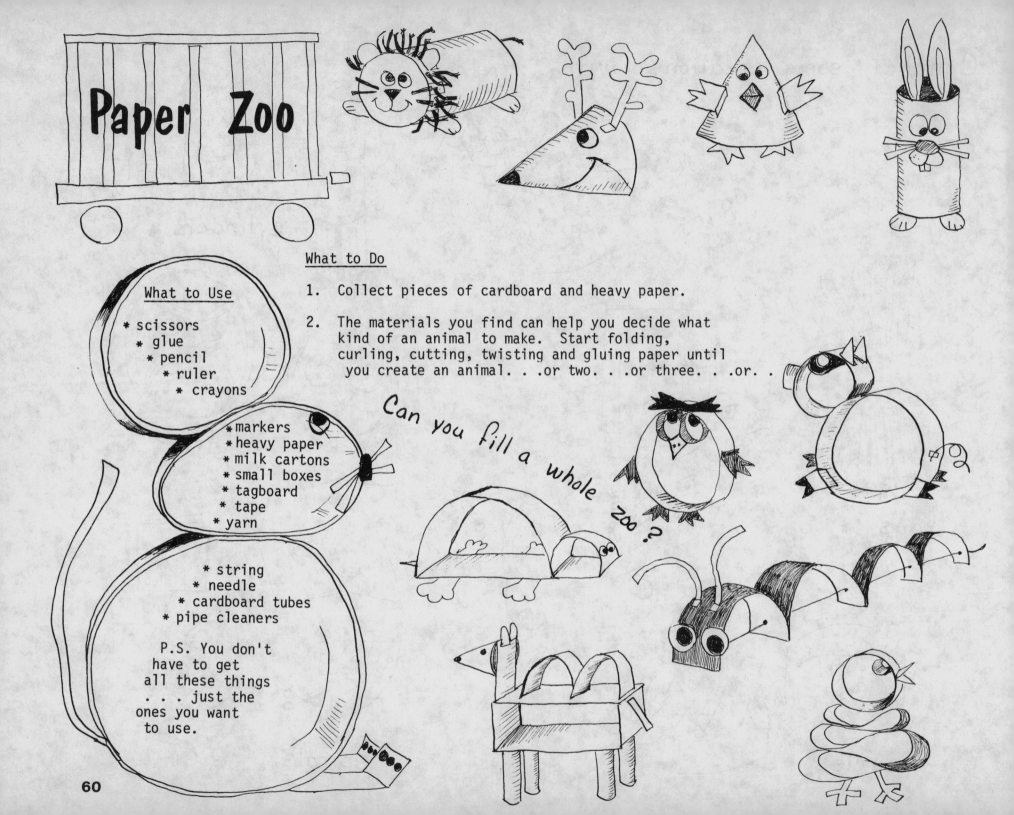

Paper Zoo

What to Use

* scissors
* glue
* pencil
* ruler
* crayons

* markers
* heavy paper
* milk cartons
* small boxes
* tagboard
* tape
* yarn

* string
* needle
* cardboard tubes
* pipe cleaners

P.S. You don't have to get all these things . . . just the ones you want to use.

What to Do

1. Collect pieces of cardboard and heavy paper.

2. The materials you find can help you decide what kind of an animal to make. Start folding, curling, cutting, twisting and gluing paper until you create an animal. . .or two. . .or three. . .or. .

Can you fill a whole zoo?

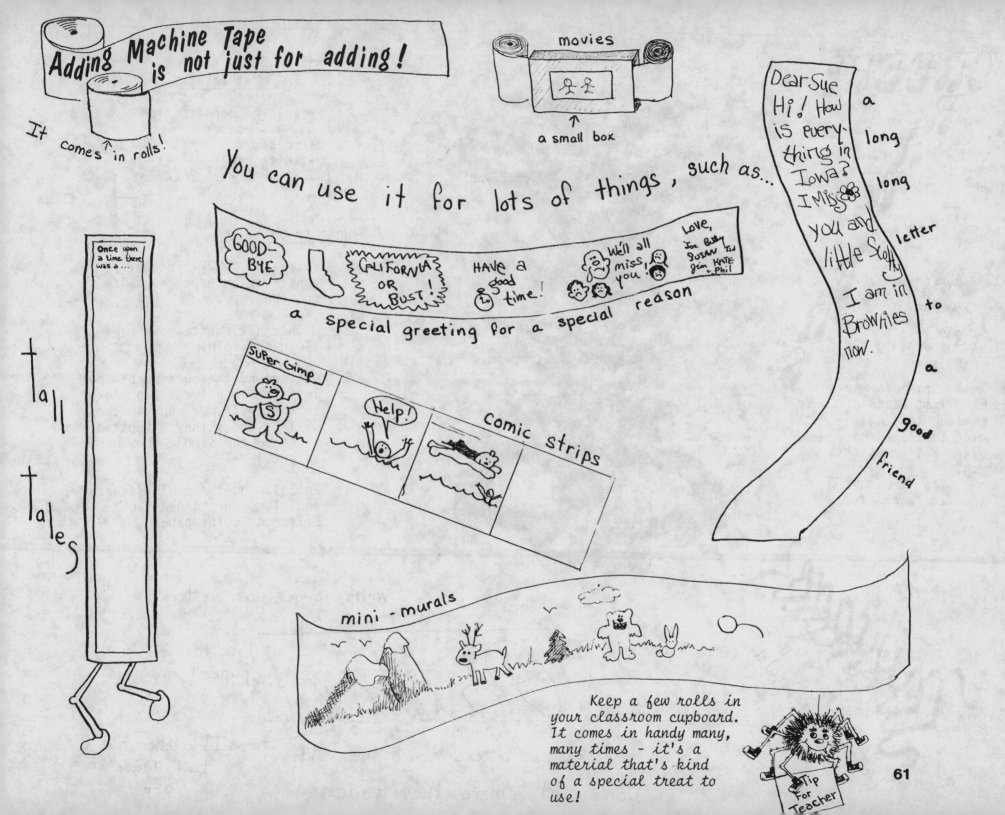

Adding Machine Tape is not just for adding!

It comes in rolls!

movies

a small box

Dear Sue
Hi! How is everything in Iowa? I miss you and little Scotty. I am in Brownies now.

a long long letter to a good friend

You can use it for lots of things, such as...

GOOD-BYE

CALIFORNIA OR BUST!

HAVE a good time!

We'll all miss you,

Love, Joe Betty Ted Susan Kate Jim + Phil

a special greeting for a special reason

Once upon a time there was a...

Super Gimp

Help!

comic strips

Tall Tales

mini - murals

Keep a few rolls in your classroom cupboard. It comes in handy many, many times - it's a material that's kind of a special treat to use!

Tip For Teacher

61

CREEPY CRAWLERS

Students who have just learned cursive writing will love showing off their names this way.

Try it with spelling words too!

Glue dots on seperately!

What to Use

* colored construction paper
* scissors
* white chalk
* glue or rubber cement

What to Do

1. Fold a 9" X 12" piece of construction paper in half the long way.

2. With chalk, write your name along the fold.

3. Cut around the outside of the letters. Don't cut too close to the chalk, or your letters will be too skinny. (Dotted lines on the sample show where to cut.)

4. Put glue on the chalky side, and glue your "insect" on a different color paper.

Write large, fat letters.

Fill the paper!

FOLD

Make your letters touch the fold.

If a letter has a tail, leave it off!

Don't cut where they touch!

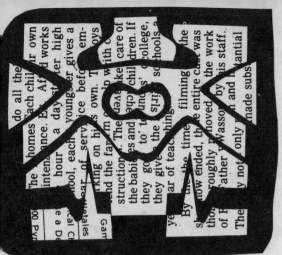

Indian cut-apart designs

What to Use

* plain-colored or printed
    paper such as
    construction paper
        or
    colored foil
        or
    wrapping paper
    (maybe even newspaper)
* pencil
* scissors

What to Do

1. Cut a shape from colored or patterned paper. It can be a regular or an irregular shape.

2. Use a pencil to mark lines for cutting the shape into a design.

3. Cut apart the shape   (see examples on this page).

4. Lay the pieces on a contrasting background, leaving some space between the pieces. (Contrasting means a color that is different.)

5. Glue the pieces of the design in place.

wampum beads

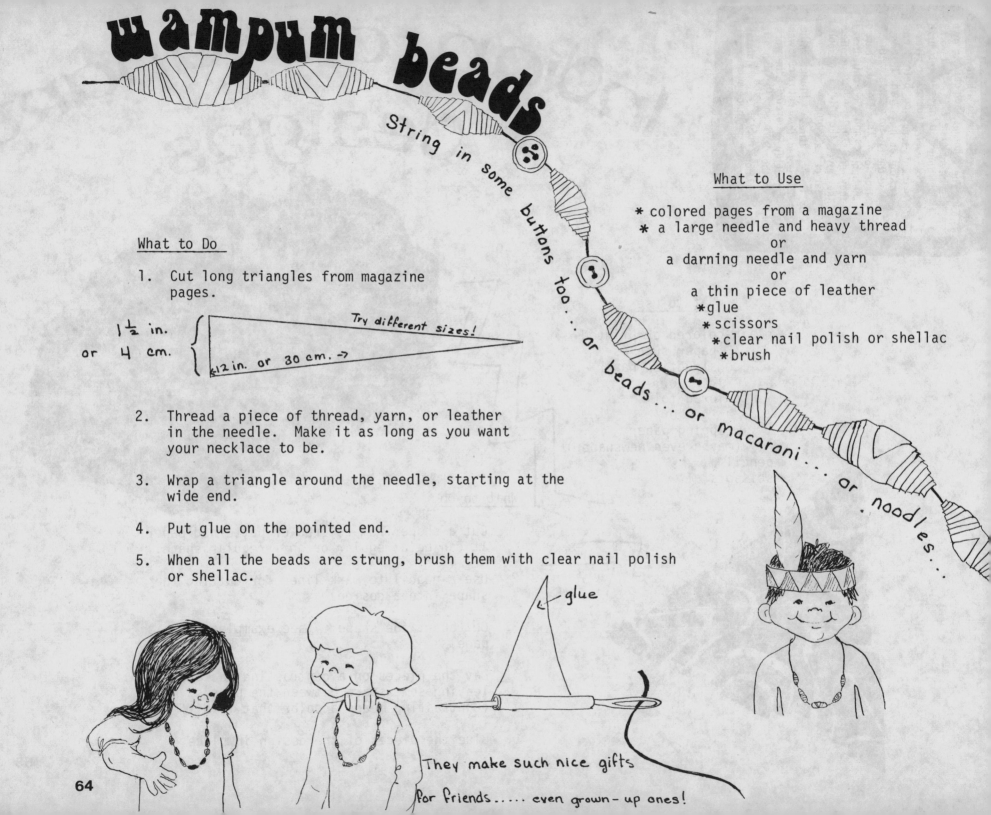

String in some buttons too... or beads... or macaroni... or noodles...

What to Use

* colored pages from a magazine
* a large needle and heavy thread
  or
  a darning needle and yarn
  or
  a thin piece of leather
* glue
* scissors
* clear nail polish or shellac
* brush

What to Do

1. Cut long triangles from magazine pages.

1½ in.
or   4 cm.

Try different sizes!

←12 in. or 30 cm.→

2. Thread a piece of thread, yarn, or leather in the needle. Make it as long as you want your necklace to be.

3. Wrap a triangle around the needle, starting at the wide end.

4. Put glue on the pointed end.

5. When all the beads are strung, brush them with clear nail polish or shellac.

glue

They make such nice gifts for friends..... even grown-up ones!

64

STAINED GLASS
(with paper)

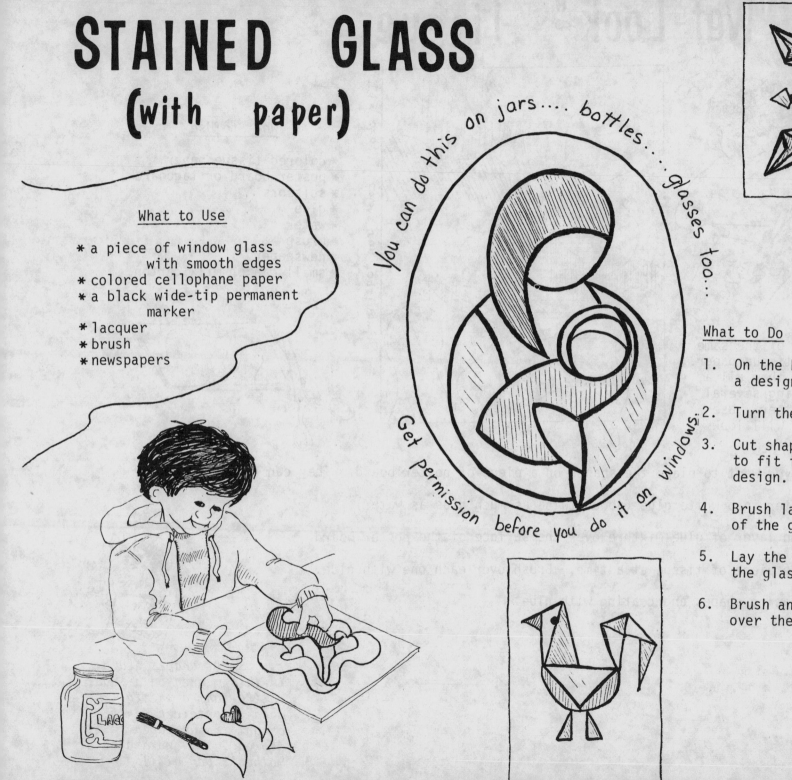

You can do this on jars.... bottles.... glasses too...

Get permission before you do it on windows.

What to Use

* a piece of window glass with smooth edges
* colored cellophane paper
* a black wide-tip permanent marker
* lacquer
* brush
* newspapers

What to Do

1. On the back of the glass, draw a design with a black marker.

2. Turn the glass over.

3. Cut shapes from cellophane to fit into the spaces of the design.

4. Brush lacquer over the front of the glass.

5. Lay the cellophane pieces onto the glass.

6. Brush another coat of lacquer over the whole design.

65

"Wet-Look" Tissue

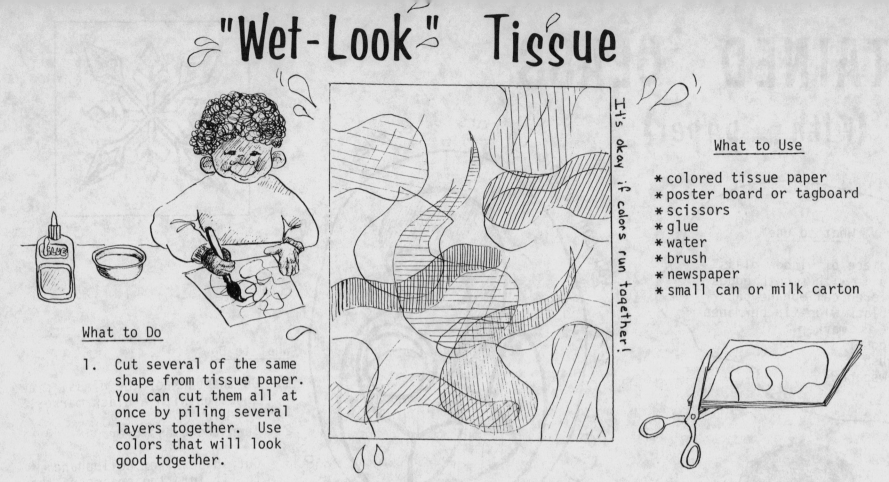

It's okay if colors run together!

What to Use

* colored tissue paper
* poster board or tagboard
* scissors
* glue
* water
* brush
* newspaper
* small can or milk carton

What to Do

1. Cut several of the same shape from tissue paper. You can cut them all at once by piling several layers together. Use colors that will look good together.

2. Decide how you want to place the shapes on a piece of poster board. They can overlap.

3. Mix some water into white glue (about twice as much glue as water).

4. Brush a thin layer of glue mixture over the surface of the poster board.

5. Lay down one piece of tissue at a time. Brush over each one with glue.

6. Continue placing shapes and coating with glue.

Tip For Teacher

Small shapes glued in this manner on a soda bottle form a pretty mosaic container for a bright tissue paper flower . . . and a nice Mother's Day gift!

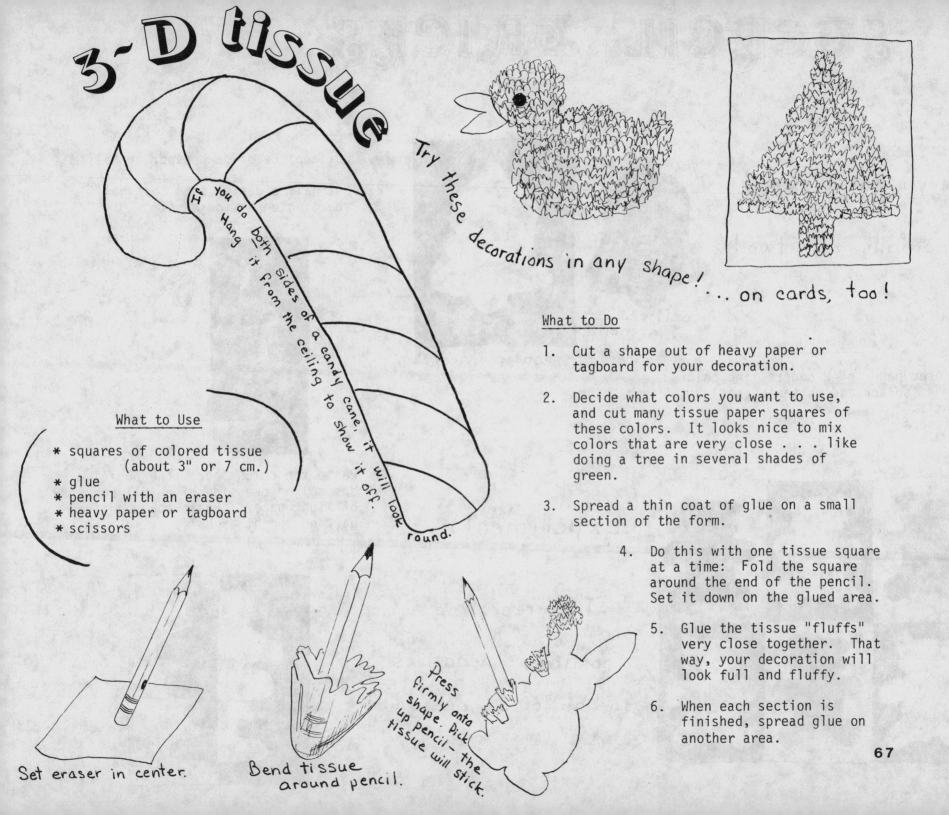

3-D tissue

Try these decorations in any shape!

... on cards, too!

If you do both sides of a candy cane, it will look round. Hang it from the ceiling to show it off.

What to Use

* squares of colored tissue (about 3" or 7 cm.)
* glue
* pencil with an eraser
* heavy paper or tagboard
* scissors

Set eraser in center.

Bend tissue around pencil.

Press firmly onto shape. Pick up pencil – the tissue will stick.

What to Do

1. Cut a shape out of heavy paper or tagboard for your decoration.

2. Decide what colors you want to use, and cut many tissue paper squares of these colors. It looks nice to mix colors that are very close . . . like doing a tree in several shades of green.

3. Spread a thin coat of glue on a small section of the form.

4. Do this with one tissue square at a time: Fold the square around the end of the pencil. Set it down on the glued area.

5. Glue the tissue "fluffs" very close together. That way, your decoration will look full and fluffy.

6. When each section is finished, spread glue on another area.

67

STENCIL TRICKS

When you cut a stencil,

you actually get two!

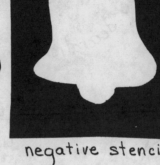

positive stencil

negative stencil

What to Use

* colored paper of 2 contrasting colors
      (black and white is good)
* pencil
* scissors

What to Do

1. Cut a piece of dark paper in half.

2. Cut half a design from that half starting on a side edge.

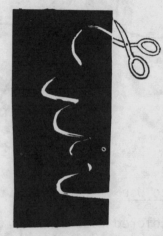

3. Paste the cutout part (the positive design) on one side of a full sheet of light paper. Paste the negative part on the other half.

Experiment!

Try repeating positives and negatives to build a design.

or, try this "shadow effect" using a positive and negative stencil.

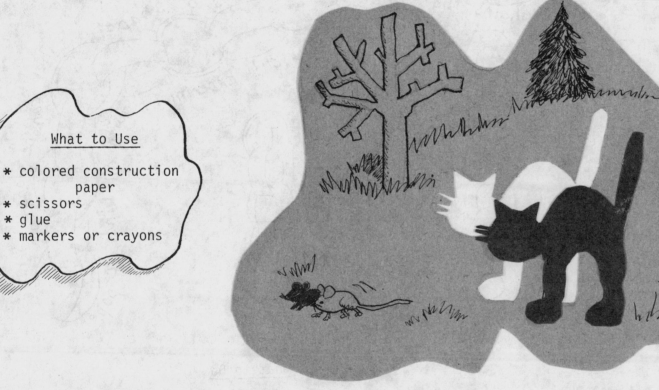

What to Use

* colored construction
      paper
* scissors
* glue
* markers or crayons

What to Do

1. Cut a shape or picture out of 2 colors at once. (One of them should be a dark color.)

2. Paste the negative design of the lighter color onto another sheet of paper.

3. Paste the positive design of the darker color a little a-side of the other shape.
   You might try pasting a lump of cardboard behind the shadow so that it stands out
   from the paper.

4. Add scenery or other objects to the picture with marking pens.

::CHAINS::CHAINS::

Paper chains can be made with links of many colors, sizes, or shapes.
Make some chains that look good to you! Experiment with all kinds of paper. They can be long or short.

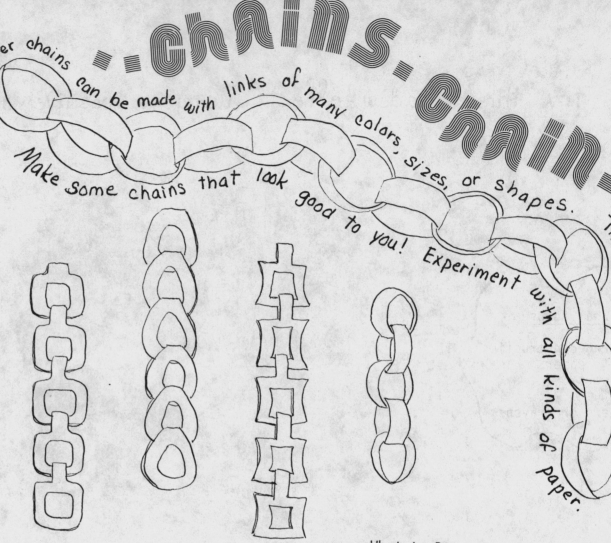

What to Use

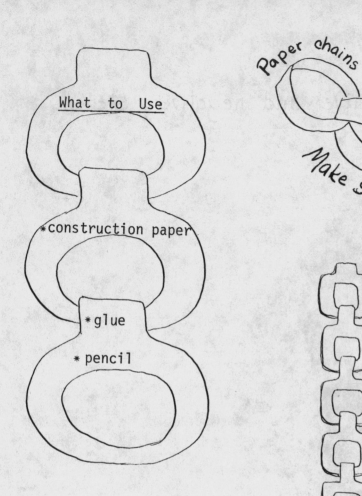

*construction paper

*glue

*pencil

Cut them like this. ↓

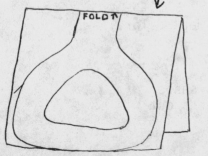

FOLD

Link them like this!

What to Do

1. Make links by cutting strips of paper, or by cutting your own shape. Be sure to cut them double with a fold across the top edge.

2. Link the pieces together or join the ends with a little glue.

What to Do

1. Choose an idea for your collage.

2. Collect "pieces" that relate to the idea . . . you can write or draw them, cut them out of magazines and newspapers, or form them from other materials. You might want to use cut-out letters or words, or bits of poetry, music, colored fabric.

3. Lay the pieces on cardboard or wood and move them around until you like the arrangement.

4. Then, glue them in place.

5. Give your collage a title, if you wish.

6. In case someone asks, be ready to tell what is important about each piece.

What to Use

* large piece of wood or cardboard
* glue
* pictures or photos
* printed matter
* sketches
* fabric
* string, yarn
* drawings etc.

collage talk

A collage is a work of art made by combining pieces that have to do with one topic or idea.

Many different kinds of materials can be used, but each piece is put into the collage for a reason — it _fits_ there!

Choose a theme for your collage. It might be about yourself, something you've learned, a feeling you want to represent, an idea that's important or interesting . . . or it might be a combination of colors or textures that are just pleasing to the eye.

71

Paper Weaving

What to Use

* construction paper
* scissors
* ruler
* glue

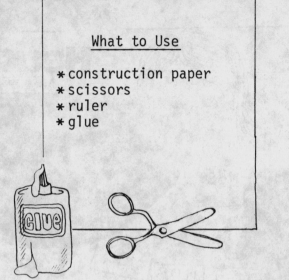

Slits can be straight, wiggly, or even diagonal!

What to Do

1. Start with 2 different colors of the same size paper.

2. Cut one piece into strips.

3. Fold the other sheet in half.

4. Starting at the fold, cut slits across the paper, stopping about an inch or 2 centimeters from the edge. The slits don't have to be straight or even.

5. Weave the short strips in and out of the slits you've cut. Start the first one going over one slit, under the next one. The second strip should start under, then go over...and so on. Glue each strip at the ends so it doesn't slide around.

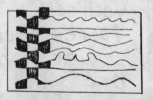

Try using 2 colors of strips!

T.O.'s You-won't-believe-it's-paper! Jewelry

What to Use

* construction paper of
    several colors
* pencil
* scissors
* white glue
* sandpaper
    (or electric sander)
* shellac or clear nail polish
* brush
* a friend with a drill
* a leather thong, a chain
    or a piece of twine

Try pins, earrings, and rings too.....

What to Do

1. Sketch a shape that you would like for the pendant on your necklace.

2. Cut several shapes (exactly the same) from colored construction paper.
    Cut about 30 using whatever colors you like.

3. Glue the shapes on top of each other. Make sure each one is thoroughly
    "stuck" to the one beneath it.

4. Wait a day until the glue is completely dry.

5. Sand around the edges at an angle. You don't have to sand evenly. You can sand farther around onto
    the front in some places.

6. Sand some spots on the top. Sand through a few layers so that different colors show. <u>The sanding</u>
    <u>will take time</u> (unless you have an electric sander), so work on it a little each day. . . and
    be patient! The more time you spend sanding. . . the more beautiful the pendent will be.

7. Coat the pendant with 2 layers of shellac or clear nail polish.

8. Drill a hole and hang on a leather thong, chain, or piece of twine.

T.O. is a good friend who showed me how to make this jewelry.
That's why I call it T.O.'s construction paper jewelry.
I think it's beautiful, T.O.!

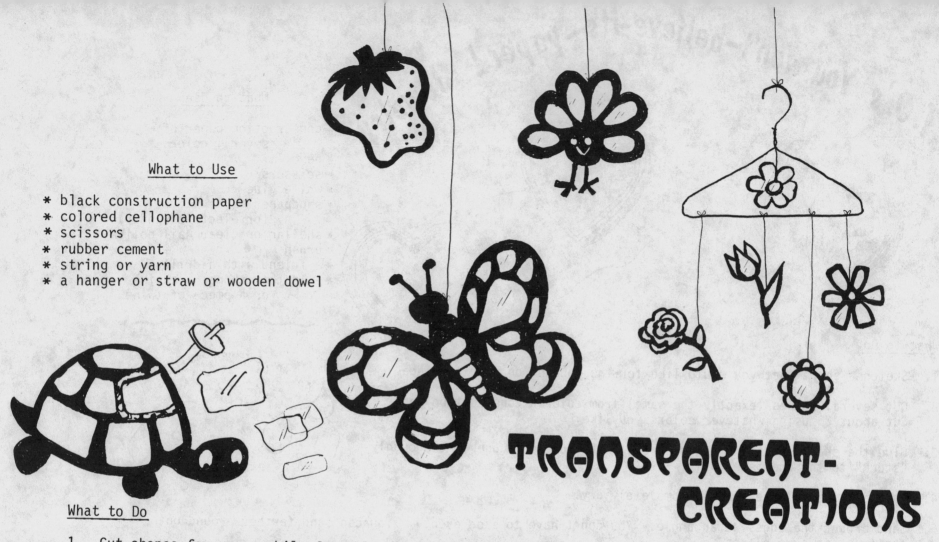

What to Use

* black construction paper
* colored cellophane
* scissors
* rubber cement
* string or yarn
* a hanger or straw or wooden dowel

TRANSPARENT-
CREATIONS

What to Do

1. Cut shapes for your mobile from black construction paper. Cut each one double (2 at the same time) so you end up with 2 exactly the same.

2. Cut large holes in each shape in the spots you want to see through.

3. Cut pieces of colored cellophane large enough to <u>cover</u> each hole.

4. On one of the shapes, brush rubber cement around the outside edge of each hole and lay the cellophane pieces over the holes. Press on them until they stick.

5. After each hole is covered with cellophane, brush rubber cement around the edge of the shape. (The cement should be put on the same side that you pasted the colored cellophane.)

6. Lay the second shape on top of the one with the wet cement, and press them together.

7. Punch a hole near the top, and hang the shape from yarn or string.

74

PUNCH-A-SCENE

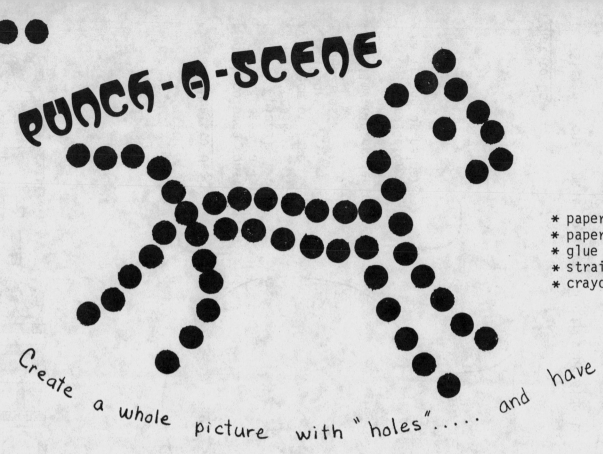

What to Use

* paper (white or colored)
* paper punch
* glue
* straight pin
* crayons

Create a whole picture with "holes"..... and have fun punching too!

What to Do

1. Punch lots of circles. Collect them on a sheet of paper!

2. Glue the circles into a design on a sheet of construction paper.

3. Use crayons to add to the picture or design.

SELF-SILHOUETTE

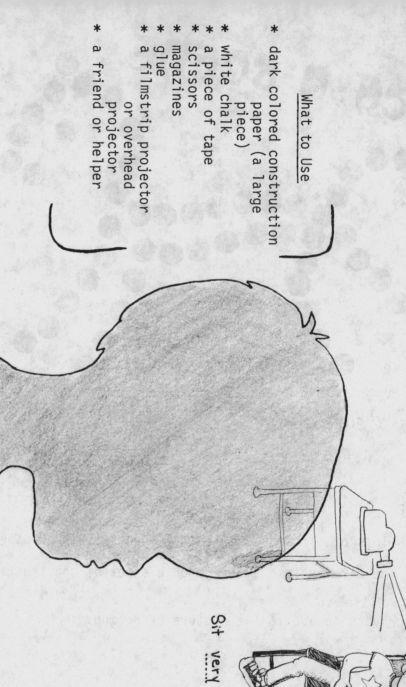

Sit very still!

* dark colored construction paper (a large piece)
* white chalk
* a piece of tape
* scissors
* magazines
* glue
* a filmstrip projector or overhead projector
* a friend or helper

What to Do

1. Sit in a chair next to a wall (with your side to the wall).

2. Tape the construction paper to the wall at the same level as your head.

3. Set up a source of light (projector) and shine it right on the paper.

4. Return to your chair and sit very still while a friend traces around the shadow of your profile with a piece of chalk. Then you draw while your friend poses!

5. Carefully cut out the silhouette. You might want to paste it onto a card, bright paper, or a piece of wood.

6. You can do this part too, if you wish:

   Cut pictures and words out of magazines that tell something about you. Paste them on the head (not over the face) of your silhouette to show "what's inside your head"!

Tip For Teacher

Accompany this with written auto-biographies.

or

Paste silhouettes on hearts, and give as valentines!

or

Prepare silhouettes of famous persons.

Chapter 3

Things to print & paint

fingerprints

Go creative with fingerprints!

What can you make?

What to Use

* stamp pad
* paper
* fingers
* magnifying glass
* fine point markers

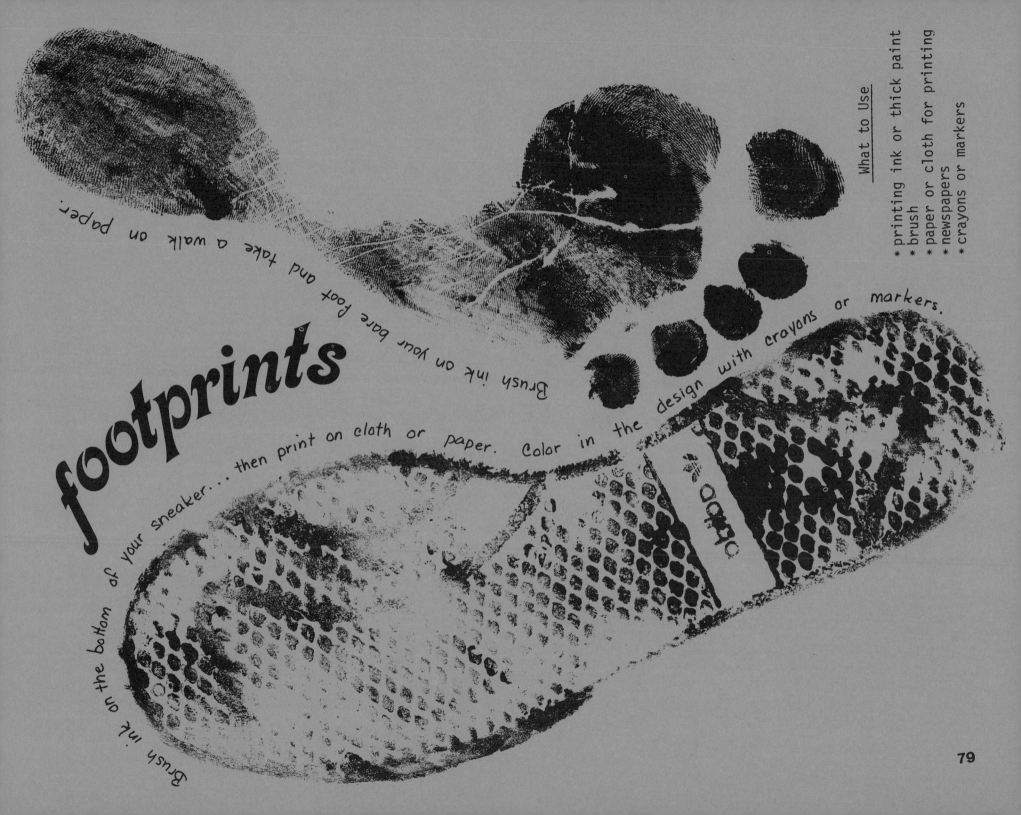

footprints

Brush ink on the bottom of your sneaker... then print on cloth or paper. Color in the design with crayons or markers.

Brush ink on your bare foot and take a walk on paper.

What to Use

* printing ink or thick paint
* brush
* paper or cloth for printing
* newspapers
* crayons or markers

lemon

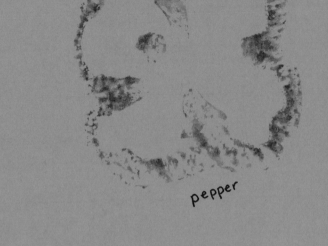

pepper

cauliflower

Cut fruits and vegetables.
Dip them in ink...
and....
print.

Fruit & Vegetable

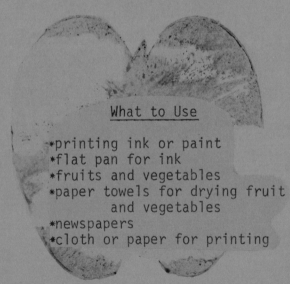

What to Use

*printing ink or paint
*flat pan for ink
*fruits and vegetables
*paper towels for drying fruit
    and vegetables
*newspapers
*cloth or paper for printing

onion

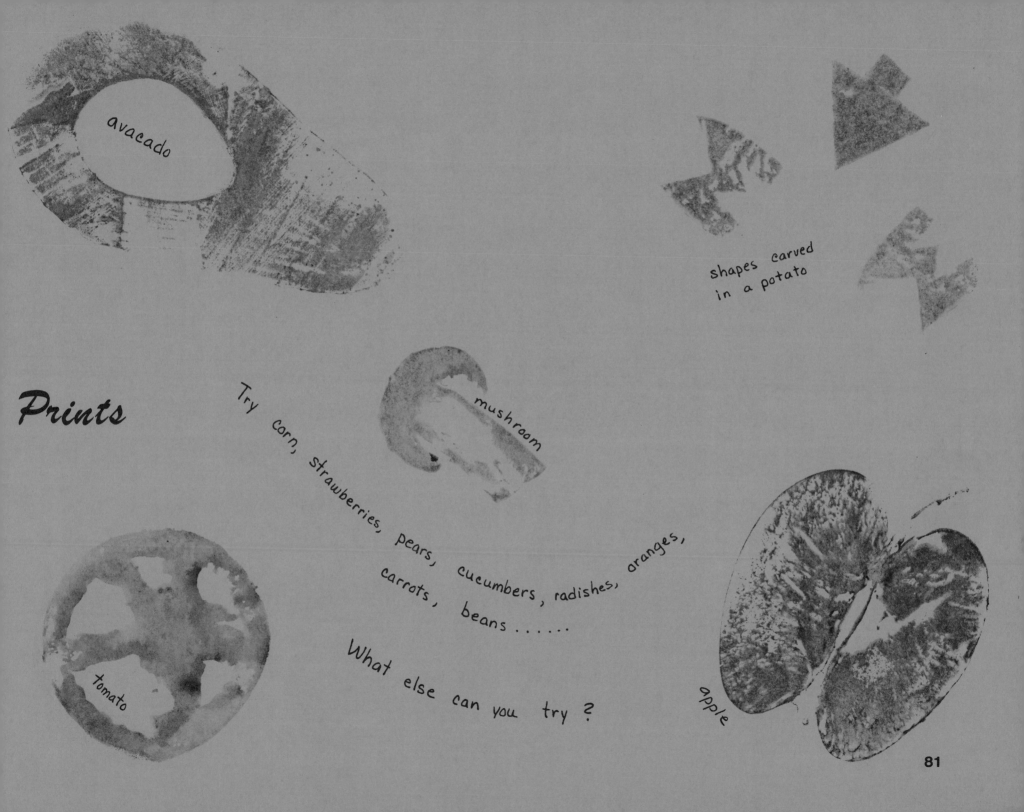

avacado

shapes carved
in a potato

Prints

mushroom

Try corn, strawberries, pears, cucumbers, radishes, oranges, carrots, beans . . . . . .

What else can you try?

tomato

apple

81

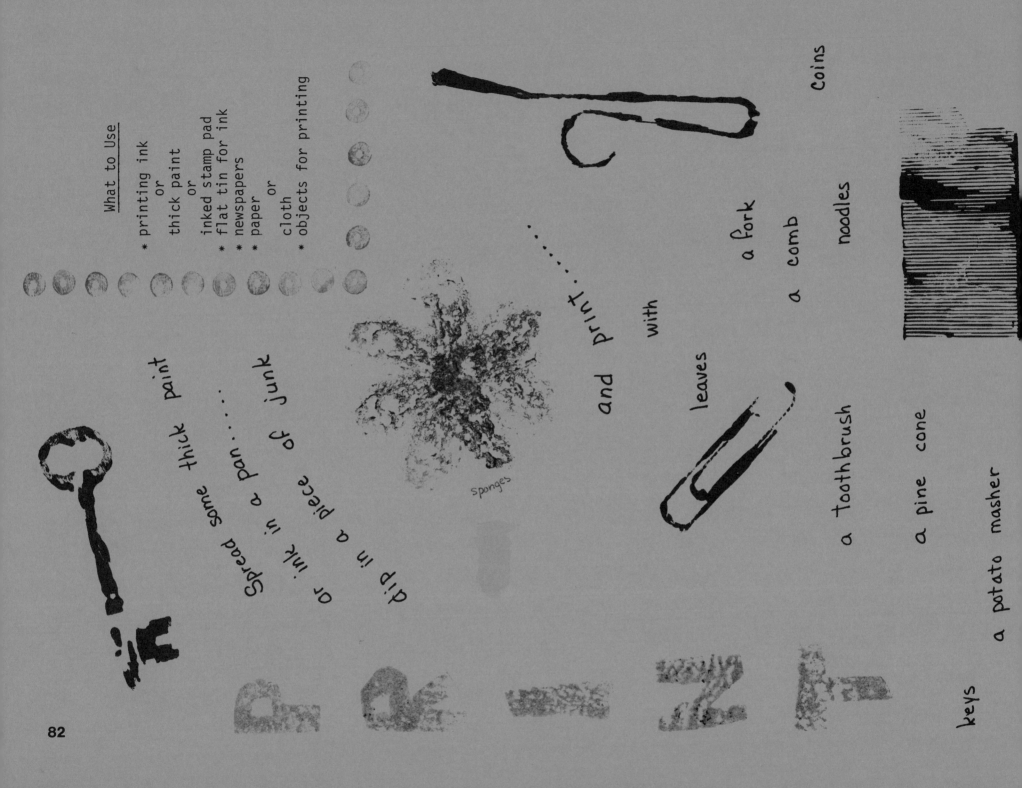

<u>What to Use</u>

* printing ink
  or
  thick paint
  or
  inked stamp pad
* flat tin for ink
* newspapers
* paper
  or
  cloth
* objects for printing

Spread some thick paint

or ink in a pan......

or a piece of junk

dip in a

and print ......

with

leaves

a fork

a comb

noodles

Coins

a toothbrush

a pine cone

a potato masher

keys

Sponges

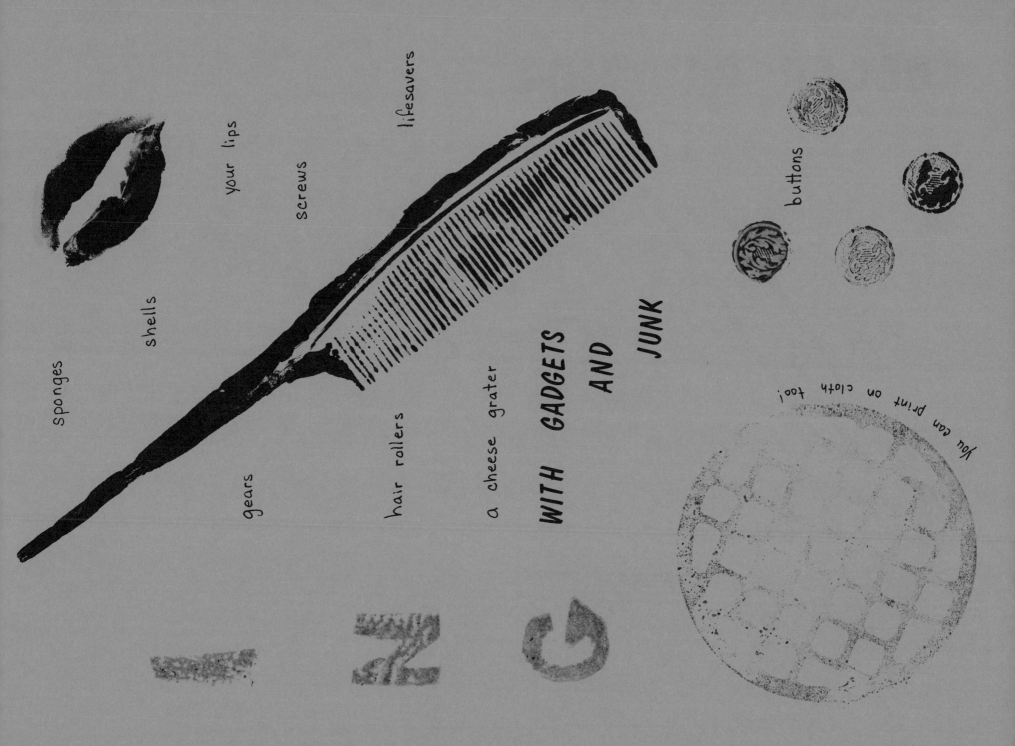

your lips

lifesavers

shells

screws

buttons

sponges

gears

hair rollers

a cheese grater

WITH GADGETS AND JUNK

You can print on cloth too!

ROLLER PRINTING

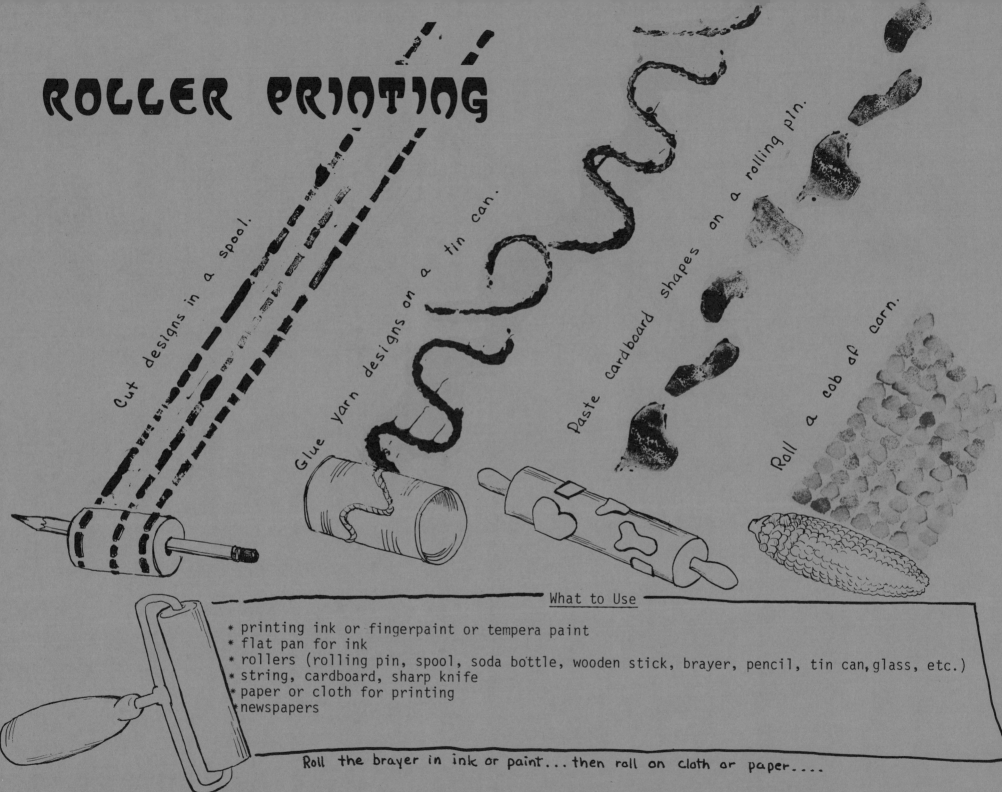

Cut designs in a spool.

Glue yarn designs on a tin can.

Paste cardboard shapes on a rolling pin.

Roll a cob of corn.

<u>What to Use</u>

* printing ink or fingerpaint or tempera paint
* flat pan for ink
* rollers (rolling pin, spool, soda bottle, wooden stick, brayer, pencil, tin can, glass, etc.)
* string, cardboard, sharp knife
* paper or cloth for printing
* newspapers

Roll the brayer in ink or paint . . . then roll on cloth or paper . . . .

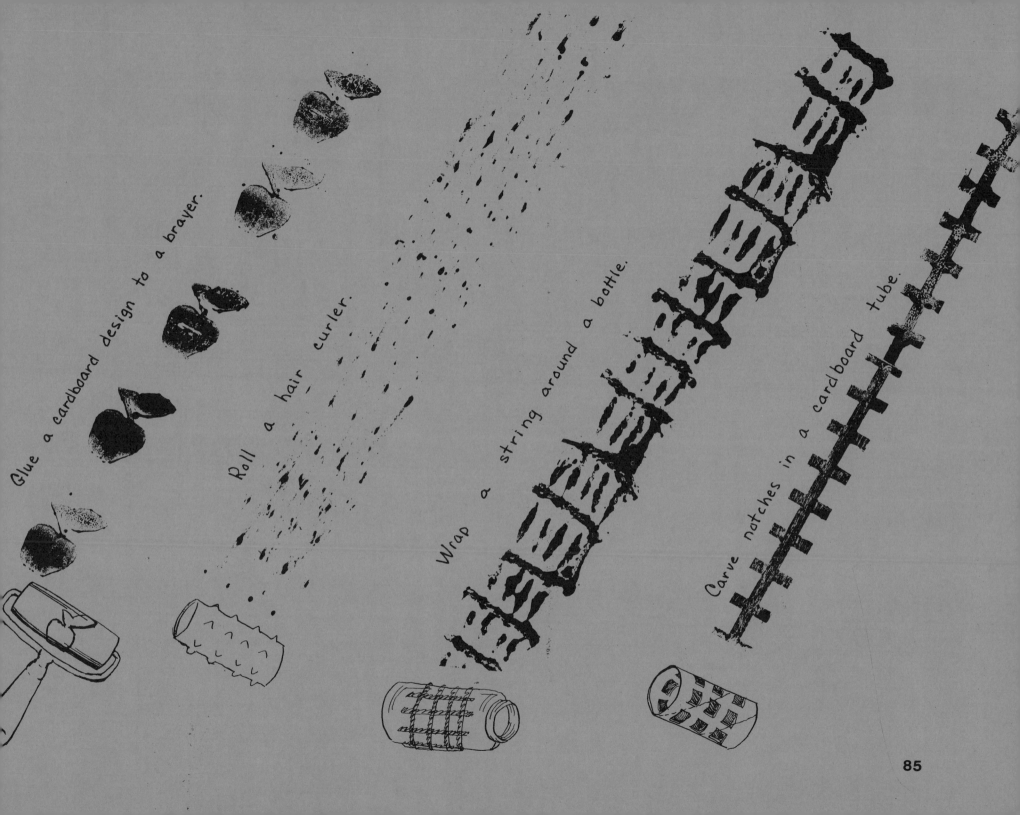

Glue a cardboard design to a brayer.

Roll a hair curler.

Wrap a string around a bottle.

Carve notches in a cardboard tube.

85

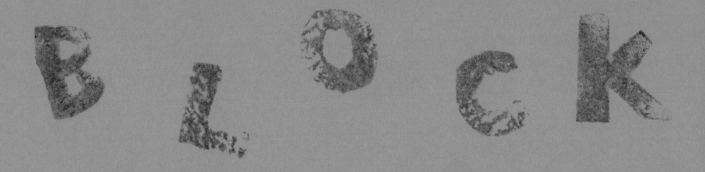
BLOCK

What to Do

For whatever kind of block you choose, the process is about the same.

1. Cover your work area with newspapers.

2. Plan a picture or design that will fit your block. Prepare the block in one of the ways shown here...(or try your own idea!)

3. Put some ink on the tile or glass. (We'll call this your ink slab.) Spread the ink on the slab with the roller until it is smooth.

4. Roll ink onto the printing block covering it evenly.

5. Print by placing a piece of paper over the block. Rub over the paper with your hand or with the back of a spoon.

OR

Print by pressing the inked block onto the paper.

6. Roll ink on the block for each time you print.

7. Wash all the tools or clean them with turpentine.

Carve a design

in soap

in wood

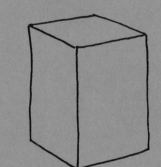
in a block of plaster

in a linoleum block

in wax

PRINTING

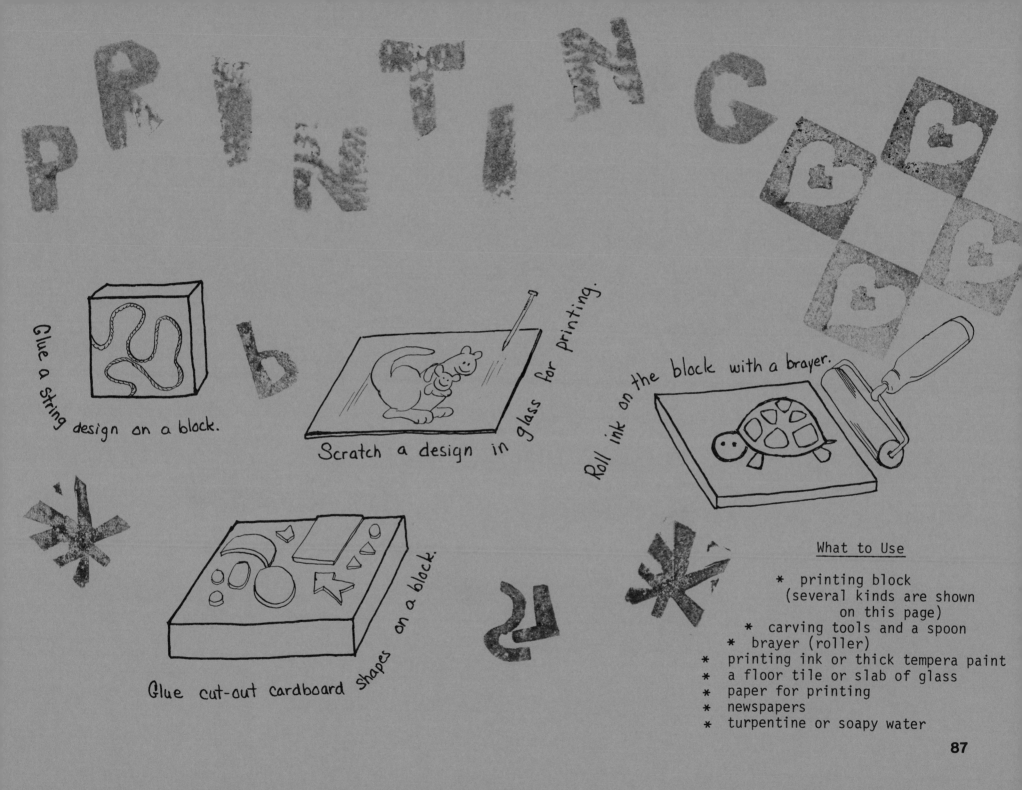

Glue a string design on a block.

Scratch a design in glass for printing.

Roll ink on the block with a brayer.

Glue cut-out cardboard shapes on a block.

What to Use

* printing block
  (several kinds are shown
    on this page)
* carving tools and a spoon
* brayer (roller)
* printing ink or thick tempera paint
* a floor tile or slab of glass
* paper for printing
* newspapers
* turpentine or soapy water

87

You can do Wonderful, Surprising Things

You can paint with skinny brushes

fingers or toes

fat brushes

sponges

cotton balls

Q-tips

rags

feathers

with Paint!

You can paint on boxes

on foil
(add a few drops of liquid detergent to paint)

No Stic Cellophane

Tin Foil

on paper plates

on old license plates (use acrylics)

-MINN-
YO·123

on stones

on wood (use acrylics)

on Shingles
(use acrylics)

on tissue paper

on paper bags

on bricks

on tin cans (with acrylics)

on glass
(with acrylics)

on cardboard

SOAP PAINTING

Paint-a-scene on a bar of soap!

Try any size, shape, or color soap.

What to Use

* bar of soap
* water color paints
* small brush
* large needle
* yarn

Try painting on some already-been-used bars too!

Create a soap-on-a-rope.
Dig a hole with a large needle and hang the bar from a rope of yarn.

The sad part about soap scenes is: they wash off!

SCREEN PAINTING

Try it with white shoe polish on black paper!

What to Use

* a piece of screen
  or a metal strainer
* tempera paints
  or food coloring
  or ink
* an old toothbrush
* dishes for paint
* drawing paper
* newspapers

What to Do

1. Cover your work area with newspaper.

2. Hold the screen over a piece of paper.

3. Dip the toothbrush in paint and brush it on the screen so that the paint splatters onto the paper.

4. Wash the brush and "splatter" with a new color.

OR

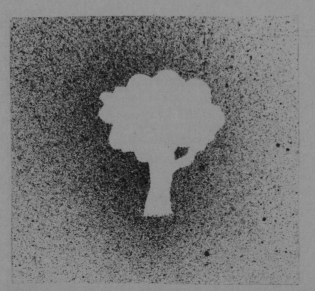

1. Lay a cut-out shape (or objects or leaves) on top of the paper.

2. Splatter paint over the paper. The part you have covered will stay free from paint.

3. You can move the objects and repeat with a different color.

Squashed Paint

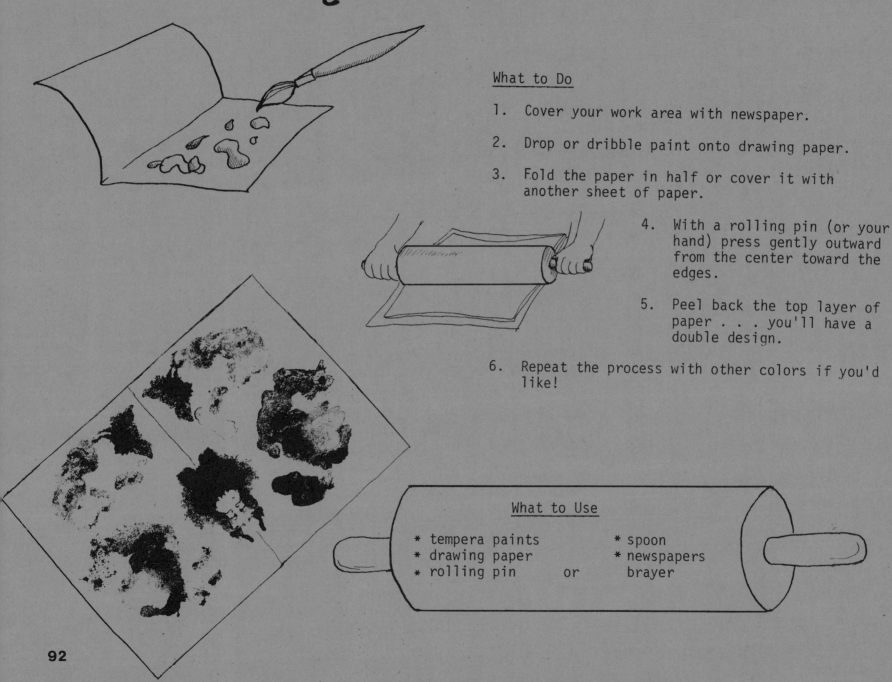

What to Do

1. Cover your work area with newspaper.

2. Drop or dribble paint onto drawing paper.

3. Fold the paper in half or cover it with another sheet of paper.

4. With a rolling pin (or your hand) press gently outward from the center toward the edges.

5. Peel back the top layer of paper . . . you'll have a double design.

6. Repeat the process with other colors if you'd like!

What to Use

* tempera paints   * spoon
* drawing paper   * newspapers
* rolling pin   or   brayer

Body Painting

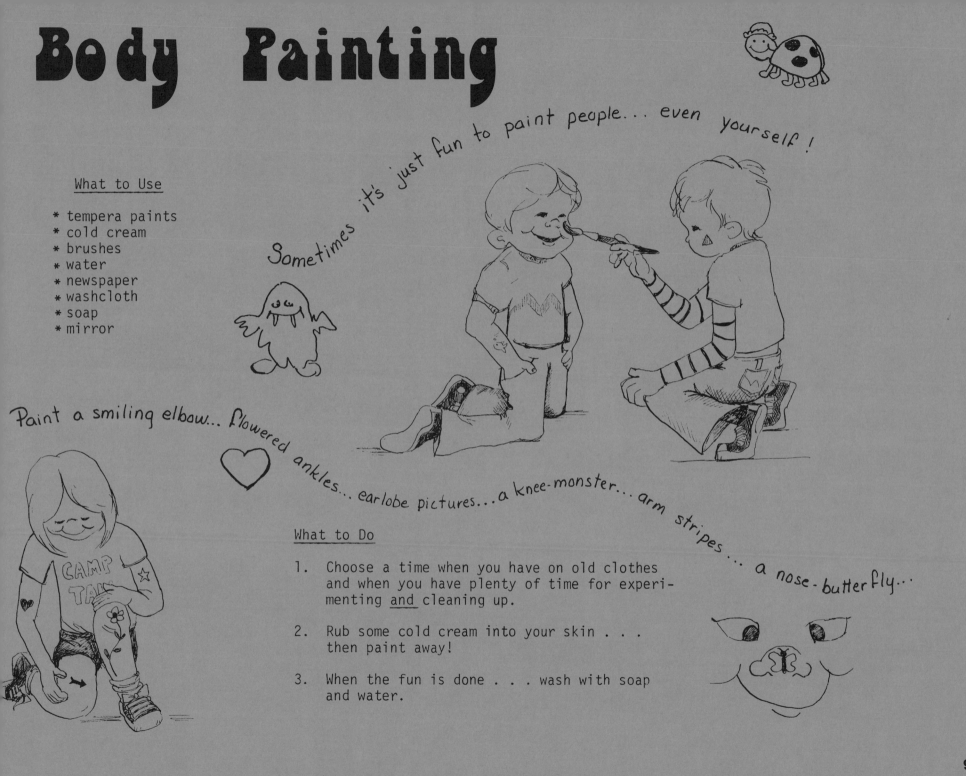

Sometimes it's just fun to paint people... even yourself!

What to Use

* tempera paints
* cold cream
* brushes
* water
* newspaper
* washcloth
* soap
* mirror

Paint a smiling elbow... flowered ankles... earlobe pictures... a knee-monster... arm stripes... a nose-butterfly...

What to Do

1. Choose a time when you have on old clothes and when you have plenty of time for experimenting and cleaning up.

2. Rub some cold cream into your skin . . . then paint away!

3. When the fun is done . . . wash with soap and water.

Wet Watercolors

1. Soak a piece of drawing paper in water. Hold it up to drip for a few seconds.

2. Place the wet paper on newspaper.

3. Paint right away on the wet paper with watercolors. The colors will blend together and blur as you paint.

4. When the painting is dry, you can add fine lines and details with a dark pen.

What to Use

* water color paints
* drawing paper
* brush
* pan of water
* newspapers
* fine-point marking pen

Use your feet!

If you can fingerpaint...
why can't you footpaint?
Try it!
You'll like it!

Don't forget to take off your shoes and socks!

What to Use

* tempera paints
  or
* finger paints
* flat pan
* wrapping paper
  or
* shelf paper
* your feet
* sponge
* newspapers

What to Do

1. Spread a big piece of shelf or wrapping paper on top of newspapers.

2. Pour some paint into a flat pan.

3. Dip your toe in and use it as a painting tool.
   OR
4. Make prints with your whole foot.

4. Clean off your foot with a wet sponge.

Foot paint to music!

Mothers and fathers and teachers will be happiest if you get permission before you start this!

And please don't forget to wash your feet and clean up any footprints that wandered off the paper!

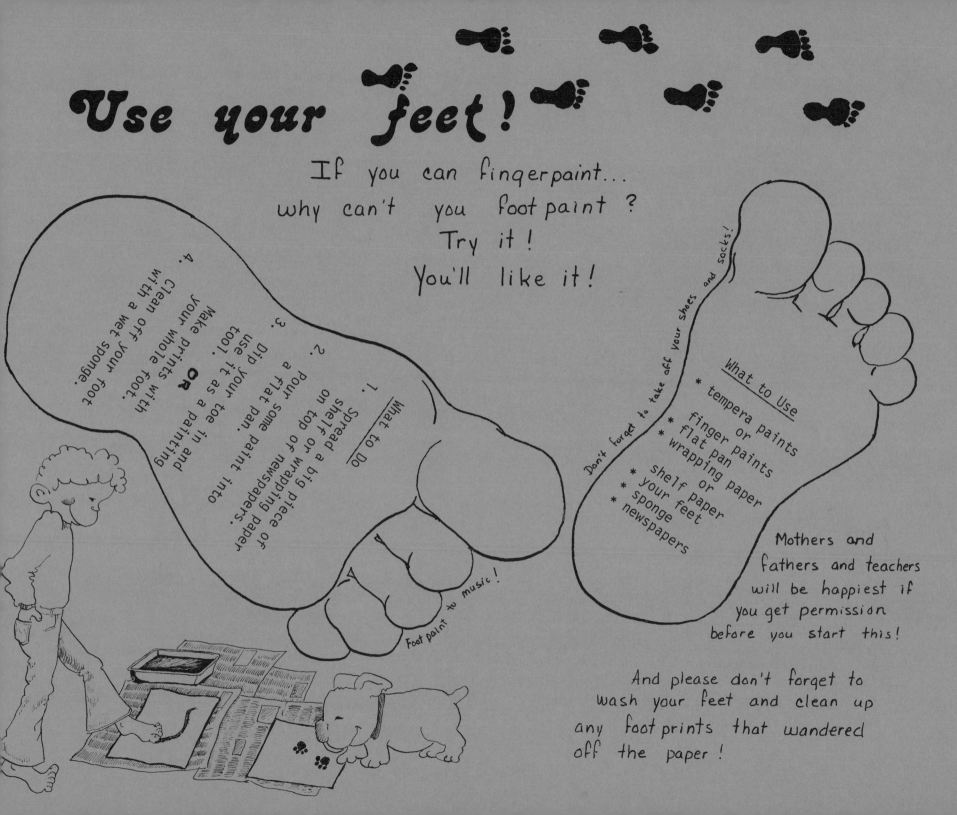

95

STRING PAINTINGS

What to Use

* drawing paper
* tempera paints
* string
* paint
* container
* brush
* newspaper

Try white paint on dark paper, too!

What to Do

1. Fold the drawing paper in half. Then open it up.

2. Cover a piece of string with paint. Use the brush to coat the string.

3. Lay the paint-y string on one half of the paper, leaving the ends hanging over the edge. Curl and twist the string as you lay it on the paper.

4. Fold the other half of the paper over the string. Hold it down firmly with one hand.

5. Use your other hand to pull the string out from between the layers of paper. You may pull one or both ends at the same time.

6. If you want another color, repeat the steps after the first color is dry.

96

Paint with Bubbles!

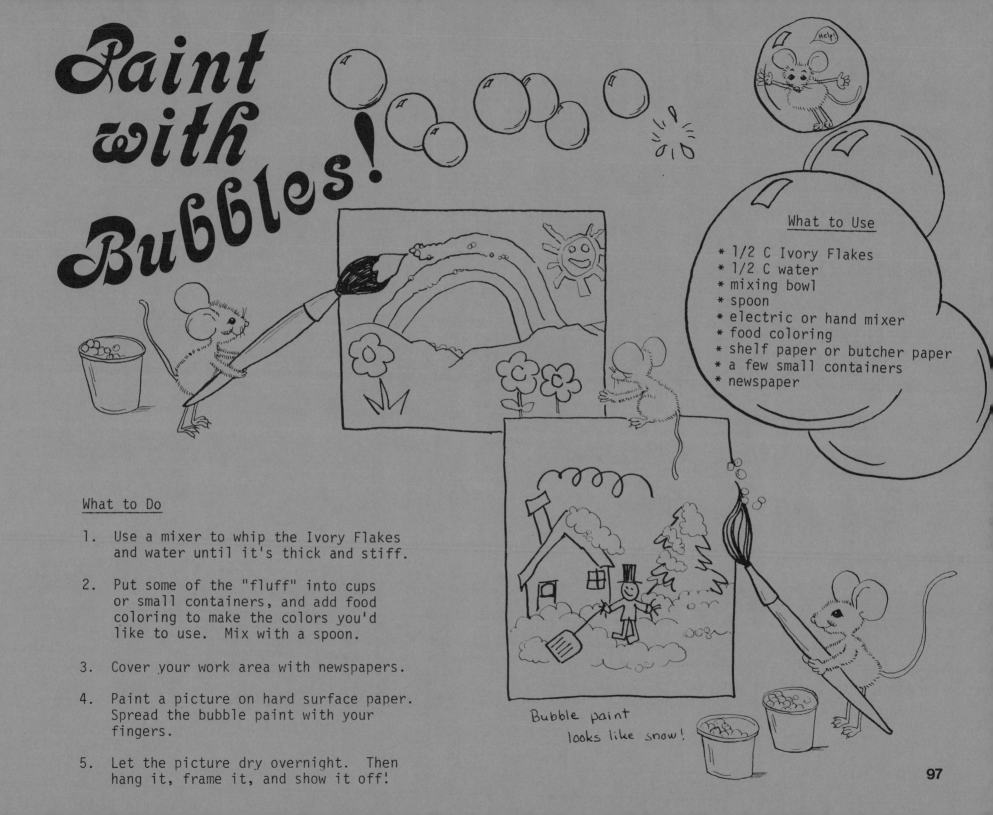

What to Use

* 1/2 C Ivory Flakes
* 1/2 C water
* mixing bowl
* spoon
* electric or hand mixer
* food coloring
* shelf paper or butcher paper
* a few small containers
* newspaper

What to Do

1. Use a mixer to whip the Ivory Flakes and water until it's thick and stiff.

2. Put some of the "fluff" into cups or small containers, and add food coloring to make the colors you'd like to use. Mix with a spoon.

3. Cover your work area with newspapers.

4. Paint a picture on hard surface paper. Spread the bubble paint with your fingers.

5. Let the picture dry overnight. Then hang it, frame it, and show it off!

Bubble paint looks like snow!

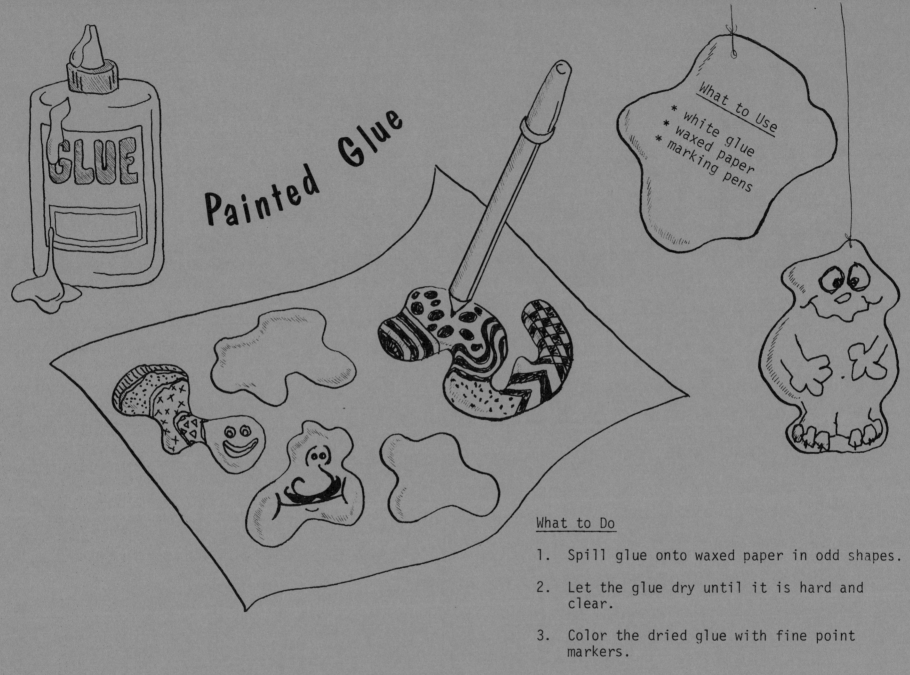

Painted Glue

What to Use
* white glue
* waxed paper
* marking pens

What to Do

1. Spill glue onto waxed paper in odd shapes.

2. Let the glue dry until it is hard and clear.

3. Color the dried glue with fine point markers.

4. Remove the shapes from the paper. You can hang them in windows . . . from mobiles . . . even around your neck!

Here's a mud-luscious way
to create crazy designs,
build beautiful blobs, and
scoop together scrumptious scenes!

And the mess doesn't matter
...if you work outside!

MUD-ART

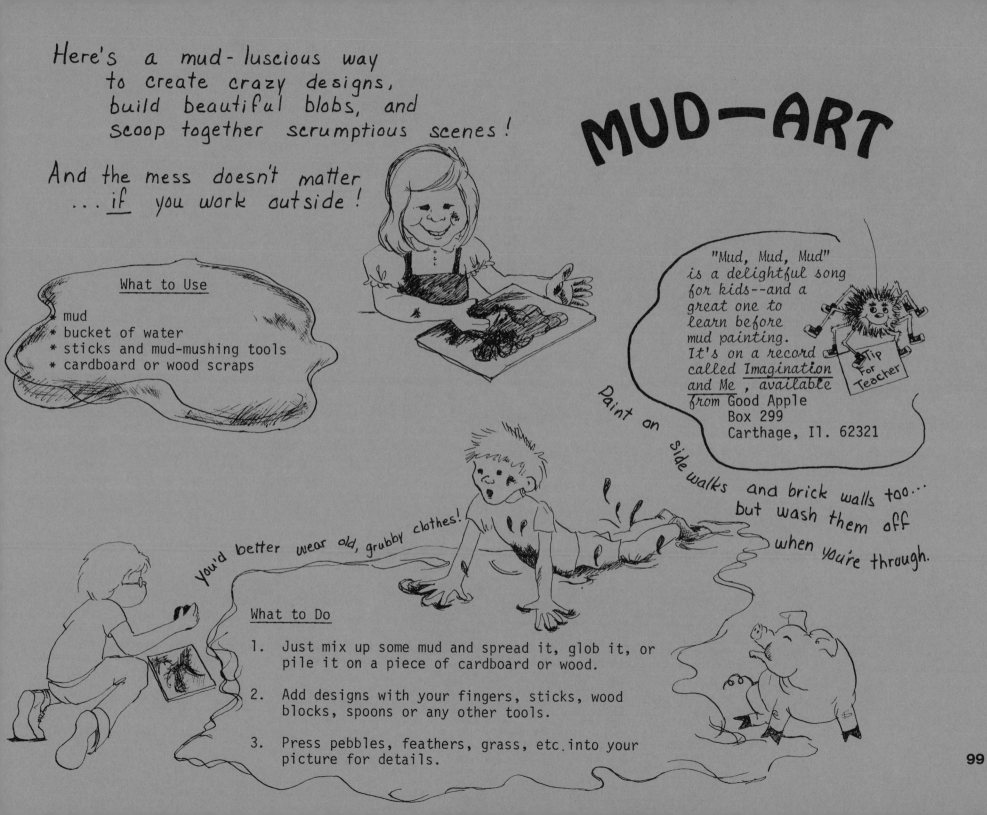

What to Use

* mud
* bucket of water
* sticks and mud-mushing tools
* cardboard or wood scraps

"Mud, Mud, Mud"
is a delightful song
for kids--and a
great one to
learn before
mud painting.
It's on a record
called Imagination
and Me , available
from Good Apple
Box 299
Carthage, Il. 62321

Tip For Teacher

Paint on sidewalks and brick walls too...
but wash them off
when you're through.

You'd better wear old, grubby clothes!

What to Do

1. Just mix up some mud and spread it, glob it, or
   pile it on a piece of cardboard or wood.

2. Add designs with your fingers, sticks, wood
   blocks, spoons or any other tools.

3. Press pebbles, feathers, grass, etc. into your
   picture for details.

finger painting

Make designs with your whole hand or your fingers or your fingernails or your fist or the side of your hand.

What to Do

1. Mix food coloring or tempera into liquid starch to make different colors of finger paint.

2. Dip your paper in water to wet it, and lay it on newspaper.

3. Spread the paint with your fingers.

Use other tools too... a sponge ...a comb... a brush ... a table knife.... erasers.... a fork ... elbows ...

4. Use your finger painting to
   wrap a gift
   or . . . cover a book
   or . . . fold around important papers
   or . . . frame a special poem
   or . . . wallpaper a door
   or . . . cut into flowers
   or . . . what else can you think of?

There are more finger paint
recipes in the appendix
of this book.

Squeeze Painting

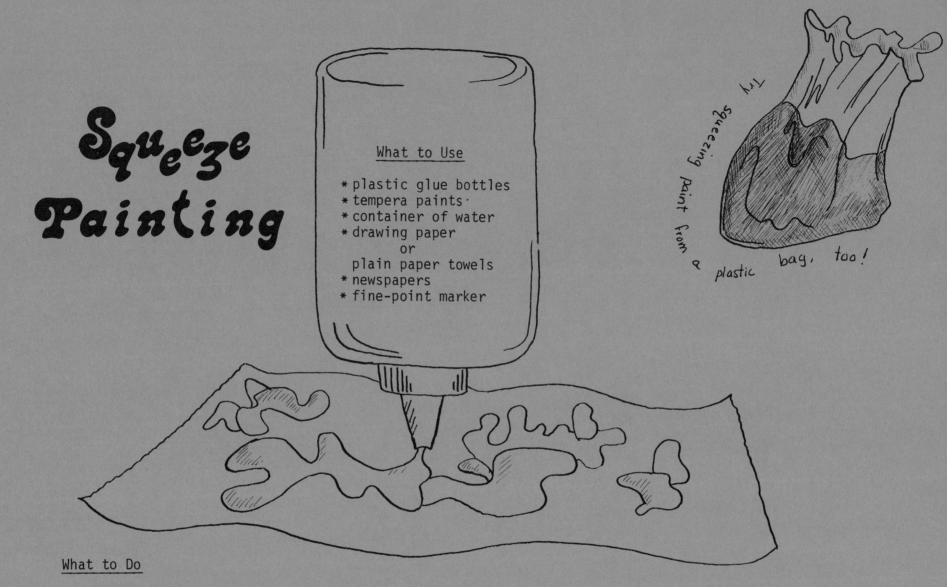

What to Use

* plastic glue bottles
* tempera paints
* container of water
* drawing paper
    or
  plain paper towels
* newspapers
* fine-point marker

Try squeezing paint from a plastic bag, too!

What to Do

1. Dampen a piece of paper or paper toweling and lay it on newspaper.

2. Squeeze some "globs" of paint from a plastic bottle.

3. Let the paint soak and spread for a few seconds, then add other colors.

4. When the paint and paper are dry, add designs or details with a fine point marker.

SPRAY SCENES

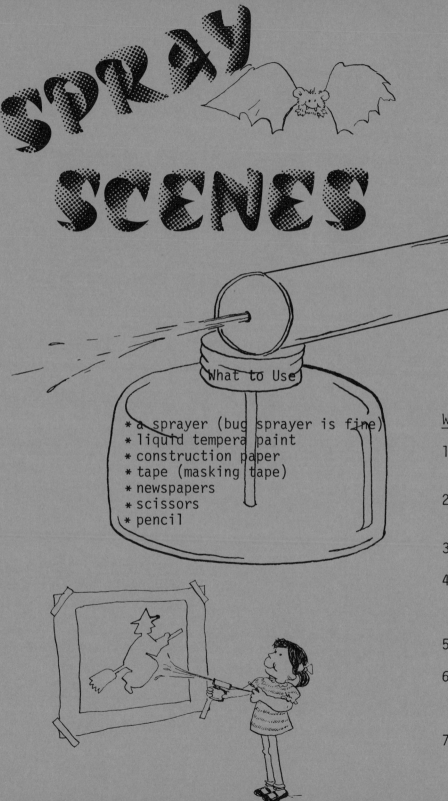

One of the finest spray paintings
I've ever seen was a huge Halloween
scene done by a fourth grade class...
sprayed with iridescent poster paints
and topped with an original spooky poem.

Tip
For
Teacher

Cut holes for eyes.

What to Use

* a sprayer (bug sprayer is fine)
* liquid tempera paint
* construction paper
* tape (masking tape)
* newspapers
* scissors
* pencil

What to Do

1. Tape some newspapers to a wall or to some windows.

2. Fill a sprayer with liquid paint (or you can use spray paint from a can).

3. Cut a shape from scrap paper.

4. Roll a piece of tape, stick it to the back, and place the shape on a piece of construction paper.

5. Tape the construction paper to the newspaper.

6. Stand about a foot away and spray the picture. You can spray different parts with different colors or one color on top of another.

7. When the paint is dry, remove the cut-out shape.

patriotic paintings

Stars and stripes make grand designs... and they don't always have to be in flags!

What to Use

*bright red tempera paint
*bright blue tempera paint
*white tempera paint
*brush and water
*paper *pencil
*scissors *newspapers

What to Do

1. Cut any shape from drawing paper.

2. Paint a bright, bold, red-white-and-blue design using stripes and stars.

If you live in a country other than the United States, use the colors and symbols from your flag.

104

Foil Etchings

What to Use

* tape
* cardboard
* tin foil
* dark-colored tempera paint
* liquid soap
* brush
* nail or pencil
* colored paper or fabric for frame
* glue
* Q-tips

Try wrinkling the foil first!

What to Do

1. Tape a piece of tin foil to lightweight cardboard.

2. Add 2 or 3 drops of liquid soap to dark-colored tempera paint.

3. Brush paint over the whole piece of foil.

4. Let the paint dry.

5. Use a nail or pencil to scratch a picture or design through the paint. Don't scratch so hard that you tear the foil.

6. Cut a frame from colorful paper or fabric and glue it around your scratched masterpiece!

Oil Swirls

...an extra fancy, colorful way to decorate paper or bottles...

Try it with eggs.

What to Use

* oil paints
* turpentine
* dishpan or pail of water
* stick or spoon for stirring
* small cans or milk cartons
* paper
    or
  a bottle
    or
  hard boiled eggs and a wire for
      dipping eggs
* lots of newspaper

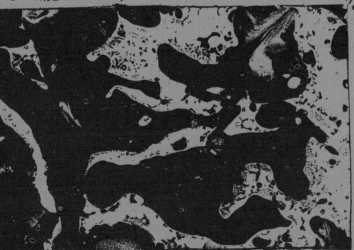

You can use more than one color at a time... or dip more than once in different colors.

What to Do

1. Spread lots of newspaper over your work
    area.

2. Mix a little turpentine with oil paint until it is thin
    enough to pour.

3. Pour some paint on the water and stir (but don't stir much!)

4. Lay a piece of paper on the surface of the water and gently
    pick it up. Lay it on newspaper to dry.

OR

Dip a bottle or an egg all the way into the water, and
quickly remove it.

106

Try these ideas, too!

Dip up some oil-y water and drip it onto an old sheet. This makes good monster shapes!

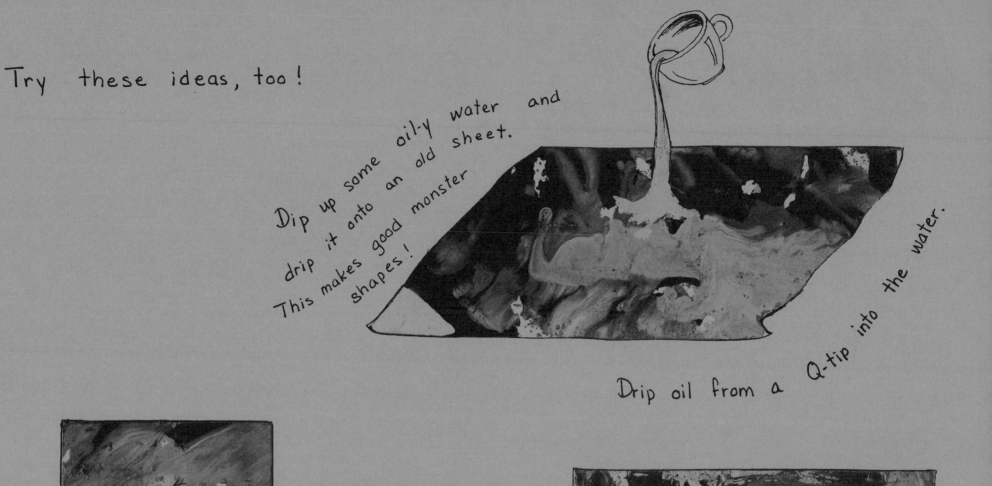

Drip oil from a Q-tip into the water.

Draw a scene on swirl paper when it's dry or outline figures with black ink.

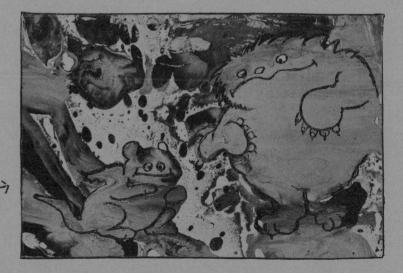

Pudding Painting

Fingerpaint with pudding....

and eat the "paint" while you work!

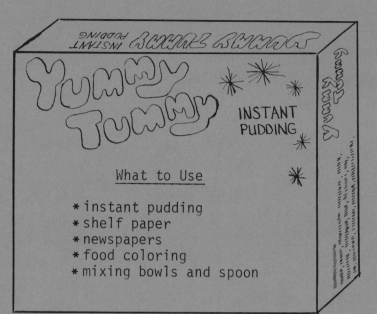

What to Use

* instant pudding
* shelf paper
* newspapers
* food coloring
* mixing bowls and spoon

What to Do

Mix instant pudding - any flavor - according to the directions on the package. Then use the pudding the way you'd use fingerpaint.

Don't forget to cover your work place with newspapers.

Clean up is easy! Just lick the bowl and then your fingers.

Add food coloring to vanilla pudding to get lots of colors.

Chapter 4

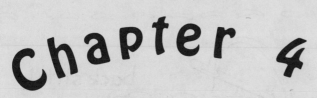

Things to do

with

cloth,

yarn,

& string

Stitchery

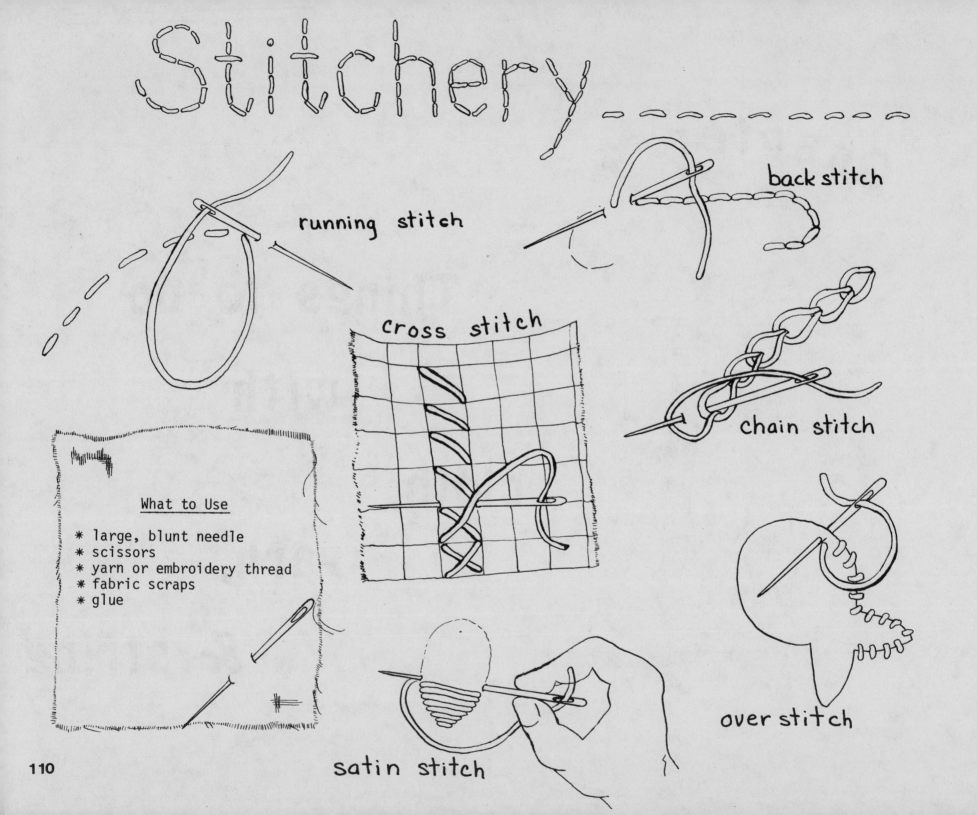

running stitch

back stitch

cross stitch

chain stitch

What to Use

* large, blunt needle
* scissors
* yarn or embroidery thread
* fabric scraps
* glue

over stitch

satin stitch

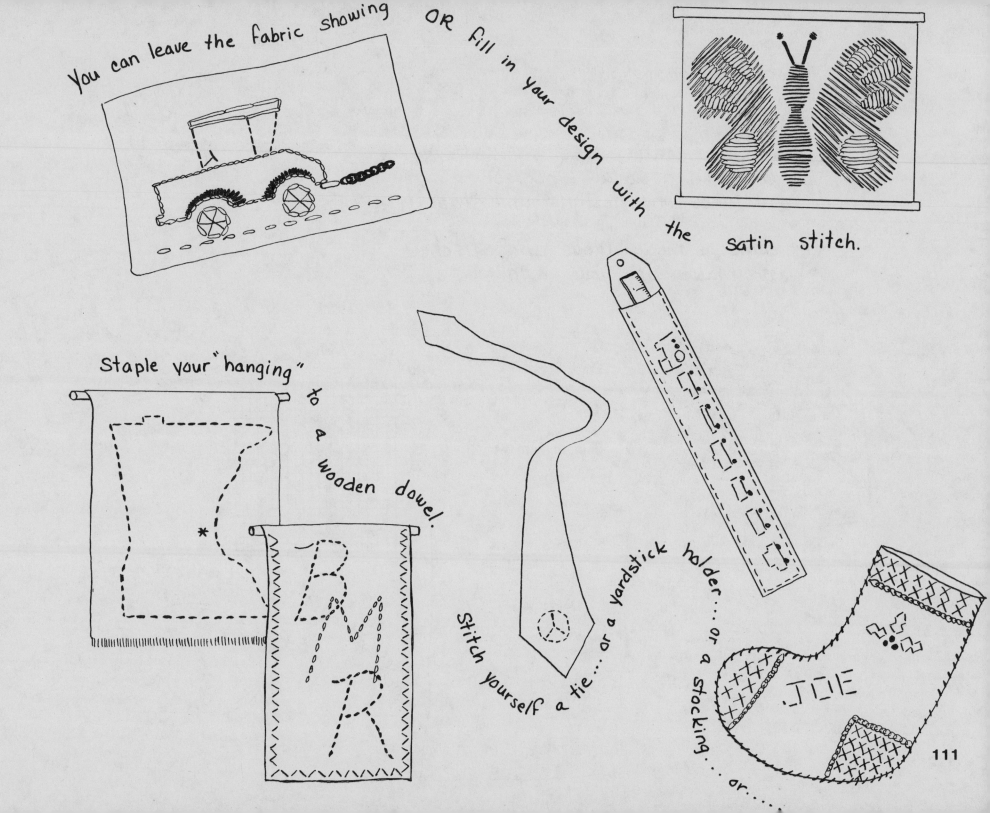

You can leave the fabric showing OR fill in your design with the satin stitch.

Staple your "hanging" to a wooden dowel.

Stitch yourself a tie... or a yardstick holder...or a stocking... or.....

111

and more stitchery

You can stitch up all kinds of
pictures and designs and tapestries.

Try some of these ideas and stitches,
or make up your own.

Try stitching on cotton or burlap or velvet or felt or wire or even on styrofoam meat trays!

Glue shapes on fabric and stitch around them.

Stuff parts of the picture with cotton before you sew the bottom edge.

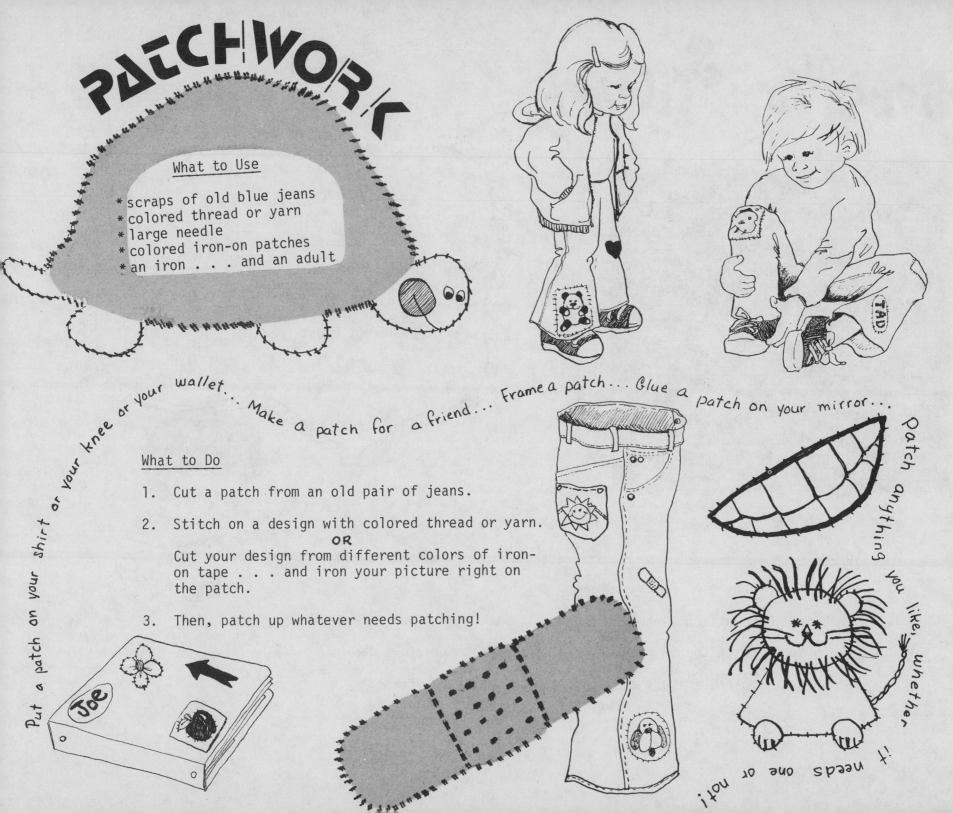

PATCHWORK

What to Use

* scraps of old blue jeans
* colored thread or yarn
* large needle
* colored iron-on patches
* an iron . . . and an adult

Put a patch on your shirt or your knee or your wallet... Make a patch for a friend... Frame a patch... Glue a patch on your mirror... Patch anything you like, whether it needs one or not!

What to Do

1. Cut a patch from an old pair of jeans.

2. Stitch on a design with colored thread or yarn.

   OR

   Cut your design from different colors of iron-on tape . . . and iron your picture right on the patch.

3. Then, patch up whatever needs patching!

Scribble Stitchery

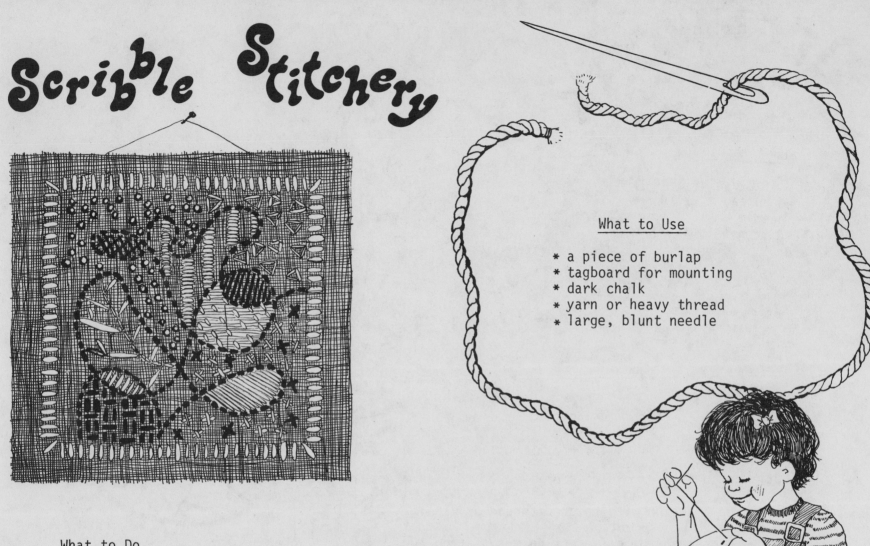

What to Use

* a piece of burlap
* tagboard for mounting
* dark chalk
* yarn or heavy thread
* large, blunt needle

What to Do

1. Use chalk to "scribble" on the burlap.

2. With black yarn, stitch along the chalked lines. Use a running stitch.

3. Fill in some of the spaces with colored stitching to create a design.

4. Glue your scribble stitchery to a tagboard or cardboard "frame."

FABRIC BLOSSOMS

Make your own garden of flowers that never die...

...all from scraps and bits of fabric.

What to Use

* fabric scraps
* pipe cleaners
* scissors
* white glue
* pencil
* paper
* green floral tape

What to Do

1. Draw a pattern for the petals and cut it out of paper.

2. Trace around the pattern onto the fabric and cut 6 petals.

3. Choose pipe cleaners of a color that matches the fabric. Glue a pipe cleaner around the edge of each petal you've drawn.

4. Leave one long end on each pipe cleaner. Cut away the fabric from the outside of each petal.

5. Make a center for the flower: cut a circle of material, wrap it around a bit of material, or cotton.

6. Put the flower together: hold the stem ends and group the petals around the center.

7. Wrap one end of a long pipe cleaner tightly around the stems.

8. Wrap tape around all the wires.

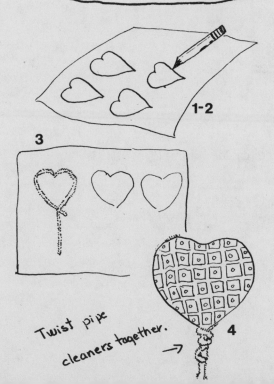

1-2

3

Twist pipe cleaners together. ➔

4

6-7

5

Flower center - circle stuffed with cotton.

115

THE SHEET SCENE

What to Use

* a piece of an old sheet
       or
  an old pillow case
* tempera paints
* brush
* water
* newspaper
* cardboard
* piece of printed fabric
* glue

What to Do

1. Wrap a piece of printed fabric around a square of cardboard. Staple, tape, or glue the edges on the back.

2. Paint a picture on a piece of sheet with thick tempera paint. Use a piece of sheet smaller than the fabric-covered cardboard frame you've just made.

3. When the painting is dry, spread glue around the edges on the back and glue it on the frame.

3-D creations

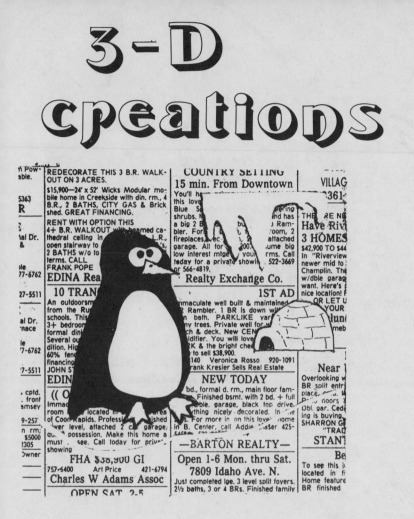

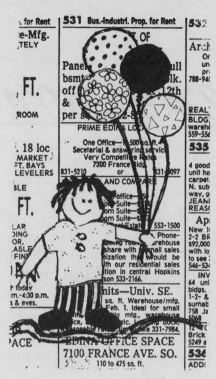

What to Use

* cardboard
* newspaper (a page with small print)
* scraps of fabric
    yarn
    braid
    rick rack
    trim
* pencil
* glue

What to Do

1. Cover a large cardboard shape with newspaper. Wrap the newspaper around the edges and glue it on the back.

2. Plan a picture or design. For each part of the design draw and cut a cardboard shape.

3. Wrap each cardboard shape with fabric. Glue it down on the back.

4. Glue the wrapped shapes on the newspaper-covered background.

5. Glue on braid, yarn or trim to outline the shapes or to add decoration.

SILKSCREENING

<u>What to Use</u>

* silkscreen frame
    or embroidery hoop
    or an old picture frame
    or a shoebox lid

* fabric: fine silk. old nylon
    stocking, cheese cloth
* drawing paper
* fingerpaint or a water base
    ink
* stapler
* tape
* scissors
* squeegee or a small piece
    of sturdy cardboard
* stencil knife
* clothespins
* newspapers
* rags
* water

A stencil is cut from paper.

A screen is prepared by tacking fabric to a frame.

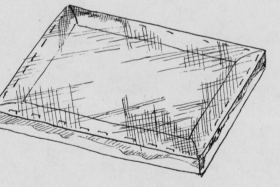

Ink or paint is pushed through the screen onto paper or fabric. The stencil, which lies between the screen and the paper, keeps ink from touching parts of the paper.

118

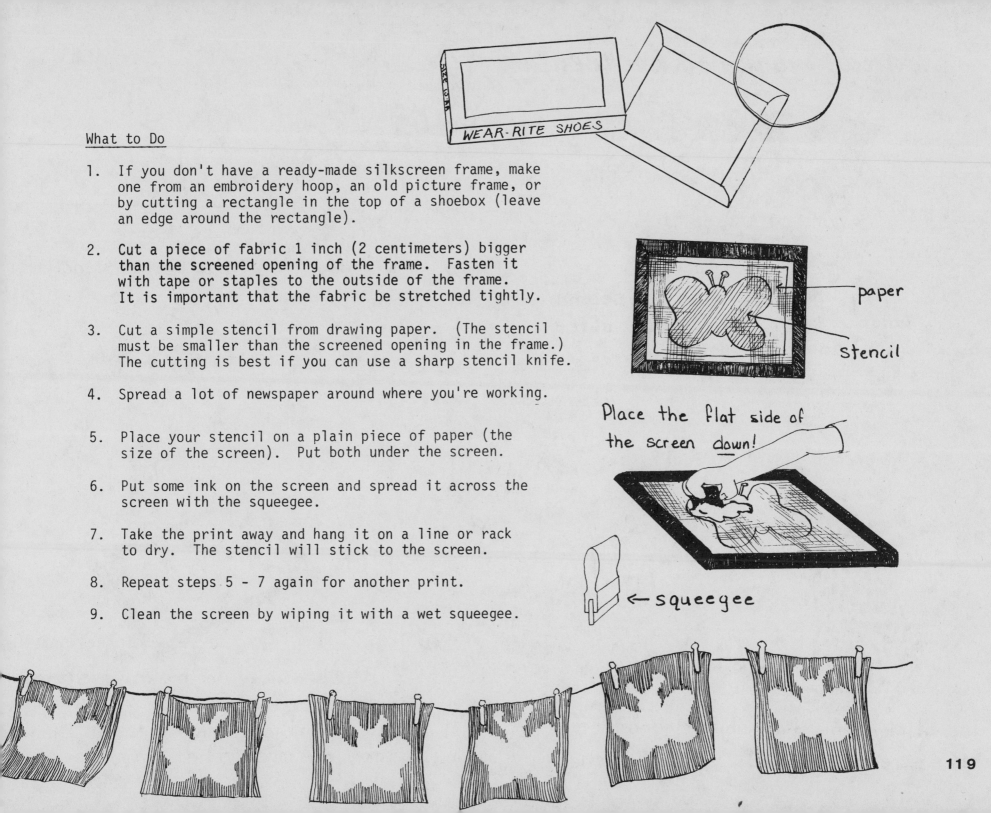

What to Do

1. If you don't have a ready-made silkscreen frame, make one from an embroidery hoop, an old picture frame, or by cutting a rectangle in the top of a shoebox (leave an edge around the rectangle).

2. Cut a piece of fabric 1 inch (2 centimeters) bigger than the screened opening of the frame. Fasten it with tape or staples to the outside of the frame. It is important that the fabric be stretched tightly.

3. Cut a simple stencil from drawing paper. (The stencil must be smaller than the screened opening in the frame.) The cutting is best if you can use a sharp stencil knife.

4. Spread a lot of newspaper around where you're working.

5. Place your stencil on a plain piece of paper (the size of the screen). Put both under the screen.

6. Put some ink on the screen and spread it across the screen with the squeegee.

7. Take the print away and hang it on a line or rack to dry. The stencil will stick to the screen.

8. Repeat steps 5 - 7 again for another print.

9. Clean the screen by wiping it with a wet squeegee.

paper

Stencil

Place the flat side of the screen down!

← squeegee

...and more silkscreening

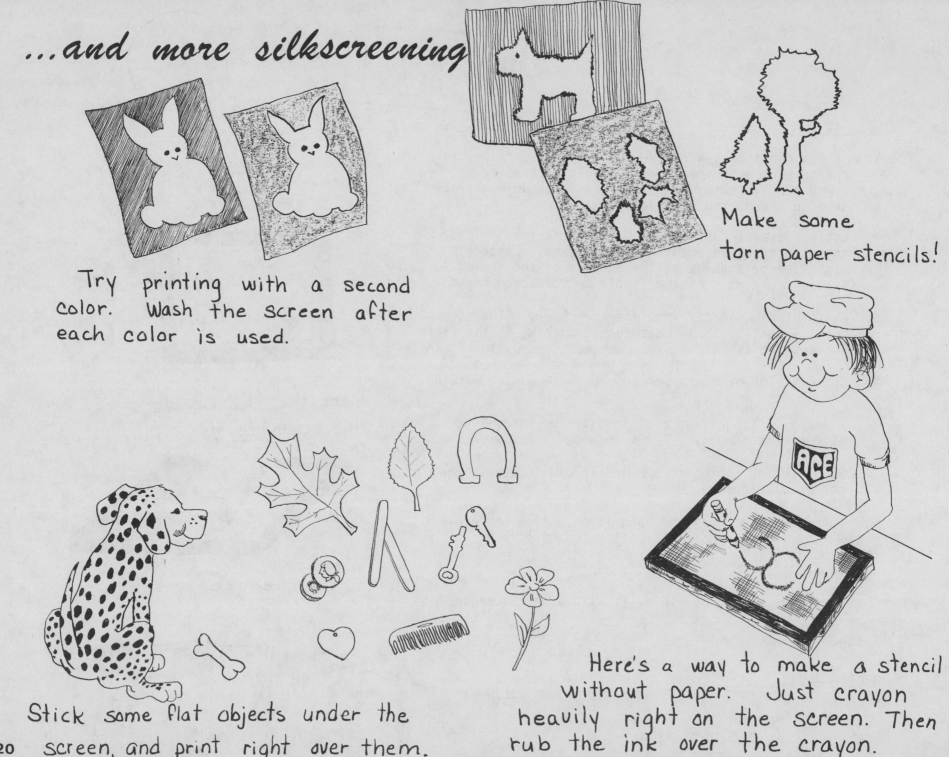

Try printing with a second color. Wash the screen after each color is used.

Make some torn paper stencils!

Stick some flat objects under the screen, and print right over them.

Here's a way to make a stencil without paper. Just crayon heavily right on the screen. Then rub the ink over the crayon.

ACE

OJOs

Ojo de Dios means "eye of God" in Spanish. The Mexican Indians made them for good luck pieces. Weave a colorful Ojo for yourself!

What to Use

* 2 ice cream sticks
  or 2 pencils
  or 2 sticks
  or 2 Q-tips
* colored yarn or string

What to Do

1. Cross the two sticks.

2. Tie the yarn in a knot around the sticks where they cross.

3. Weave the yarn over one stick, then around and under, then over the stick toward the next stick.

   Do this on each stick. Continue around the square doing the same thing for all the rows.

4. You can change colors whenever you'd like to. Start a new color by tying it to one of the sticks.

121

String Art

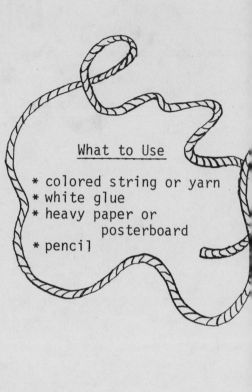

What to Use

* colored string or yarn
* white glue
* heavy paper or posterboard
* pencil

What to Do

1. Choose a piece of paper or posterboard for the background, and a few colors of yarn or string for the design.

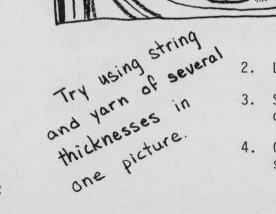

Try using string and yarn of several thicknesses in one picture.

2. Lightly sketch a pattern for the design.

3. Squirt glue along the major lines of the design (one at a time) and lay the string on the glue. Let the yarn come to the edge of the paper.

4. Continue gluing string to follow the lines of the design. You may want to leave some areas open for the background color to show through.

These Lollipops are NOT for Licking!

What to Do

1. Cut a lollipop shape from cardboard.

2. Spread a layer of glue on the cardboard.

3. Decorate the "lollipop" with yarn, rick rack, felt, ribbon, buttons or other trims.

4. Glue a stick to the back.

5. Please don't try to eat this lollipop! But you might write a happy message on the back and give it to a friend. Or you could make several small ones and hang them on a tree for decoration!

SUPER SPINNER

To make it spin:

Hold one end in each hand. Twist the strings to wind it up.
Spread your arms apart...
Bring them together...
Apart...
Together...
and
your spinner
will
spin!

* string
* cardboard
* a fat needle
* crayons, paints or markers
* a compass for making a circle
* scissors

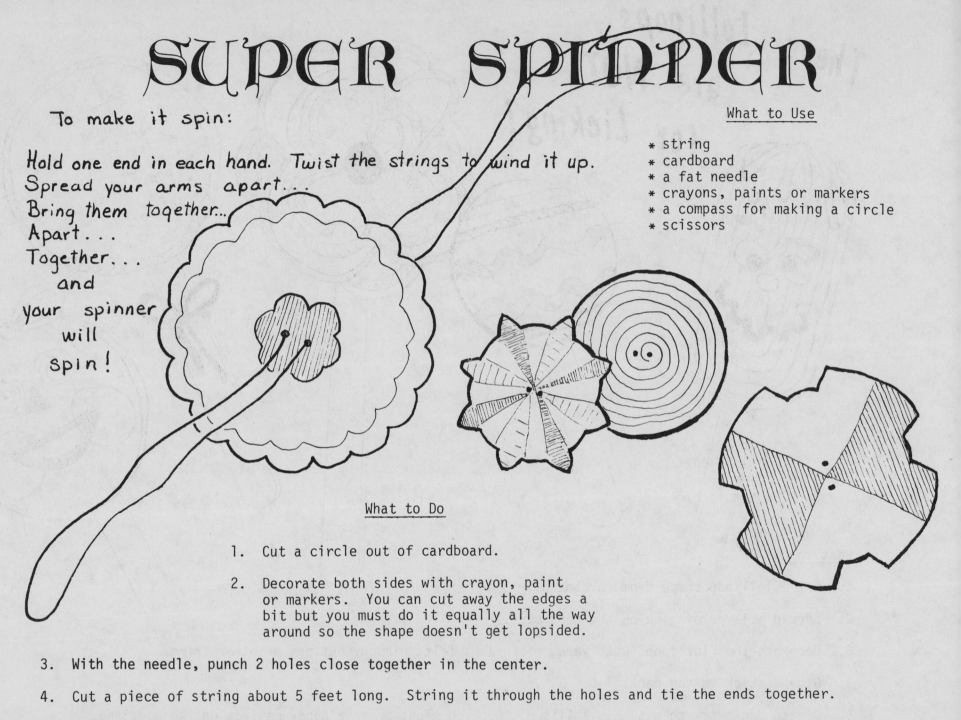

What to Do

1. Cut a circle out of cardboard.

2. Decorate both sides with crayon, paint or markers. You can cut away the edges a bit but you must do it equally all the way around so the shape doesn't get lopsided.

3. With the needle, punch 2 holes close together in the center.

4. Cut a piece of string about 5 feet long. String it through the holes and tie the ends together.

5. Keep the spinner in the center . . . and spin!

Wet Yarn Sculpture

What to Use

* fat yarn (rug yarn)
* white glue
* water
* can or cup
* waxed paper
* pencil
* drawing paper
* newspaper
* paper clips

What to Do

1. Draw a simple picture or design on paper. Every line in the design <u>must</u> touch other lines!

like this —   NOT like this —

2. Mix 2 parts glue with 1 part water in a cup or can.

3. Spread newspaper on your work area.

4. Lay waxed paper over your drawing. Clip the papers together.

5. Cut a piece of yarn the length of the outside edge.

6. Soak the yarn in the glue. Squeeze it out some so that it doesn't drip.

7. Lay the wet yarn over the outline.

8. Cut, soak, and lay yarn for the other lines.

MAKE SURE THE ENDS OF EACH PIECE OF YARN OVERLAP SLIGHTLY WITH ANOTHER PIECE. OTHERWISE YOUR SCULPTURE WILL NOT STICK TOGETHER WHEN IT DRIES. The sculpture will be sturdier if the yarn lines are double or triple.

9. Let the yarn picture dry overnight. The next day, remove it from the waxed paper. It will be stiff enough to hang.

If any spots are not sticking tightly together, lay it back on waxed paper, squeeze a big blob of glue on that spot, and let it dry.

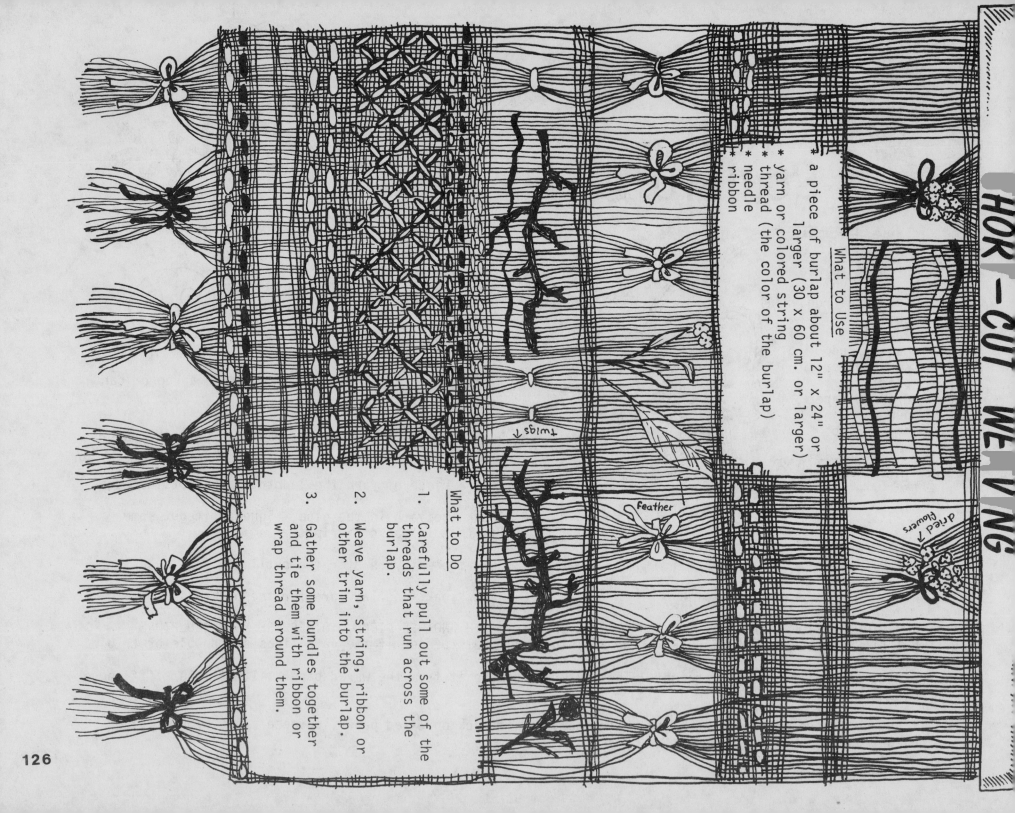

What to Use

* a piece of burlap about 12" x 24" or larger (30 x 60 cm. or larger)
* yarn or colored string
* thread (the color of the burlap)
* needle
* ribbon

What to Do

1. Carefully pull out some of the threads that run across the burlap.

2. Weave yarn, string, ribbon or other trim into the burlap.

3. Gather some bundles together and tie them with ribbon or wrap thread around them.

twigs

feather

dried flowers

126

GEOMETRIC STRING DESIGNS

You only use straight lines... but the designs look curved!

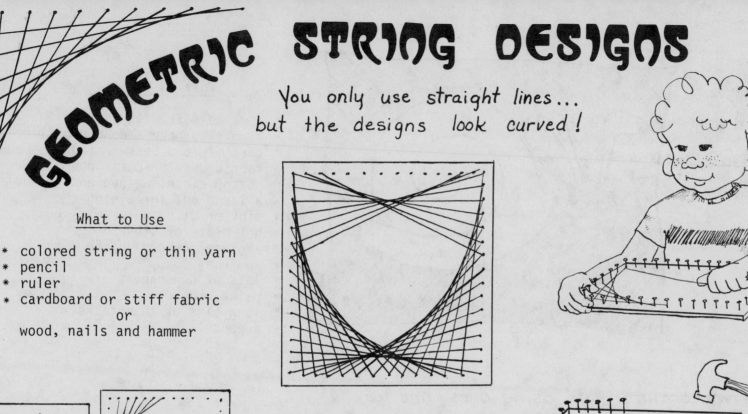

What to Use

* colored string or thin yarn
* pencil
* ruler
* cardboard or stiff fabric
  or
  wood, nails and hammer

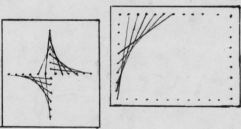

What to Do

You can string the lines
through holes on cardboard
or cloth.

OR

You can string the lines
from nails pounded around
the edges of a piece of wood.

1. With a pencil mark points around the edges of cardboard or wood or cloth piece.
   The points need to be an equal distance apart.

2. Pound a nail or poke a hole at each point.

3. Choose the colors of string you want to use.

4. Thread each string through a hole across to the second hole and tie it securely
   or wrap the string between 2 nails.

* some help from an adult
* 2 pots to make a double boiler
* paraffin and beeswax (equal amounts)
* fabric dyes or batik dyes
* cotton cloth (washed and ironed)
* a large pot for dyeing
* sink or dishpan for rinsing
* hot plate or stove
* a place for drying the cloth
* an iron
* lots of newspapers
* paint brushes
* long pins or thumbtacks
* a pencil

Batik is a method of decorating cloth using dyes and wax.

You paint melted wax on the cloth, and when the cloth is dyed, the waxed areas stay un-colored.

Please be careful when you batik... hot wax burns!

What to Do

1. Boil water in the bottom pot. Put the wax in the top pot to melt.

2. Tack a piece of fabric to a stack of newspapers. Sketch a simple design on the fabric. Use a pencil for the sketching.

3. Start with the lightest color. Brush melted wax over all the spots that you want to keep from getting touched by that color. Make sure the wax soaks all the way through the fabric.

128

4. Mix the dye in water. . .following the directions on the package. Add a pinch of salt.
   Start with the dye of the lightest color. Dye the darkest color last.

5. Soak the waxed cloth until it is as dark as you want it.

6. Rinse in cold water, blot on newspapers and hang up to dry.

7. Then brush with wax the areas you want to stay the color of your first dye.

8. Dye again, rinse and dry.

9. Wax the areas you want to stay the color of the second dye, rinse and dry. On the last dye,
   wrinkle the cloth before you dip it.

10. When you are finished dyeing, lay the cloth on a thick pad of newspapers and put a newspaper over
    the cloth. Press with a hot iron to remove the wax. Keep changing to a new newspaper until all
    the wax is melted out. Be careful not to iron right on the cloth . . . . You don't want a wax-y iron!

Tie-Dyeing

What to Do

Before you start:
- Spread newspapers all over your work area.
- Cover yourself with a smock.
- Make sure the cloth has been washed.
- Soak it in cold water for a few minutes then squeeze and blot the water out of it.
- Experiment with the dye . . . try it out on some small pieces.

1. Tie up the cloth. It needs to be tied tightly so the dye doesn't soak inside.

What to Use

* cotton cloth
* a large pot for dyeing (not aluminum)
* commercial dyes for fabric
* string or heavy thread
* large spoon
* water
* scissors
* newspapers
* clothespins
* adult help

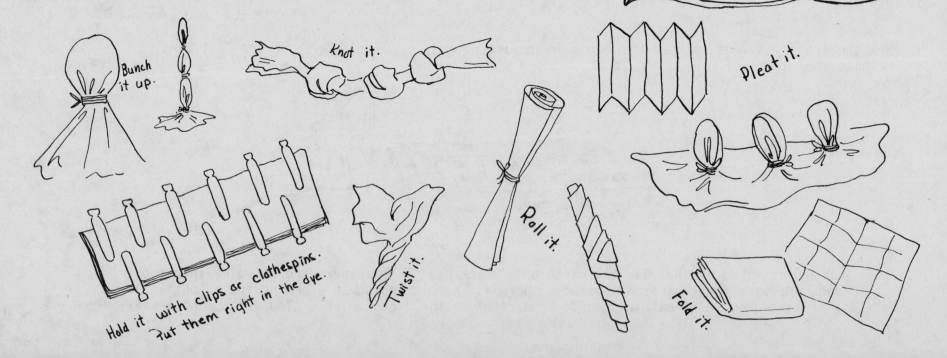

Bunch it up.

Knot it.

Pleat it.

Hold it with clips or clothespins. Put them right in the dye.

Twist it.

Roll it.

Fold it.

2. Dye the cloth according to the directions that come with your dye. Use a large spoon or stick to stir and handle the cloth.

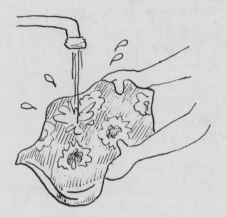

3. After dyeing rinse the cloth thoroughly in cold water. Untie it and rinse again. Squeeze out the water and drain the cloth on newspaper.

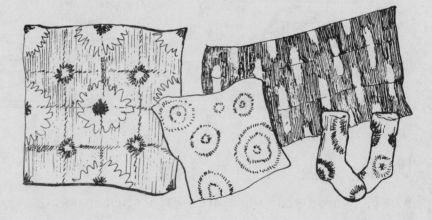

4. You can re-tie the cloth and dye it again with another color.

5. When you're finished dyeing, untie the cloth, rinse well; then cover the cloth with a newspaper and iron it.

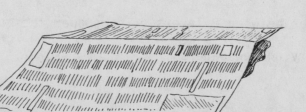

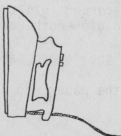

131

Dip & Dye

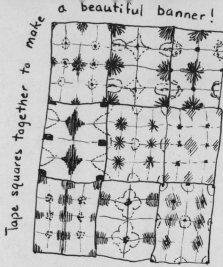

Tape squares together to make a beautiful banner!

Cover a book or frame a picture.

What to Use

* a muffin tin
* vegetable dyes (food coloring)
* rice paper
    or paper toweling
    or squares of an old sheet

* water
* newspapers

What to Do

1. Cover your work area with newspapers.

2. Pour food coloring into the muffin tin. For a lighter color, add a small amount of water.

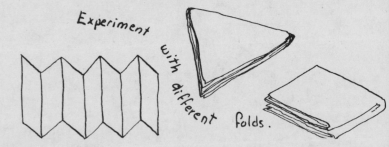

Experiment with different folds.

3. Fold squares of paper or cloth . . . . Experiment with different kinds of folds.

4. Dip a corner into the food coloring. Hold it a few seconds while the color soaks up. Turn it and dip another section.

5. Press the folded paper between 2 layers of newspaper to squeeze out extra dye.

6. Open the paper and dry on newspapers.

Chapter 5

Things to carve, mold & sculpt

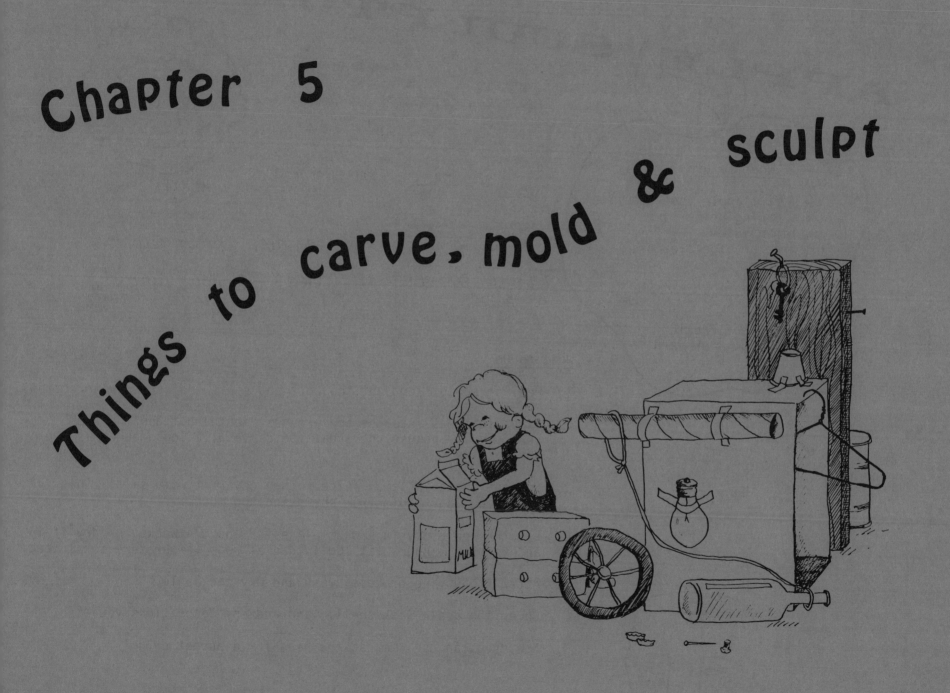

APPLE SCULPTURE

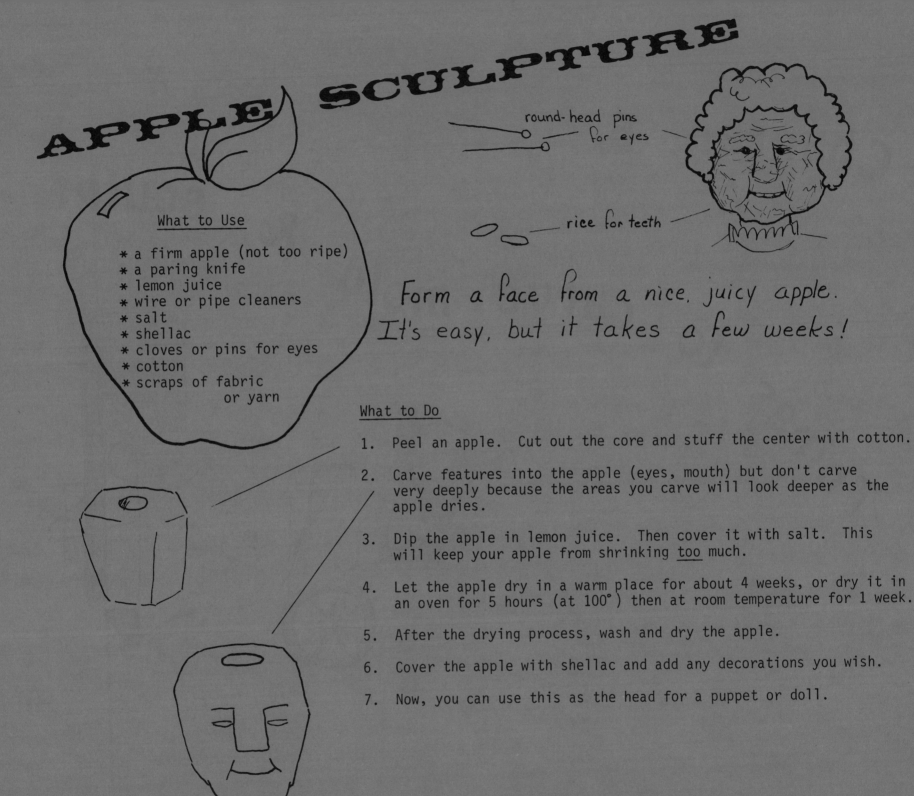

round-head pins for eyes

rice for teeth

What to Use

* a firm apple (not too ripe)
* a paring knife
* lemon juice
* wire or pipe cleaners
* salt
* shellac
* cloves or pins for eyes
* cotton
* scraps of fabric
       or yarn

Form a face from a nice, juicy apple.
It's easy, but it takes a few weeks!

What to Do

1. Peel an apple. Cut out the core and stuff the center with cotton.

2. Carve features into the apple (eyes, mouth) but don't carve very deeply because the areas you carve will look deeper as the apple dries.

3. Dip the apple in lemon juice. Then cover it with salt. This will keep your apple from shrinking <u>too</u> much.

4. Let the apple dry in a warm place for about 4 weeks, or dry it in an oven for 5 hours (at 100°) then at room temperature for 1 week.

5. After the drying process, wash and dry the apple.

6. Cover the apple with shellac and add any decorations you wish.

7. Now, you can use this as the head for a puppet or doll.

How to work with clay

1. Keep the clay tightly covered when it's not in use.

2. While you're working, keep the clay moist by dipping your hands into water.

3. When you model an object, try to squeeze it into shape. If you do this instead of "sticking" pieces onto one another, your object will have a better chance of drying without cracking.

4. When you must stick two pieces of clay together, do it this way:

   Mix some clay with water until you've made a liquid-like clay called a "slip". Paint surfaces of clay with this slip before you attach them together. Then smooth the joints with a wet finger.

5. Start your sculpture by molding a ball, rolling some coils, or rolling a flat slab of clay. Use a rolling pin to make slabs about 1/2 inch or 1 centimeter thick.

6. Allow your finished clay object to dry for a few days.

7. When it's thoroughly dry, you can paint clay with tempera paints and "glaze" over the paint with shellac.

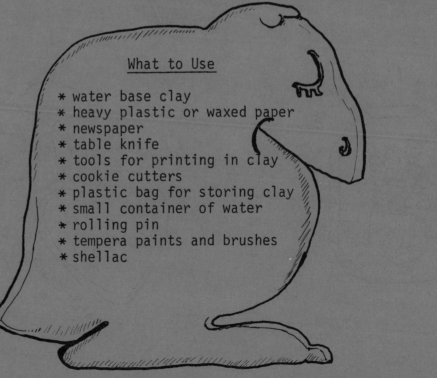

What to Use

* water base clay
* heavy plastic or waxed paper
* newspaper
* table knife
* tools for printing in clay
* cookie cutters
* plastic bag for storing clay
* small container of water
* rolling pin
* tempera paints and brushes
* shellac

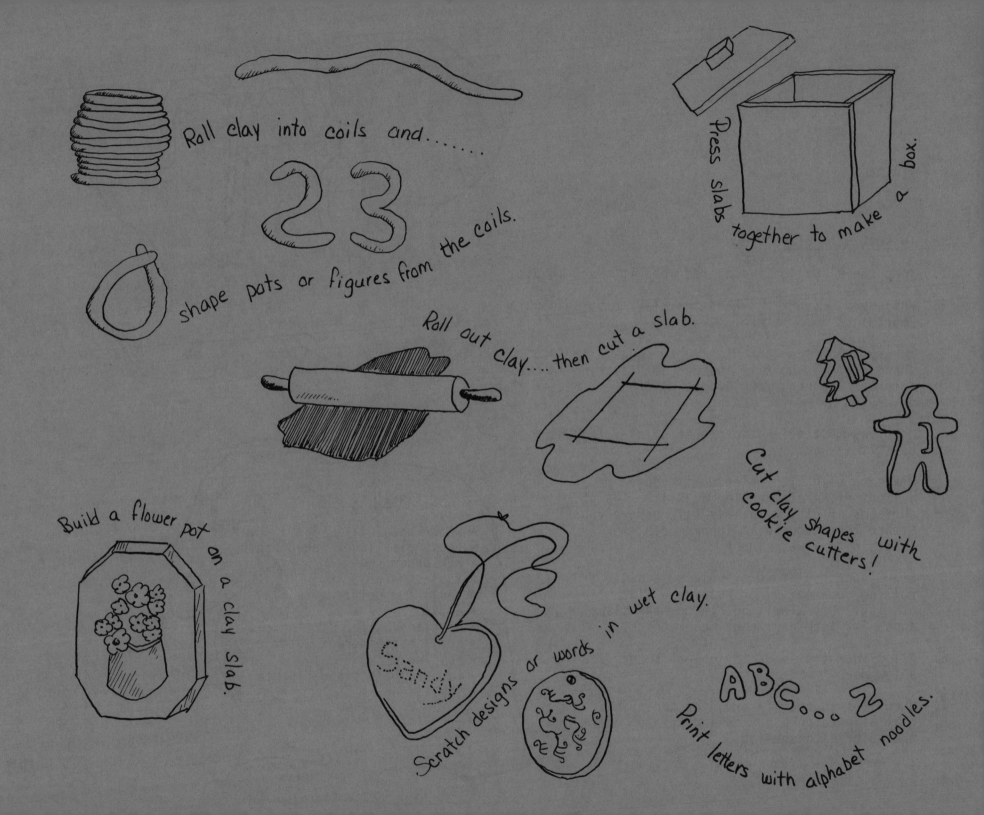

Roll clay into coils and ....

23

shape pots or figures from the coils.

Press slabs together to make a box.

Roll out clay.... then cut a slab.

Cut clay shapes with cookie cutters!

Build a flower pot on a clay slab.

Scratch designs or words in wet clay.

Sandy

ABC... Z

Print letters with alphabet noodles.

Design a clay tile to use for block printing.

Press a coil on top of a clay slab.

Mold a relief map!

Shape a planter.... or a pet!

Roll clay balls into animals.

Make jewelry with lumps of clay.

137

Please! Don't Eat the Lunch!

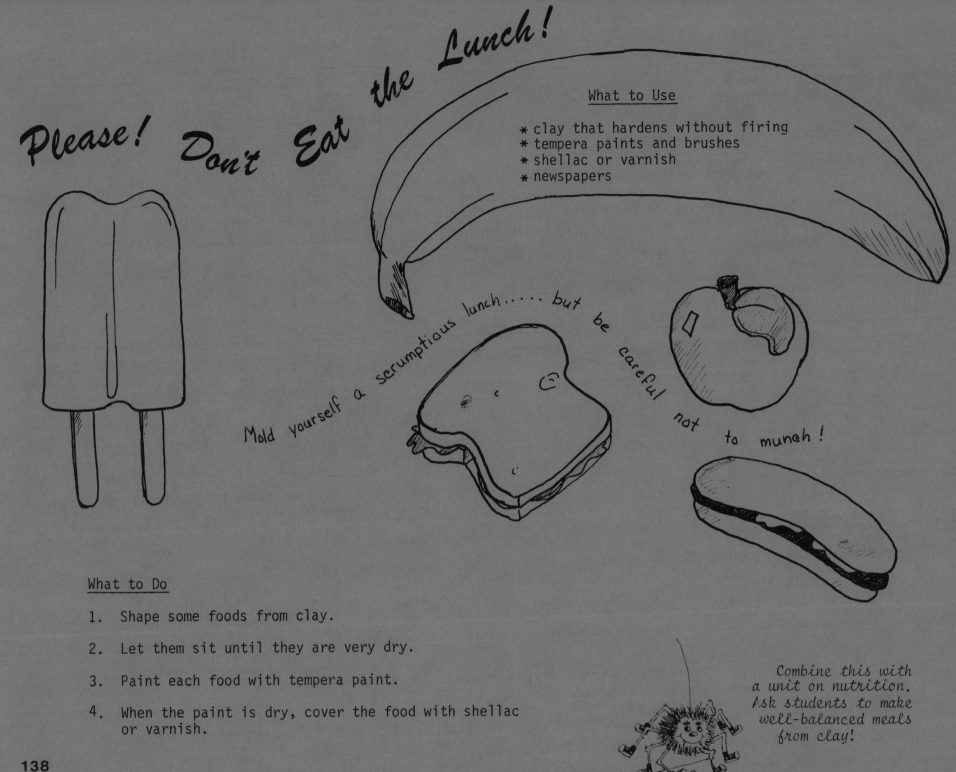

What to Use

* clay that hardens without firing
* tempera paints and brushes
* shellac or varnish
* newspapers

Mold yourself a scrumptious lunch..... but be careful not to munch!

What to Do

1. Shape some foods from clay.

2. Let them sit until they are very dry.

3. Paint each food with tempera paint.

4. When the paint is dry, cover the food with shellac or varnish.

Combine this with a unit on nutrition. Ask students to make well-balanced meals from clay!

Tip For Teacher

138

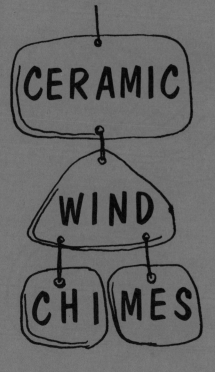

CERAMIC WIND CHIMES

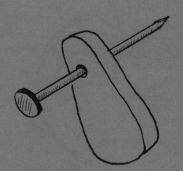

What to Use

* clay
* rolling pin
* waxed paper
* knitting needle
* tempera paints
* brushes
* shellac
* newspapers
* twine or leather strips

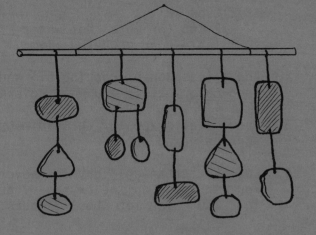

What to Do

1. Roll thick clay slabs on waxed paper.

2. Cut shapes from the slabs (any kinds of shapes you like).

3. Make a hole through each slab with a knitting needle.

4. When the shapes are dry, paint and shellac them.

5. Connect the shapes by stringing twine or leather through each one. Tie a knot beneath each piece.

6. Hang the wind chimes outdoors in a place that "catches" the wind. (For example: from a tree, on a porch, from the garage).

Dough–It–Yourself

...but don't eat it!

The alum keeps the dough from getting moldy!

Cut shapes with a knife or cookie cutters.

Scratch designs with a nail.

Roll it into coils.

What to Do

1. In a mixing bowl, mix:
   - 2 Cups flour
   - 2 Cups salt
   - 1/2 Cup (or more) hot water
   - 1 Tablespoon powdered alum

2. Add a teaspoon of cooking oil and some food coloring (if you want colored dough).

3. Model flat shapes or three-dimensional objects. Work on waxed paper.

4. Let the "creations" dry for several days. You can speed up the drying by putting them in a 250° oven for about 3 hours.

What to Use

* flour	* food coloring
* salt	* cooking oil
* water	* mixing bowl
* spoon	* newspapers
* waxed paper	* powdered alum

Add more water if dough is dry.

James

You can save leftover dough in the refrigerator. Wrap it in a plastic bag!

Dough – It – Again
...and eat all you want!

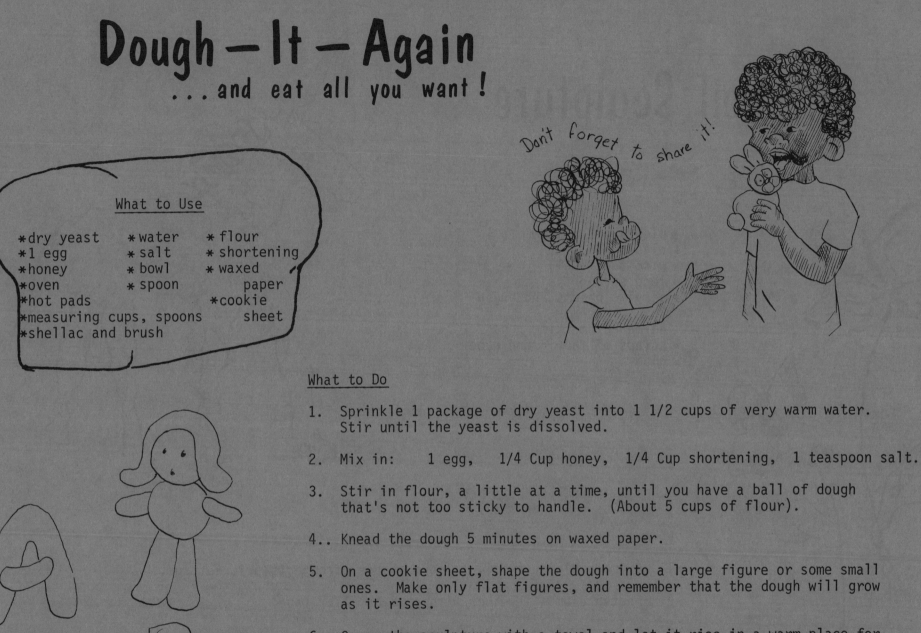

Don't forget to share it!

What to Use

- *dry yeast
- *1 egg
- *honey
- *oven
- *hot pads
- *measuring cups, spoons
- *shellac and brush
- *water
- *salt
- *bowl
- *spoon
- *flour
- *shortening
- *waxed paper
- *cookie sheet

What to Do

1. Sprinkle 1 package of dry yeast into 1 1/2 cups of very warm water. Stir until the yeast is dissolved.

2. Mix in: 1 egg, 1/4 Cup honey, 1/4 Cup shortening, 1 teaspoon salt.

3. Stir in flour, a little at a time, until you have a ball of dough that's not too sticky to handle. (About 5 cups of flour).

4.. Knead the dough 5 minutes on waxed paper.

5. On a cookie sheet, shape the dough into a large figure or some small ones. Make only flat figures, and remember that the dough will grow as it rises.

6. Cover the sculpture with a towel and let it rise in a warm place for 25 minutes. (Let it rise longer if you want it fatter.)

7. Bake about 20 minutes or until it's golden brown, in a 350° oven.

8. If you don't want to eat the sculpture, you can shellac it when it cools. Then it will keep for a long, long time.

Tin Foil Sculpture

What to Use

* plenty of aluminum foil
* clear tape
* wire (optional)
* long straight pins
* acrylic paints and brush
      or
  permanent marking pens
* scraps of fabric and paper
* glue

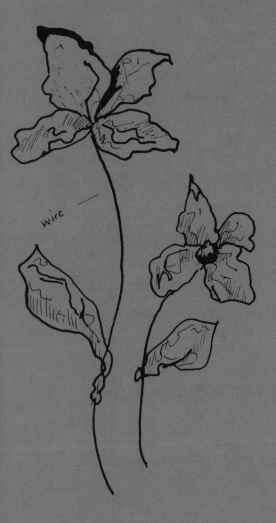

wire

What to Do

1. Crumple aluminum foil to form shapes of objects or creatures.

2. Fasten clumps together with pins or clear tape.

3. Use paint or markers to add color.

4. Glue on scraps of fabric, paper, yarn, etc. to add details.

Tin Foil plus Junk

What to Use

* aluminum foil
* white glue
* scissors
* small can
* brush
* India ink or tempera paint
* liquid detergent
* cloth
* scraps and junk for sculpture:
  yarn   screws
  nails   washers
  paper clips   beads
  cardboard cut out shapes
  coins   heavy string
      etc.
          etc.
              etc.

What to Do

1. Plan a design or picture which will make use of junk you have collected or shapes you've cut from cardboard.

2. Glue objects on a piece of heavy cardboard.

3. When the glue is dry, mix more glue with some water in a small container. Mix 2 parts glue to 1 part water. Paint this glue over the whole surface of the cardboard, even over all the objects.

4. Lay a sheet of foil over the surface of the design. Gently crumple, wrinkle and mold it to cling to all the bumps and lumps of the sculpture.

5. Glue the edges of the foil down securely or wrap them over the sides of the cardboard.

6. If you want a dark antique-look finish, mix a few drops of liquid detergent with some tempera paint or India ink. Paint this over the surface.

7. The next day, gently "polish" the sculpture with a cloth.

WOOD CARVING

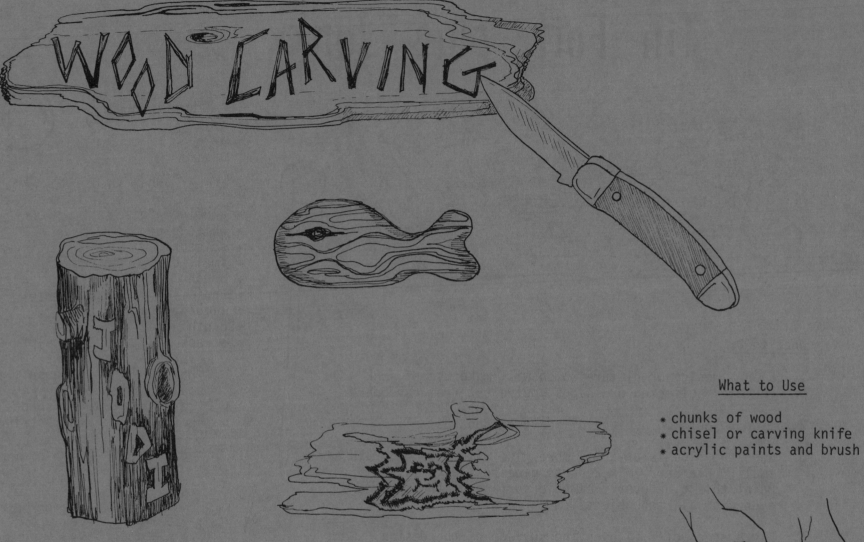

What to Use

* chunks of wood
* chisel or carving knife
* acrylic paints and brush

What to Do

Use a sharp tool to dig or carve out features on
a piece of wood. Try to leave some of the natural
surface of the wood showing. Let the natural design
and contours of the wood help you decide how to
carve. Paints can be used to add touches of color
to your wood carving.

...and more carving

Some other good carving materials are....

sponges

cork

blocks of wax

* **Tools You Might Use**

nail	scissors
knife	sharp stick
spoon	single-edge
file	razor blade
chisel	paints
	brushes
	glue or cement

chunks of styrofoam

plaster and vermiculite
mixed in equal amounts

plaster and sawdust
mixed in equal amounts

PLASTER

* powdered plaster for molding
* large bowl for mixing plaster
* water
* a mold (clay, cardboard, plastic, balloon)
* tools for carving or modeling
* petroleum jelly for greasing molds
* tempera paints and shellac
    or India ink or food coloring or stain
* brushes
* newspapers
* string

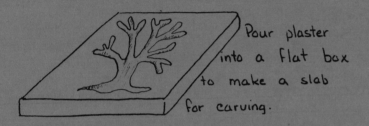

Pour plaster into a flat box to make a slab for carving.

Wet the plaster block before you carve it.

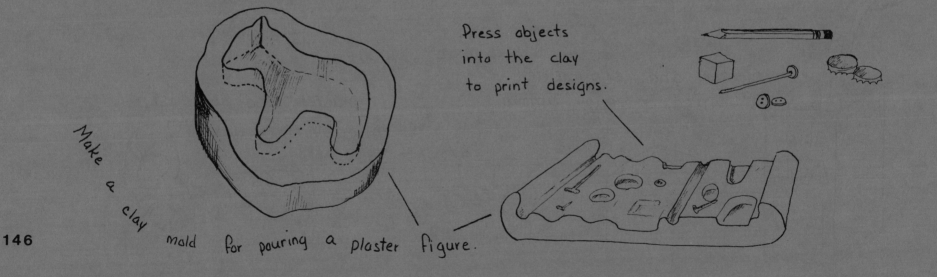

Make a clay mold for pouring a plaster figure.

Press objects into the clay to print designs.

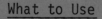

146

SCULPTURE

What to Do

1. Cover your work area with newspapers.

2. Prepare a mold from clay, cardboard or a plastic container. Coat the inside of the mold with petroleum jelly.

3. Mix the plaster by carefully and slowly pouring it into warm water. Stir it with your hand as you pour. Break up all the lumps.

4. Pour the liquid plaster into the mold. Shake the mold to release any air bubbles in the plaster.

5. Let the plaster dry and harden. You may insert a wire or unbent paper clip while the plaster is soft.

6. When the plaster is hard, remove it from the mold. It is now ready for carving or painting.

Pour plaster into containers to get big chunks for carving. Soak a plaster chunk in water for a minute before you carve it.

Use plastic containers as molds. Cut away the plastic when the plaster is hard.

Soak string in plaster and wrap it around a balloon. When the plaster hardens, break the balloon.

147

RINGS

Wrap around markers to make rings.

Form beads around a pencil.

'N'

Try it with papier mâché too!

THINGS

What to Use

* plaster
* water
* bowl for mixing plaster
* gauze strips
* clear tape
* heavy string
* waxed paper
* cylinders such as:
   pencils, crayons, fat marking pens
   cans, bottles
* newspaper
* tempera paints and brushes
* shellac
* very fine sandpaper

Smooth off the jewels with sandpaper before painting!

Bottles and cans are good for bracelets!

What to Do

1. Tape waxed paper around a cylindrical object.

2. Mix plaster in a bowl. (See Appendix for tips on mixing plaster).

3. Soak strips of gauze in plaster and wrap them around the cylinder.

4. When the rings and things are dry and hard, paint and shellac them.

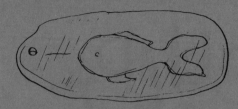

SCRIMSHAW

The Eskimos made whale-bone carvings called scrimshaw.

You can use plaster to make carvings that look like scrimshaw.

What to Use

* plaster
* water
* bowl for mixing plaster
* waxed paper
* nail or sharp tool for scratching
* dark tempera paint
* brush
* shellac
* yarn for pendants

What to Do

1. Mix plaster with water. See hints for mixing plaster in the Appendix of this book.

2. Drop globs of plaster onto waxed paper. Flatten them with your fingers.

3. Make a hole in the globs that you wish to hang.

4. When the plaster is hard, scratch a design in the glob.

5. Mix some dark paint with water so that the paint is very thin.

6. Brush one coat of paint over the plaster.

7. Shellac the scrimshaw when the paint is dry.

SQUEEZE and SCULPT

What to Use

* plaster
* water
* bowl for mixing plaster
* sturdy plastic bag
* string
* newspapers
* fine sandpaper
* optional: paint and brush

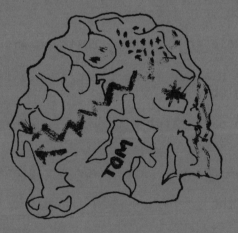

What to Do

1. Mix plaster into warm water. See hints for mixing plaster in the Appendix of this book.

2. Pour plaster into a plastic bag and tie it shut tightly with string.

3. When the plaster begins to thicken squeeze the bag with both hands.

4. Hold the "squeeze" for 5 to 10 minutes until the plaster is hard enough to hold its shape.

5. When it is completely hard, tear away the plastic bag and lightly sand the rough edges (if you want to).

6. Paint your sculpture if you'd like it colored!

Rock Sculpture

Turn a rock into something special!

Paint a design that follows the natural markings of the rock!

Add color with paints or markers.

Decorate with seeds, string, buttons, felt, foil, cardboard, bottle caps, wire, flowers, or . . . .

SCHOOL BUS

Glue rocks together with epoxy glue.

151

WIRE SCULPTURE

What to Use

* copper wire
    or aluminum wire
    or colored telephone wire
* wire-cutting tool

* Optional:

    wood block for base
    hammer and nails
    scraps of paper, wood, metal
      or fabric for detail

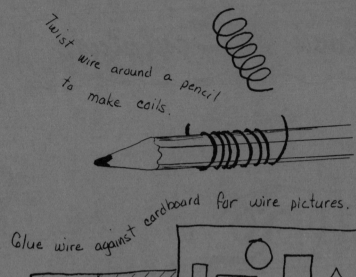

Twist wire around a pencil to make coils.

Glue wire against cardboard for wire pictures.

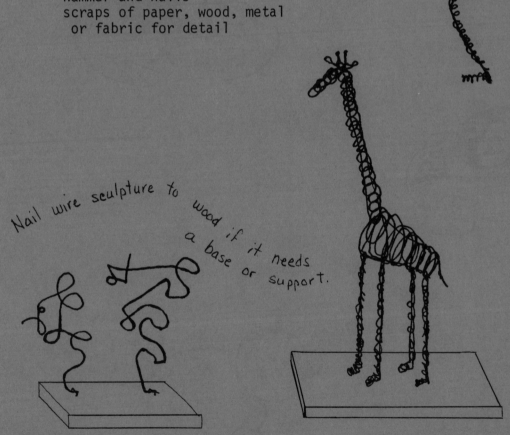

Nail wire sculpture to wood if it needs a base or support.

What to Do

1. Choose a figure or plan a design for a sculpture.

2. Shape the wire until you are happy with the figure you've created.

3. Add color, details or a new texture by using bits of other materials as part of your sculpture. Try wood scraps or snips of tin or cloth.

WRAPPED-WIRE SCULPTURE

What to Use

* flexible wire
* wire-cutting tool
* gauze strips or old nylon stocking
* plaster of Paris
* container for mixing plaster
* water
* newspapers
* scissors

What to Do

1. Build a figure or design with wire.

2. Attach the wire to a base if it needs support. Nail it to wood, or stick it into a block of styrofoam or cork.

3. Mix plaster into warm water in a bowl.

4. Soak strips of gauze or nylon in plaster and wrap them around the wire figure.

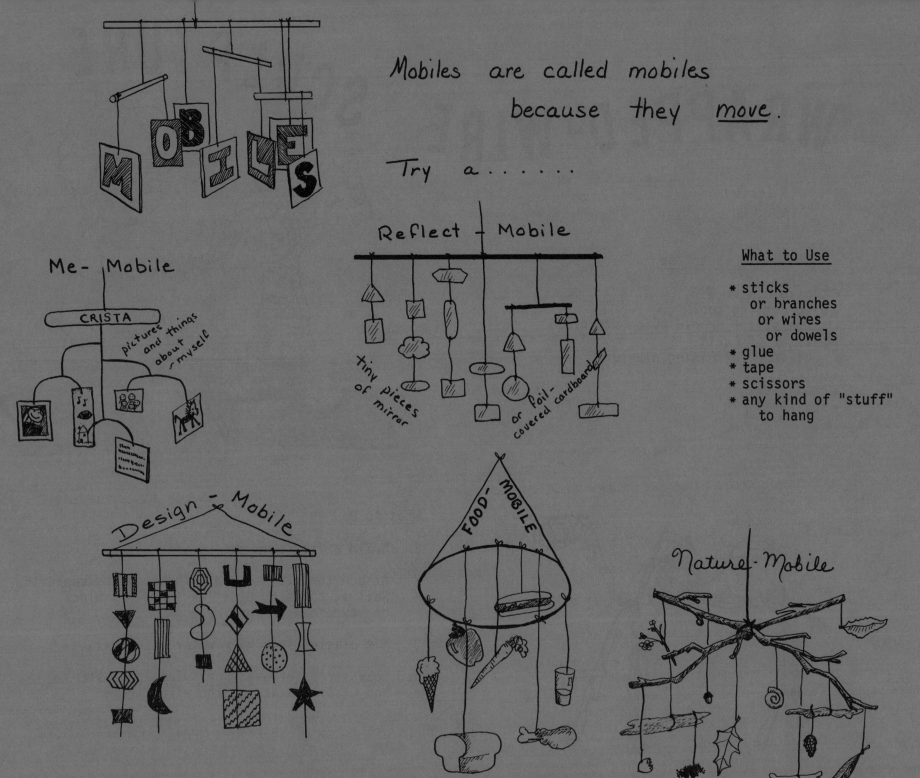

Mobiles are called mobiles because they _move_.

Try a ......

MOBILES

Me - Mobile

CRISTA

pictures and things about myself

Reflect - Mobile

tiny pieces of mirror

or foil - covered cardboard

What to Use

* sticks
  or branches
    or wires
      or dowels
* glue
* tape
* scissors
* any kind of "stuff"
  to hang

Design - Mobile

FOOD - MOBILE

Nature - Mobile

Mobile means "move·able". Make a sculpture with move·able parts!

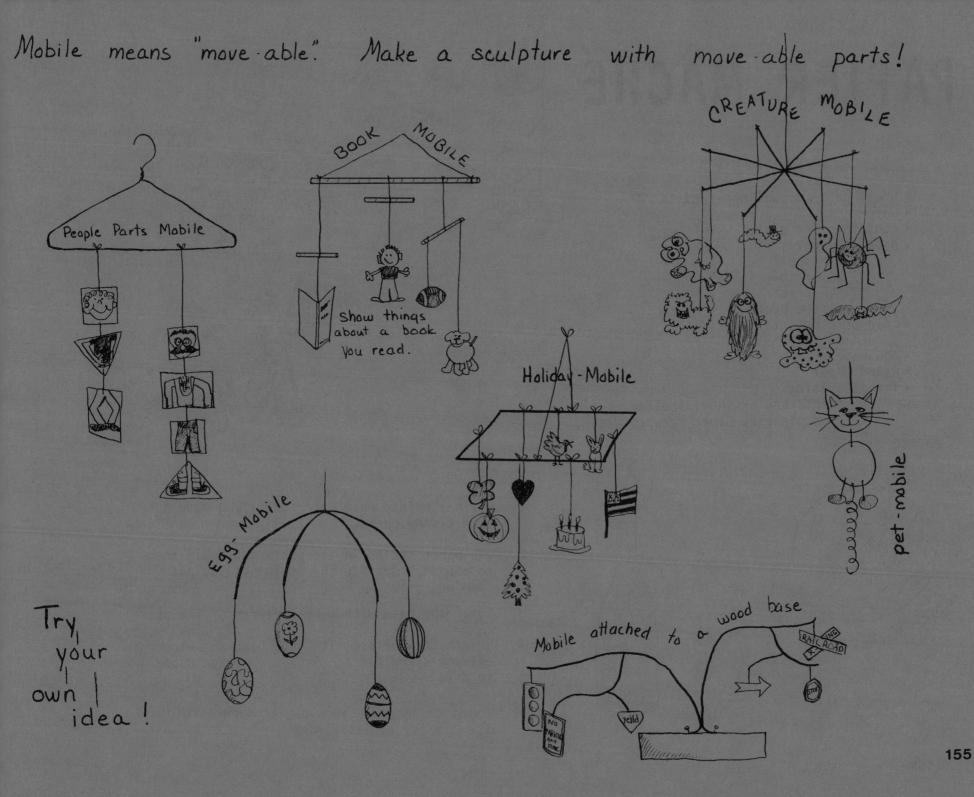

People Parts Mobile

BOOK MOBILE

Show things about a book you read.

CREATURE MOBILE

Holiday-Mobile

pet-mobile

Egg-Mobile

Try
your
own
idea!

Mobile attached to a wood base

NO PARKING ANY TIME

yeild

RAIL ROAD

STOP

PAPIER MÂCHÉ

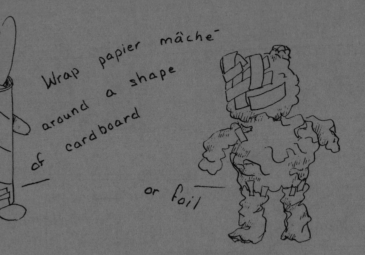

Wrap papier mâché around a shape of cardboard

or foil

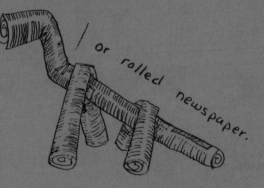

or rolled newspaper.

What to Use

* wheat paste or wallpaper paste
* water
* container for paste
* paper strips:
        newspaper
        paper towels
        newsprint
        tissue paper
* mold or a base to cover with
        mâché
* newspapers
* waxed paper
* for decorating:
        paints and brushes, shellac
        yarn, fabric, paper scraps, etc.

Papier mâché a balloon or a bottle.

What to Do

1. Mix paste into warm water until you have a thin creamy paste.

2. Dip paper strips in the paste and apply them to a base. Overlap the strips as you put them on.

3. Cover the base with 2 or 3 layers of strips.

4. Smooth the surface with your hand and wipe off any extra paste. Set it on waxed paper to dry.

5. Paint or decorate your papier mâché sculpture when it is completely dry.

TRY PAPER MASH!

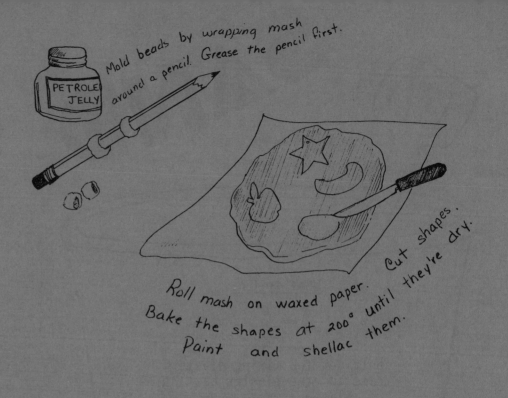

Mold beads by wrapping mash around a pencil. Grease the pencil first.

Roll mash on waxed paper. Cut shapes. Bake the shapes at 200° until they're dry. Paint and shellac them.

What to Do

1. Shred or tear paper into tiny pieces.

2. Soak the shredded pieces in a wheat paste-water mixture overnight.

3. Squeeze out the liquid. Then mold the mash or spread it over a form.

4. When the mash is wet, or after it has begun to dry, you can carve or mold the surface with various tools.

5. Let the sculpture dry completely, then paint or decorate.

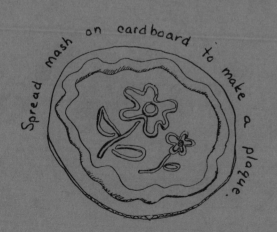

Spread mash on cardboard to make a plaque.

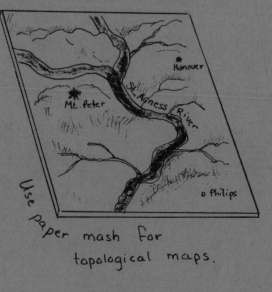

Use paper mash for topological maps.

What to Use

* newspaper or paper towels
* wheat paste
* water
* bowl for mixing mash
* waxed paper
* tools for applying and carving mash such as:

spoon	nail
knife	stick
rolling pin	

* paints and brush
* shellac
* vaseline

SAND CASTING

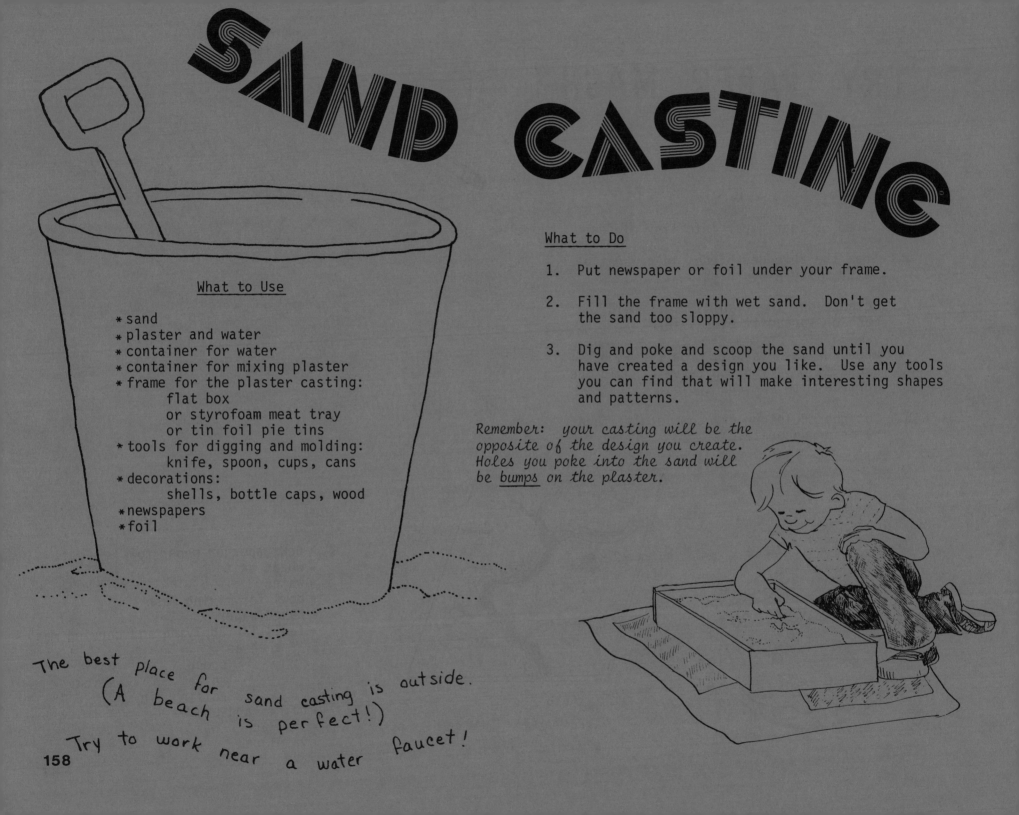

What to Use

* sand
* plaster and water
* container for water
* container for mixing plaster
* frame for the plaster casting:
    flat box
    or styrofoam meat tray
    or tin foil pie tins
* tools for digging and molding:
    knife, spoon, cups, cans
* decorations:
    shells, bottle caps, wood
* newspapers
* foil

What to Do

1. Put newspaper or foil under your frame.

2. Fill the frame with wet sand. Don't get the sand too sloppy.

3. Dig and poke and scoop the sand until you have created a design you like. Use any tools you can find that will make interesting shapes and patterns.

Remember: your casting will be the opposite of the design you create. Holes you poke into the sand will be <u>bumps</u> on the plaster.

The best place for sand casting is outside. (A beach is perfect!)

Try to work near a water faucet!

4. Mix the plaster by pouring it into warm
   water (if warm water is available).
   Stir and mix the plaster with your hands
   until it is creamy and thick.

5. Pour the plaster into a
   mold. You should pour it
   at least 1 inch or 2
   centimeters thick.

6. Wait about an hour. Then carefully
   pick up the casting and shake off the
   loose sand.

To hang a plaque,
press a bent
wire into
wet plaster.

STICK-SCULPTURE

You can have a good out-of-doors time

scrounging sticks

and twigs

and branches
(dead ones only)

What to Use

* sticks and twigs
* masking tape
* wood glue or household cement
        or
    hammer and nails
* string or twine

and creating a work of art under a blue (or grey) sky!

You can even use the ground as a base for a sculpture

Try wrapping string around a tree!

What to Do

1. Gather some good-looking twigs and sticks.

2. Plan and sculpt a design. Tape or tie the wood pieces together to hold them in place.

3. Squeeze glue to join the sticks permanently (or you might nail them together). When they're firmly together, remove the tape or string from the sculpture.

Cylinder Scenes

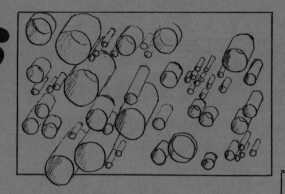

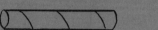

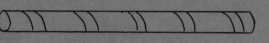

What to Use

*cylinders
such as:

tubes
paper cylinders
cardboard
    rolls
straws
wood dowels

*scissors

*glue

*saw for wood

*tape

*plywood
    or
cardboard for
    base

*optional:

paint and
    brushes

What to Do

1. Cut tubes, straws or other cylinders into different lengths.

2. Set the cylinders onto the base to form a design. Mark a place for each one.

3. When your design is planned, spread a layer of glue over the base and set the tubes on it. Don't move the sculpture until the glue is dry.

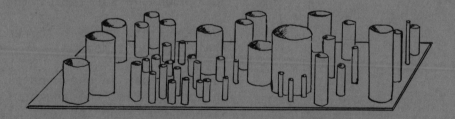

4. If you want to, you can paint some of the tubes or open areas of the background.

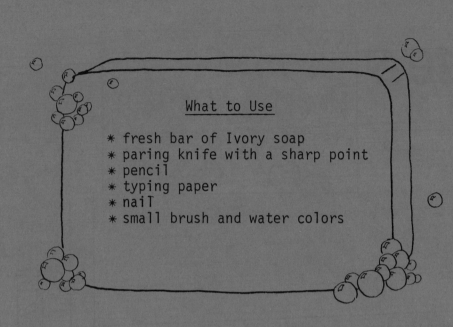

What to Use

* fresh bar of Ivory soap
* paring knife with a sharp point
* pencil
* typing paper
* nail
* small brush and water colors

SOAP SCULPTURE

Soap carving is good, clean fun.........

Keep away from subjects
that are too complicated
or have narrow parts.

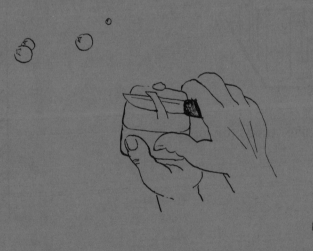

What to Do

1. Choose a simple object or subject to carve. Plan your design by sketching it on paper.

2. Use the point of a nail or a sharp stick to scratch the design on the surface of the soap.

3. Cut down into the bar to remove the parts of the soap that you won't need.

4. Hold the soap in one hand as if you were going to peel an apple. Rest the thumb of the other hand against the side of the soap and wrap the other four fingers around the knife.

5. Begin to carve the soap. Gently pull the knife toward you. Work slowly.

6. When the sculpture has the shape you want, gently scrape the surface of the soap until it's smooth.

7. The soap can be painted with watercolors, if you wish.

JUNK MASTERPIECES

Build a sculpture with things you find in garages, attics, basements and junk piles.

What to Use

* cardboard tubes
* wood scraps
* nails
* metal scraps
* nuts and bolts
* string
* straws
* jar lids
* old pots
* sponges
* cardboard
* noodles
* pebbles
* keys
* fabric scraps
* spools
* cans
* hangers
* egg cartons
* paper cups
* flower pots
* feathers
* old silverware
* kitchen utensils
* bottles
* boxes
* toothbrushes
* combs

* Tools: sharp knife
scissors
glue
tape
hammer and nails

What to Do

Make any design that is pleasing to you. Fasten together pieces of "junk".
Your sculpture doesn't have to look like anything you've ever seen before. It can be your very own original creation!

pretzel sculpture

Did you ever think of a pretzel as an angel? a fisherman? 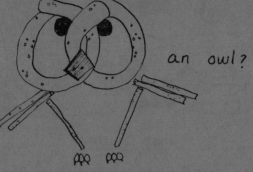 an owl?

There are lots of sculpture possibilities with pretzels!

What can you do with one?

or two?

or three?

What to Do

1. Brush pretzels with shellac.

2. Plan a pretzel picture by placing pretzels on a piece of wood or heavy cardboard.

3. Glue the pretzels in place.

4. Add details with string, felt or paper.

What to Use

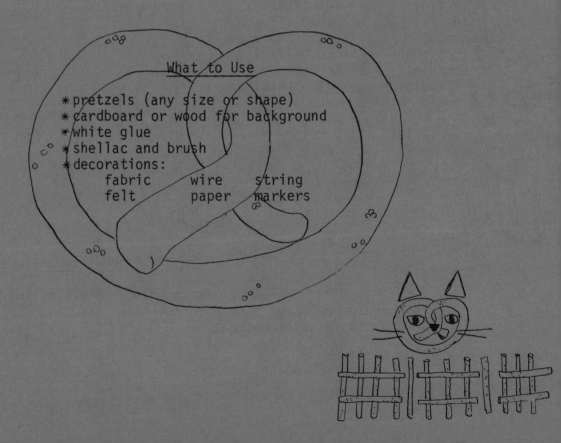

* pretzels (any size or shape)
* cardboard or wood for background
* white glue
* shellac and brush
* decorations:
  fabric   wire   string
  felt   paper   markers

Try bagel sculpture too!

Chapter 6
Things to do with food

Tips to Teachers of Young Cooks

Organization and forethought are the secrets to successful classroom cooking experiences (and to the sanity of teachers).

Have students help collect ingredients and utensils far in advance. Then (always!) introduce the activity to everyone and make a plan together for proceeding. Before you ever begin, the group should decide:

who brings what
who does what
what to do when it's not your turn
where to work, and when

how long it will take
when the eating part comes
how to clean up

Many recipes work well as whole-class activities. Students working around 2 long tables pushed together or in groups of 5 or 6 at small tables can do such things as:

peel apples for baking
pull and shape taffy
shape caramel corn or yummy gooey mixup treats
mix a bag of gorp
roll dough ropes and form pretzels
dish up parfaits
paint cookies

Some food preparation is not sensible or workable with a large group - and needs to be done with a few at a time, ie: baking cookies, folding fortune cookies, decorating marshmallows, blending smoothies. For these foods a good plan of action might be:

1. Discuss and plan the cooking and start it together.
2. Put the group to work on another activity.
3. Call small groups or individuals to an area where they take turns "fixing" food.
4. Join everyone together for eating, enjoying and cleaning up.

Sometimes in the fun of eating and cooking or in the haste of getting ready and cleaning up, it's easy to overlook the value of such good experiences. If you're alert to the possibilities, you can see and encourage a great deal of learning in the areas of:

measuring
reading
following directions
keeping records of the activity
describing
discriminating among tastes
imagining
creating
social and motor skills

There are loads of super cook books available for children. Three of my favorites are Arts and Crafts You Can Eat, Kids Are Natural Cooks, and Betty Crocker's Cookbook for Boys and Girls. (See bibliography).

Tip For Teacher

EDIBLE RAINBOWS

What to Use

* mixing bowl and spoon
* measuring cups and spoons
* cookie sheets
* sharp knife
* waxed paper
* oven and hot pad
* 3 small bowls

* 1 Cup soft margarine
* 3/4 Cup white sugar
* 3/4 Cup brown sugar
* 2 eggs
* 1 teaspoon vanilla
* 3 Cups flour
* 1/2 tsp. soda
* 1/2 tsp. salt
* food coloring

Preheat the oven to 375°.

Try all the colors!

What to Do

1. Mix well: margarine, sugar, eggs and vanilla.

2. Blend these together: flour, soda and salt.
    Then mix them into the first mixture.

3. Divide the dough into 4 (or more) parts. Color each
    part with food coloring to make a rainbow color.

4. On waxed paper, pat each color of dough into a strip
    4 inches (or 10 centimeters) wide and 1/4 inch (or
    1/2 centimeter) thick.

5. Stack the rainbow strips on top of one another. Press down
    to help the strips stick together.

6. Wrap the pile in waxed paper and refrigerate overnight.

7. Slice the layered block of dough in 1/4 inch (1/2 centimeter)
    slices. Gently curve the slice into an arch.

8. Bake on an ungreased cookie sheet at 375° for about 7 minutes.

Makes about 3 dozen cookies.

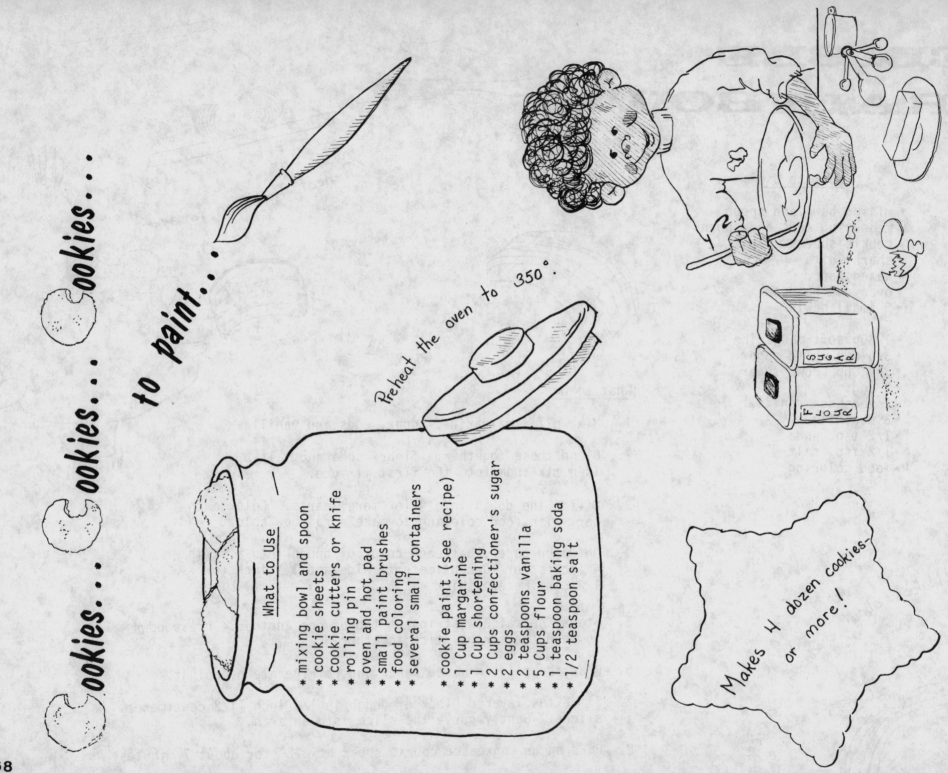

Cookies.... Cookies.... Cookies....

to paint...

Preheat the oven to 350°.

What to Use

* mixing bowl and spoon
* cookie sheets
* cookie cutters or knife
* rolling pin
* oven and hot pad
* small paint brushes
* food coloring
* several small containers

* cookie paint (see recipe)
* 1 Cup margarine
* 1 Cup shortening
* 2 Cups confectioner's sugar
* 2 eggs
* 2 teaspoons vanilla
* 5 Cups flour
* 1 teaspoon baking soda
* 1/2 teaspoon salt

Makes 4 dozen cookies—or more!

SUGAR

FLOUR

What to Do

1. Mix margarine
   shortening
   eggs
   sugar
   vanilla

   Beat it up really well with your spoon.

2. Stir in flour
   salt
   baking soda

   Add the flour a little at a time.

3. Let the dough chill for at least 3 hours.

4. Sprinkle flour on a flat surface. Roll out part of the dough to 1/4 inch or 1/2 centimeter thickness.

5. Dip cookie cutters or knife in flour and cut cookie shapes. Keep rolling out and cutting cookies until all the dough is gone.

6. Carefully lay cookies on a cookie sheet and paint them.

7. Bake at 350° for 8 minutes or until slightly brown.

8. Cool 2 minutes on the cookie sheet before removing.

... or you can paint cookies with frosting—after they're baked.

Cookie Paint

Beat 3 egg yolks with 1 tsp. water and 1 tsp. sugar. Divide this into containers. Tint each batch with a different color of food coloring.

169

STAINED GLASS COOKIES

Make a hole with a toothpick.

Preheat the oven to 350°.

What to Use

* mixing bowl and spoon
* measuring cups and spoons
* oven and hot pad
* cookie sheets
* rolling pin
* hammer
* sharp knife (cookie cutters optional)
* waxed paper

* hard candies (such as lollipops or life savers)
* 1 Cup margarine
* 1 Cup shortening
* 1 Cup sugar and 1/4 Cup honey (or 2 Cups sugar)
* 2 eggs
* 2 teaspoons vanilla
* 5 Cups flour
* 1 teaspoon baking soda
* 1 teaspoon salt

What to Do

1. Mix margarine, shortening, sugar, honey, eggs and vanilla.

2. Add flour, soda and salt. Add flour and chill the dough overnight.

3. On waxed paper roll out the dough and cut shapes with cookie cutters. Then cut out areas for "windows".

   OR

   Roll dough into "snakes". Shape the snakes into cookies--leaving some open spaces.

4. Place the cookies on a well-greased cookie sheet. Fill the openings with crushed hard candies or a whole life saver.

5. Bake at 350° for 7-8 minutes. Let cookies cool for 5 minutes before removing them from the cookie sheet.

Makes 4 dozen cookies!

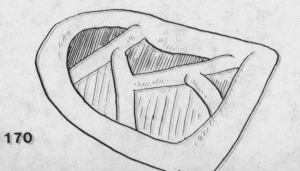

What to Use

* oven and hot pad
* cookie sheet
* mixing bowl
* wooden spoon
* measuring cups
* measuring spoons
* pancake turner
* strips of paper
* pen

* 4 egg whites
* 1 Cup sugar
* 1/2 Cup melted butter
* 1/2 Cup flour
* 1/4 teaspoon salt
* 1/2 teaspoon vanilla
* 2 tablespoons water

FORTUNE COOKIES

Beware of the second girl in the last row!

Send a secret message in a cookie!

He Who Eats No Bananas Has No Appeal!

Hide a fortune in a cookie!

At 1:15 tomorrow you will turn into a radish.

Preheat the oven to 375°.

Makes 30 cookies!

What to Do

1. Write fortunes or messages on strips of paper. Fold them.

2. Mix sugar into the egg whites and blend until fluffy.

3. Melt the butter and cool it so it's not too hot.

4. Add flour, salt, vanilla, water and butter to the sugar mixture. Beat until the batter is smooth.

5. Grease a cookie sheet <u>very</u> well. Pour batter from a spoon to form circles (about 3 in. or 8 cm.).

6. Bake at 375° for about 8 minutes.

7. Lay a message on each circle, fold it in thirds, then bend it gently in the center.
   If the cookies get too hard to bend, put them back in the oven for a minute.

NO-BAKE YUMMY GOOEY MIX-UP TREATS

What to Use

* stove or hot plate
* greased cookie sheet or waxed paper
* large saucepan and large spoon
* measuring cups and spoons

* either marshmallow or chocolate base
* all or any of these (and anything else
  you're bold enough to try):

  Rice Krispies   peanuts
  Cheerios   peanut butter
  raisins   oatmeal
  coconut   Cocoa Puffs
  marshmallows   Sugar Pops

Chocolate Goo

Mix 3 Cups of sugar
   1/3 Cup cocoa
   3/4 Cup milk
Boil for 8 minutes (keep
stirring), then add 1 stick margarine and 1 teaspoon vanilla.

Marshmallow Goo

5 Cups marshmallows
½ stick butter or margarine
Stir over medium heat until
the marshmallows are melted.

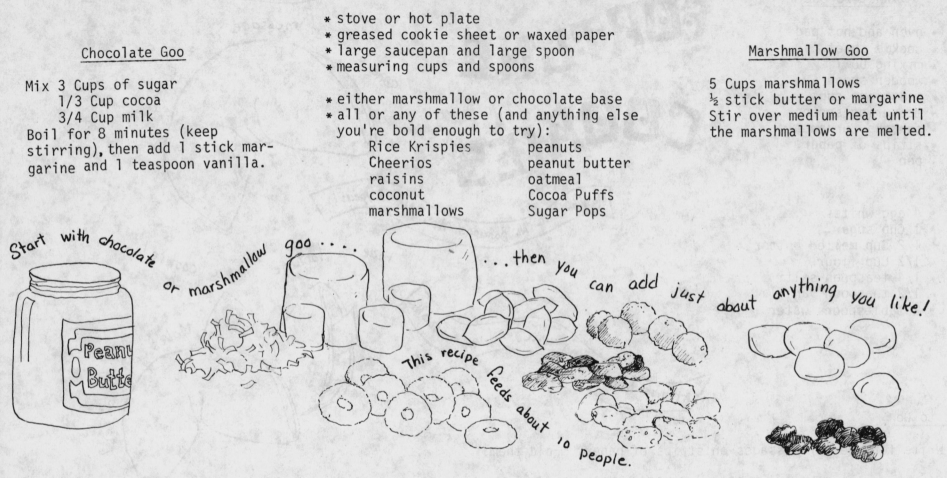

Start with chocolate or marshmallow goo . . . . . . then you can add just about anything you like!

This recipe feeds about 10 people.

What to Do

1. Prepare either chocolate or marshmallow "goo". Cool the mixture until it begins to get sticky.

2. Stir any goodies into the "goo". Try some of the suggestions or any others you think sound good.

3. Wet your hands with water, and mold the treats into balls, lollipops, flat shapes, etc.

4. Use a greased cookie sheet or waxed paper as a place to shape and cool the treats.

Luscious Lollipops

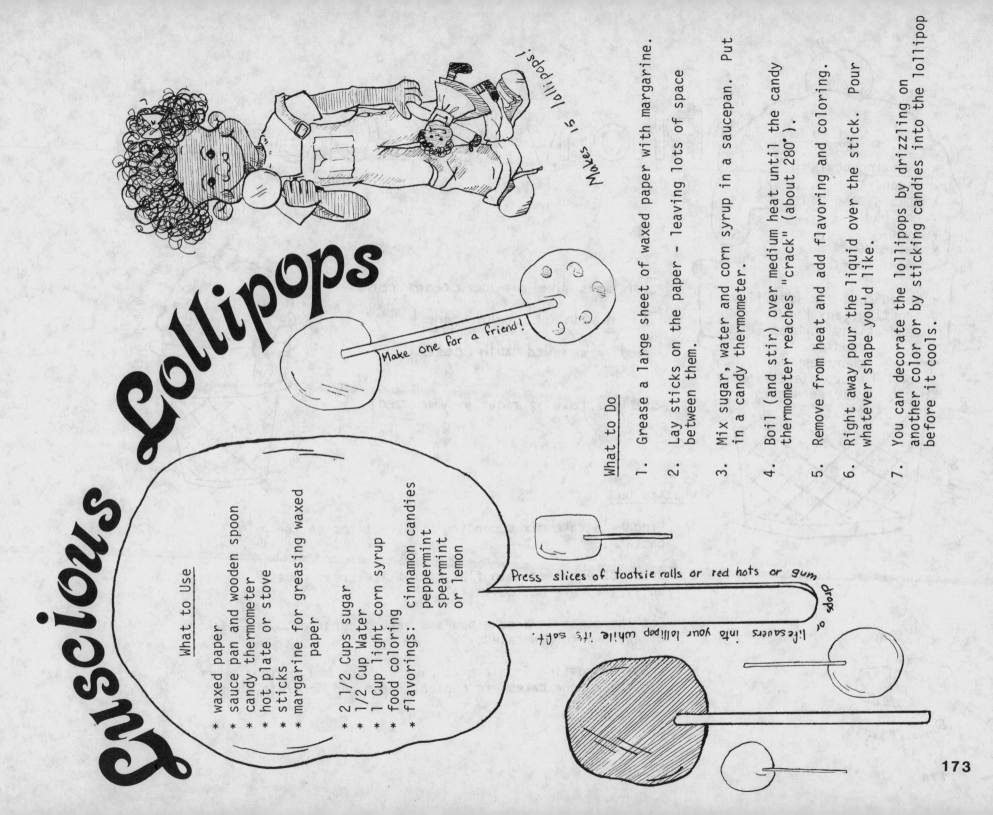

What to Use

* waxed paper
* sauce pan and wooden spoon
* candy thermometer
* hot plate or stove
* sticks
* margarine for greasing waxed paper

* 2 1/2 Cups sugar
* 1/2 Cup Water
* 1 Cup light corn syrup
* food coloring
* flavorings: cinnamon candies
  peppermint
  spearmint
  or lemon

What to Do

1. Grease a large sheet of waxed paper with margarine.

2. Lay sticks on the paper - leaving lots of space between them.

3. Mix sugar, water and corn syrup in a saucepan. Put in a candy thermometer.

4. Boil (and stir) over medium heat until the candy thermometer reaches "crack" (about 280°).

5. Remove from heat and add flavoring and coloring.

6. Right away pour the liquid over the stick. Pour whatever shape you'd like.

7. You can decorate the lollipops by drizzling on another color or by sticking candies into the lollipop before it cools.

Makes 15 lollipops!

Make one for a friend!

Press slices of tootsie rolls or red hots or gum drops or lifesavers into your lollipop while it's soft.

173

Phony Ice Cream

What to Use

* 2 mixing bowls
* spoon
* oblong cake pan
* hot pad
* oven
* table knife
* waxed paper

* boxed cake mix (any flavor)
* frosting (any kind)
* decorations such as
  candies
  cherries
  chocolate sprinkles
  colored sugars
  etc.

Makes about 12 !

It looks like an ice cream cone!
It **is** an ice cream cone !
But it's filled with cake.....

and you bake it right in your oven!

Use icing from a mix, or sift 2 cups powdered sugar into ¼ cup melted butter and mix!

What to Do

1. Prepare a cake mix according to directions on the package.

2. Spoon cake batter into flat-bottom ice-cream cones until they are not quite full.

3. Set the cones in a cake pan and bake according to the package directions for cupcakes.

4. Prepare frosting from a mix, can, or your own recipe. When the ice cream cone cakes are cooled, frost and decorate them!

Fluffy Frosting is especially yummy!

Stuffed Baked Apples

Preheat the oven to 400°.

What to Use

* baking pan
* large spoon
* teaspoon
* paring knife
* oven and hot pad

* firm baking apples
* butter or margarine
* sugar
* hot water
* fillings for apples
  (see ideas)

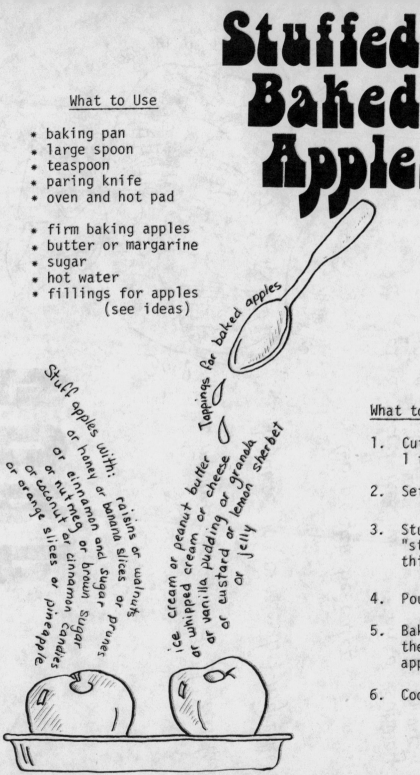

Stuff apples with: raisins or walnuts or honey or banana slices or cinnamon and sugar or prunes or nutmeg or brown sugar or coconut or cinnamon candies or orange slices or pineapple

Toppings for baked apples: ice cream or peanut butter or whipped cream or cheese or vanilla pudding or granola or custard or jelly or lemon sherbet

What to Do

1. Cut the core out of each apple and sprinkle with 1 teaspoon of sugar.

2. Set the apples in a baking dish.

3. Stuff the center of the apple. There are some "stuffing suggestions" here - but you might think of others. Try combining several!

4. Pour enough hot water in the dish to cover the bottom.

5. Bake at 400° 30 - 45 minutes or until tender. While they're baking, spoon some of the liquid over the apples every 10 minutes or so.

6. Cool the apples and eat! Try a topping.

175

GORP

Pack it in plastic bags!

Gorp

Nobody's gorp will be exactly like yours because you choose the ingredients!

Gorp is a mixture of all kinds of good foods.

Gorp can be eaten:

at a secret meeting
in a hideout
on a safari
behind the garage

on a subway
at a movie
on a hike
at parties

and many other places!

You know what else?

Gorp is good for you!

Some Things you Might Put in Your Gorp:

raisins
oatmeal
sesame seeds
granola
chocolate chips
dates
brown sugar
wheat germ
bits of hard cheese
Bugles

M & Ms
Cheerios
pretzels
sunflower seeds
Wheat Chex
Rice Chex
peanuts
walnuts
any - nuts
almost any kind of
dry cereal

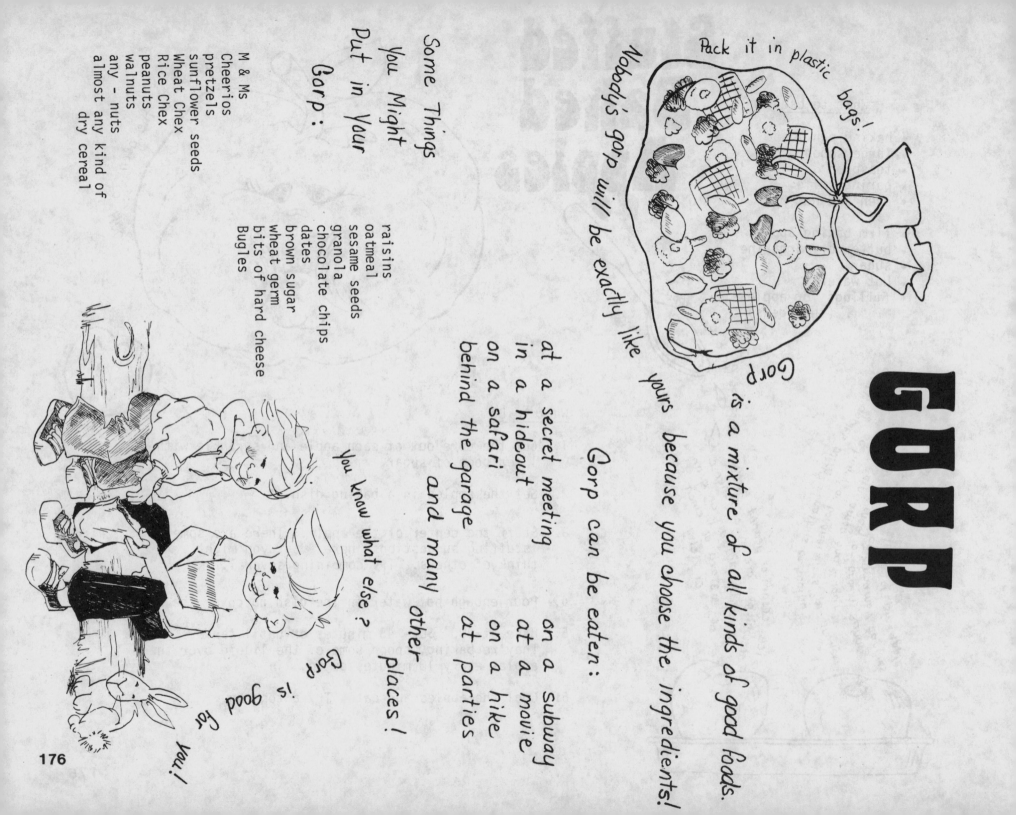

176

peanut butter

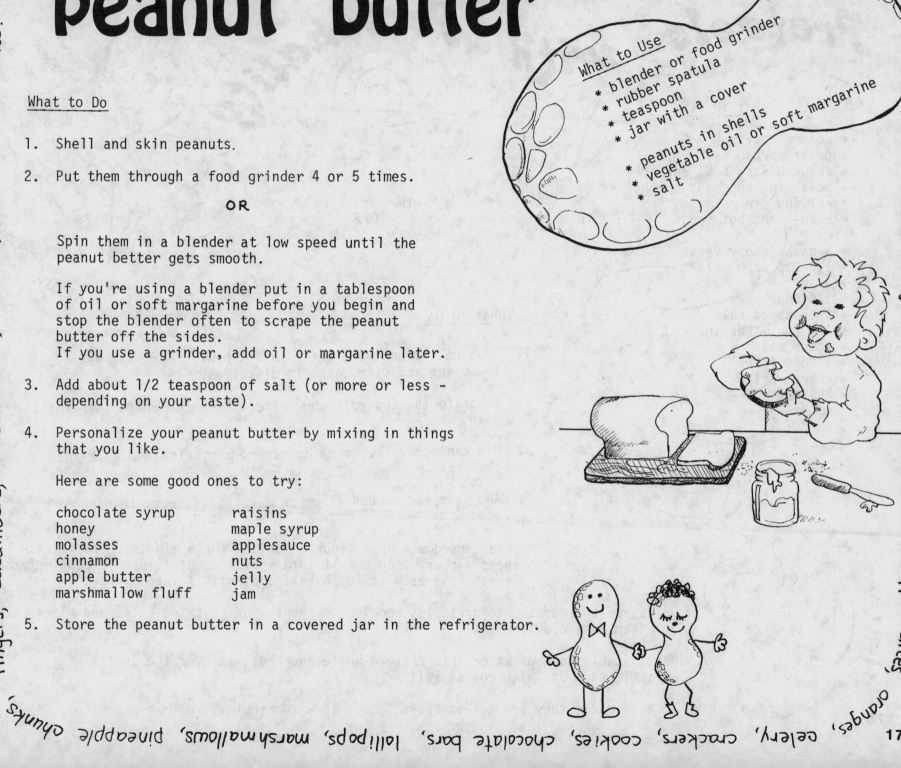

What to Use

* blender or food grinder
* rubber spatula
* teaspoon
* jar with a cover

* peanuts in shells
* vegetable oil or soft margarine
* salt

What to Do

1. Shell and skin peanuts.

2. Put them through a food grinder 4 or 5 times.

   OR

   Spin them in a blender at low speed until the peanut better gets smooth.

   If you're using a blender put in a tablespoon of oil or soft margarine before you begin and stop the blender often to scrape the peanut butter off the sides.
   If you use a grinder, add oil or margarine later.

3. Add about 1/2 teaspoon of salt (or more or less - depending on your taste).

4. Personalize your peanut butter by mixing in things that you like.

   Here are some good ones to try:

chocolate syrup	raisins
honey	maple syrup
molasses	applesauce
cinnamon	nuts
apple butter	jelly
marshmallow fluff	jam

5. Store the peanut butter in a covered jar in the refrigerator.

fingers, cucumbers, cheese slices, waffles, even in milk shakes!

celery, crackers, cookies, lollipops, marshmallows, pineapple chunks, oranges,

177

Pretzels with Personality

Preheat the oven to 425°.

What to Use

* cookie sheets
* pastry brush
* large mixing bowl and spoon
* measuring cups and spoons
* rolling pin
* oven---and hot pads

* 1 package dry yeast
* 1/2 Cup warm water
* 1 egg
* 1/4 Cup honey
* 1 teaspoon salt
* 1/4 Cup margarine
* 1 Cup milk
* 5 Cups flour
* coarse salt
* mustard

Try mustard on hot pretzels!

Makes 2 dozen pretzels.

Here's a recipe for fat, chewy pretzels to make in any shape!

What to Do

1. Measure 1/2 Cup warm water into a bowl. Sprinkle yeast on the water and stir until it dissolves.

2. Separate the egg yolk and white. Keep the white in a small dish.

3. Mix the egg yolk, honey or sugar, margarine and milk into the yeast.

4. Add salt and enough flour to make stiff, easy-to-handle dough.

5. Knead the dough on a floured surface for 5 minutes, let it rise about 1 hour, then cut it into strips about 1 inch (2 centimeters) wide. Fold each strip in half and roll it into a rope.

6. Shape the ropes into pretzels, peoples, pythons - or anything . . . and place them on a cookie sheet.

7. Beat 1 tablespoon of water into the egg white and brush it over the pretzels. Sprinkle each one with coarse salt.

8. Bake at 425° until they are golden brown (about 15 - 20 minutes).

taffy to twist

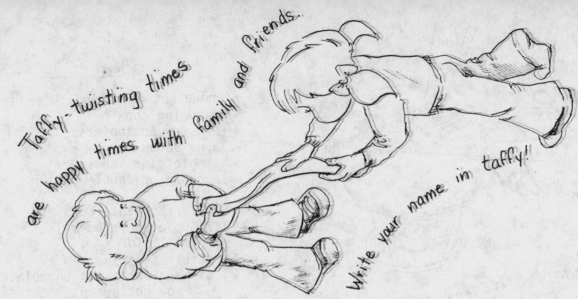

Taffy-twisting times are happy times with family and friends.

Write your name in taffy!

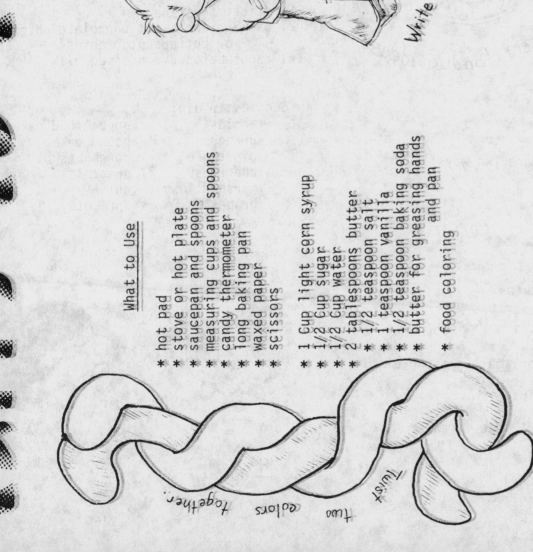

Twist two colors together.

What to Use

* hot pad
* stove or hot plate
* saucepan and spoons
* measuring cups and spoons
* candy thermometer
* long baking pan
* waxed paper
* scissors

* 1 cup light corn syrup
* 1/2 cup sugar
* 1/2 cup water
* 2 tablespoons butter
* 1/2 teaspoon salt
* 1 teaspoon vanilla
* 1/2 teaspoon baking soda
* butter for greasing hands and pan

* food coloring

What to Do

1. Generously grease a long pan.

2. Mix corn syrup, sugar and water in saucepan, put in thermometer, and boil until the mixture reaches 258°.

3. Remove from heat and stir in butter, salt, vanilla, baking soda and food coloring.

4. Pour the taffy into pan. Cool 15 minutes or until it's cool enough to handle.

5. Give a "hunk" of taffy to two people with buttered hands. Pull the taffy, fold, pull again until the taffy is light in color.

6. Twist the taffy into ropes and shapes. (A scissors will help cut it if you need to).

7. Wrap your shapes in waxed paper until you're ready to eat.

179

Do You Fondue?

If not, please do!

Here are some creamy dessert fondue ideas!

* fondue pot or ceramic dish over candle
* measuring cup
* forks or toothpicks
* large spoon
* hot plate or stove
* saucepan or double boiler

* 6 milk chocolate bars and
* 1/2 Cup evaporated milk
  OR
* 1 stick margarine
* 1 package semisweet chocolate chips
         or butterscotch chips
* 1 can sweetened condensed milk

* Goodies to dip:
apples	angel food cake
oranges	pound cake
pineapple	doughnuts
cherries	pretzels
marshmallows	nuts
grapes	apricots

What to Do

1. Make fondue sauce in a saucepan. Here are two ways:
   Use very low heat please!
   > Melt 6 milk chocolate bars.
   > Stir in 1/2 Cup milk.

   > **OR**

   > Melt 1 stick margarine with
   > 1 package semisweet chocolate chips
   >   or butterscotch chips.
   > Stir in 1 can sweetened condensed milk.

2. Keep fondue sauce warm in a fondu pot or small chafing dish.

3. Cut up fruits, cakes and goodies to dip.

4. Gather some friends and fondue together. Use forks or toothpicks for dipping!

Feeds 10 people!

"I'm fond of you, too!"

180

What to Use

* large saucepan and wooden spoon
* large bowl
* candy thermometer
* measuring cups and spoons
* hot plate or stove
* waxed paper

* 15 Cups popped popcorn
* 1 Cup molasses
* 1 Cup corn syrup
* 1/2 Cup sugar
* 1/2 Cup water
* 1/2 teaspoon salt
* 1 tablespoon butter
* 1 tablespoon vanilla
* extra butter or margarine
         for greasing hands
* Optional: decorations and
            treats to add to
            caramel corn....

candied cherries	peanuts
chocolate chips	raisins
gumdrops	hard candies
licorice bits	gum balls

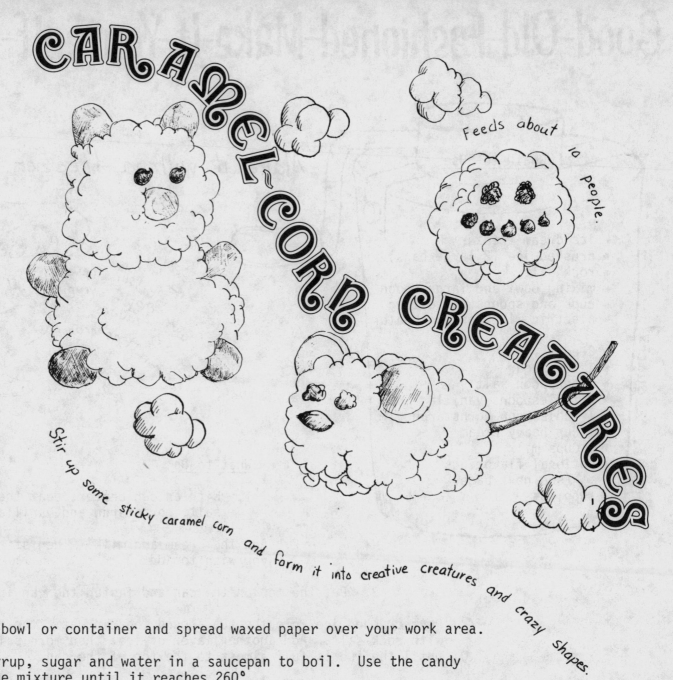

CARAMEL CORN CREATURES

Feeds about 10 people.

Stir up some sticky caramel corn and form it into creative creatures and crazy shapes.

What to Do

1. Put popcorn in a large bowl or container and spread waxed paper over your work area.

2. Place molasses, corn syrup, sugar and water in a saucepan to boil. Use the candy thermometer and boil the mixture until it reaches 260°.

3. Remove the pan from the heat and stir in salt, butter and vanilla. Cool for 3 minutes.

4. Butter your hands. Then slowly pour the syrup over the popcorn and stir with your hands.

5. Shape the caramel corn into any kind of a creature. Set it on waxed paper to dry.

Good-Old-Fashioned-Make-It-Yourself-Ice-Cream

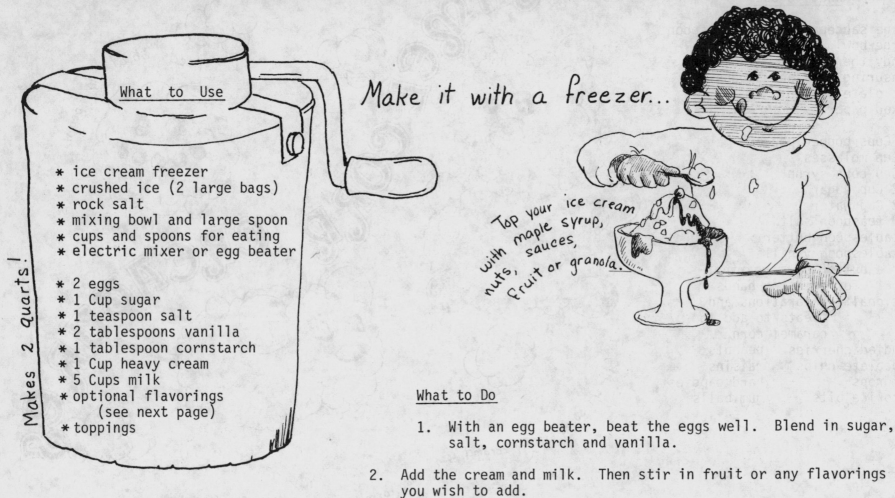

What to Use

Makes 2 quarts!

* ice cream freezer
* crushed ice (2 large bags)
* rock salt
* mixing bowl and large spoon
* cups and spoons for eating
* electric mixer or egg beater

* 2 eggs
* 1 Cup sugar
* 1 teaspoon salt
* 2 tablespoons vanilla
* 1 tablespoon cornstarch
* 1 Cup heavy cream
* 5 Cups milk
* optional flavorings
    (see next page)
* toppings

Make it with a freezer...

Top your ice cream with maple syrup, nuts, sauces, fruit or granola.

What to Do

1. With an egg beater, beat the eggs well. Blend in sugar, salt, cornstarch and vanilla.

2. Add the cream and milk. Then stir in fruit or any flavorings you wish to add.

3. Put the top on the can and fasten the can into the freezer.

4. Pour crushed ice into the tub around the can until the tub is 1/3 full. Sprinkle with rock salt. Add another layer of ice, then more salt. Layer ice and salt until the tub is full almost to the top of the can.

5. Crank the freezer until the crank becomes very hard to turn. Then remove the can. Wipe off the salty water before you open the can.

6. Take out the "dasher"--and lick it, of course! Then dish up the ice cream, add toppings, and eat!

...or, make it without a freezer !

What to Use

* 2 mixing bowls
* egg beater
* 2 ice cream trays
* measuring spoons

* saucepan and spoon
* waxed paper
* stove or hot plate
* measuring cups

* 1/2 Cup cold water
* 2 eggs
* 2 1/2 Cups milk
* 2 tablespoons vanilla
* 1 tablespoon cornstarch

* 1 teaspoon unflavored gelatin
* 1 Cup sugar
* 2 Cups whipping cream
* 1/2 teaspoon salt
* flavorings (optional)

What to Do

1. Sprinkle gelatin on cold water in mixing bowl. Let it stand 5 minutes.

2. Add eggs, sugar, salt and cornstarch. Beat with an eggbeater.

3. Stir in milk. Cook and stir over low heat JUST until it boils. BE CAREFUL NOT TO LET THE MIXTURE BURN!

4. Remove from heat, add vanilla, and pour into freezer trays.

5. Freeze for 1 hour or until the mixture is slushy.

6. Take ice cream from freezer and pour into a bowl.

7. Beat whipping cream until it's stiff and gently fold it into the ice cream.

8. Return ice cream to trays, cover with waxed paper and freeze several hours.

9. The first 2 hours, stir the ice cream often.

Makes 2 quarts!

Some Flavorings
to Add to Ice Cream
Before You Freeze It
Try One :

1/4 Cup strong coffee
honey
cinnamon candies
crushed candy canes
chocolate chips
mint flavoring
bananas
crushed pineapple
canned peaches
cranberry sauce

HOME-MADE MARSHMALLOWS

What to Use

* 9 x 9 inch baking pan
* hot plate or stove
* tea kettle or pan to boil water
* egg beater or electric mixer
* mixing bowl and spoon
* sharp knife
* measuring cups and spoons

* 1 large package of Jello
* 1½ Cups of boiling water
* ½ Cup of corn syrup
* a bowl of white sugar

Makes 25 squares!

What to Do

1. Empty the package of Jello (any flavor) into a bowl.

2. Pour in the boiling water and stir until the Jello is completely dissolved.

3. Add the corn syrup and stir well. Let the mixture sit (or refrigerate it for a while).

4. When the mixture begins to thicken, whip it with a mixer or beater until it is fluffy.

5. Pour it into a baking pan and let it set until the marshmallows are firm.

6. Cut it into small cubes, and roll each cube in sugar.

7. You can get a pretty assortment of colored marshmallows if you make several flavors!

184

SMOOTHIES... possibly the most scrumptious drink ever invented!

A smoothie is a smooth, cold, nutritious drink made with liquids, fruits and other surprises.

Nobody else's will be like yours!

What is a smoothie?

Some of the Many Smoothie Ingredients

canned, fresh or frozen fruits

berries	watermelon
melon	fruit cocktail
pineapple	apricots
oranges	apples
grapefruit	peaches
prunes	pears
grapes	bananas
applesauce	cherries

pineapple juice	malt powder
honey	syrup
ice cream	sherbet
molasses	yogurt
lemonaid	punch
prune juice	orange juice
milk	pudding
cottage cheese	grape juice
apple juice	raw egg

You can even add nuts!

* You also need: a glass jar
a spoon
a straw

What to Do

1. Spoon everything into a blender. You'll need to make sure there's _some_ liquid.

2. Spin the blender at medium speed for a minute.

3. Pour it into a tall glass!

(You might have to eat it with a spoon!)

POPSICLES

What to Use

* muffin tins, paper cups or ice cube trays
* plastic spoons or ice cream sticks
* popsicle mixture of your choice
* a freezer

Make your favorite popsicles at home, or in school.

Just freeze a mixture that sounds good!

rootbeer

pineapple juice

grape juice

cola

orange juice

lemonade mixed with milk

cider

punch

apricot nectar

yogurt and honey

orange juice and cranberry juice

thin pudding

crushed berries mixed with water and sugar

What to Do

1. Pour a popsicle mixture into ice cube trays, paper cups, or muffin tins.

2. Place a spoon or stick in each popsicle.

3. Put them in the freezer until they're frozen!

186

Pleasing Parfaits

A parfait is a dessert that's made in layers.

So..... layer up one of your own!
Try some of these, or use your very favorite ingredients.

ice cream	berries	raisins
pudding	peaches	nuts
whipped cream	pears	chocolate chips
applesauce	grapes	jelly
custard	crushed pineapple	preserves
frozen orange juice	orange slices	coconut
sherbet	cereal	cinnamon candies
chocolate syrup	marshmallows	granola
fruit cocktail	Jello	crushed peppermint candies

You don't need fancy parfait glasses.
You can pile delicious layers into any glass, tall or small!

What to Use

* hot pads
* electric frying pan
* long sticks or skewers
* mixing bowl and spoon
* rubber spatula
* measuring cups and spoons
* paper towels
* tall can or blender

* 6 hot dogs
* 2 Cups cooking oil
* 3/4 Cup flour
* 3/4 Cup cornmeal
* 1 egg
* 3/4 Cup milk
* 2 tablespoons shortening
* 1 teaspoon salt
* 1 tablespoon sugar
* 1 tablespoon baking powder
* 2 teaspoons dry mustard
* ketchup and mustard in
    squeeze bottles

corn dogs

Makes 6 corn dogs!

What to Do

1. Put oil into frying pan and heat it to 400°.

2. In a mixing bowl or blender, beat together egg, milk, sugar, shortening and salt and mustard.

3. Add flour, cornmeal, and baking powder. Mix well.

4. Pour the mixture into a glass or can (unless you have a blender).

5. Put each hot dog on a stick. Dip it into the corn mixture.

6. Fry the corn dogs in oil until they're brown (about 10 minutes).

7. Drain them on paper towels.

8. "Decorate" your corn dog with mustard and ketchup before you gobble it down!

Some special things to make

Chapter 7

Puppets... Puppets... Puppets...

There are lots and lots of ways to make puppets!

Try some of these
OR
invent some of your own.

Look at all the different things you can use!

Now, collect some junk, and turn on your imagination,

and.......

paper bag persons

*Trim puppets with:
* paper bits
* fabric scraps
* cotton
* buttons
* ribbon
* yarn and string
* seeds or noodles
* pipe cleaners
* feathers
* straws or toothpicks
* wire
    etc.

box puppets
You can cut holes and
stick out fingers for noses
or tongues.

spoon creatures

popsicle stick characters

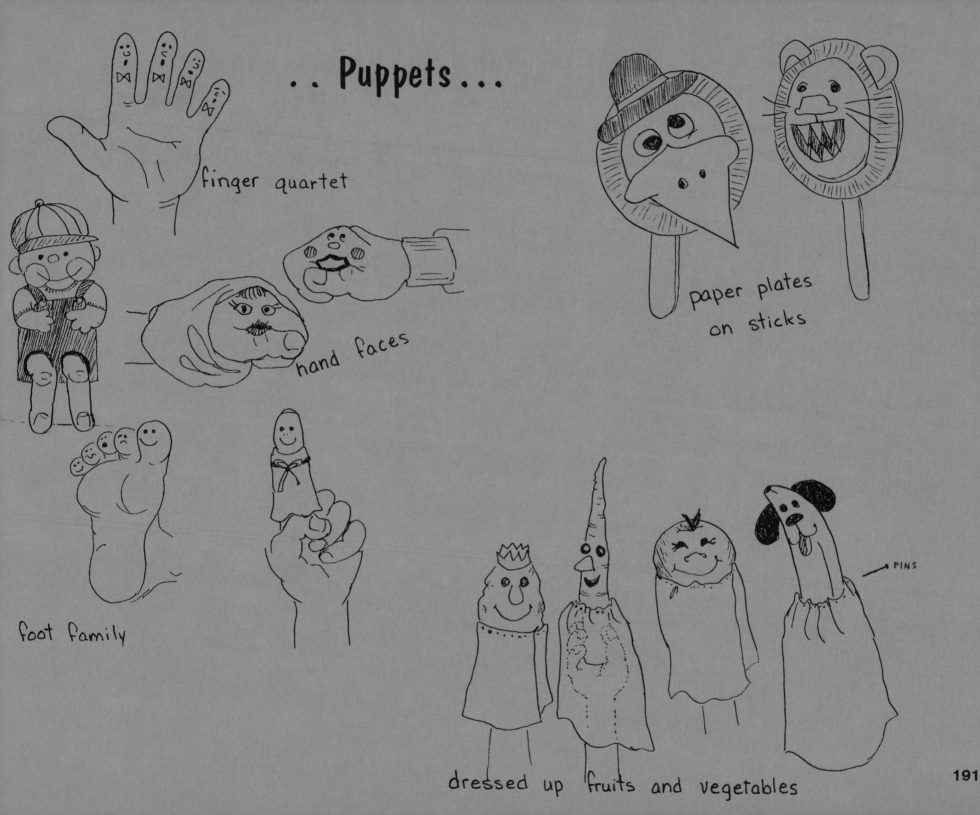

.. Puppets...

finger quartet

hand faces

paper plates on sticks

foot family

dressed up fruits and vegetables

PINS

..Puppets...

Puppets...

old socks
(with the toes
pushed in)

mitten animals

more socks

Cut a slit for the mouth.
Sew red felt
inside!

styrofoam balls
Cut a hole for
your finger. →

PINS

192

.. Puppets ..

chore-boy
(with wire legs)

Do you recognize this pair?

old hair brushes with new life

dish soap bottles

tin can puppets

butter tubs
on
sticks

193

Now, put your puppets on stage

and let them come alive!

Perform through an opening cut in an old sheet.

An old TV set (with no insides) is a super puppet theater.

Turn a chalkboard into a puppet stage.

Find a box large enough for people to get under or inside.

Peeping Periscopes

What to Use

* a long box (an aluminum foil box is good)
* 2 small mirrors
* 2 pieces of cardboard (bigger than the mirrors)
* heavy sturdy tape
* scissors and knife
* glue
* crayons, markers or paint for decorations

What to Do

1. Draw a dotted line across the corner of the box to make a triangle which has 2 sides the same length. (In the picture, side A is the same length as side B)

2. Mark both ends this way, then slice off the ends on the dotted lines you've drawn.

3. Now cut a square window near the bottom of the back.

4. Cut another square window near the top end <u>on the opposite side from the bottom</u> window.

5. Cut 2 pieces of cardboard big enough to completely cover the open ends.

6. Glue the mirror on one piece and tape that piece onto the bottom so that the mirror faces up! Tape all around the edges so that this bottom fits tightly.

7. Glue the other mirror on the second piece of cardboard and tape it to the top opening so that the mirror faces <u>down</u>.

8. Paint, draw or color your own special designs on your private periscope.

9. Try it out. . . . peek over fences, under beds around corners. You can watch without being seen. Be careful though, you might get arrested for spying!

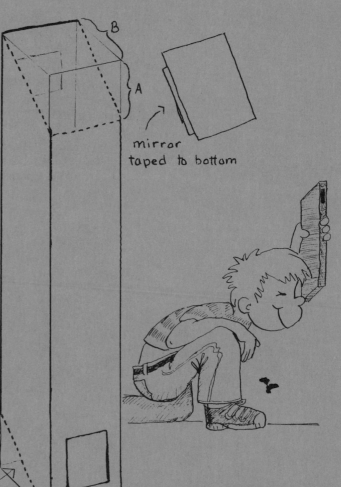

mirror taped to bottom

mirror

A Salt Sculpture

PAPER

What to Do

1. Decide what colors you want to use. You'll need a piece of chalk and a cup for each color.

2. Dump some salt on a paper towel. Rub chalk over and over the salt until the salt is all colored. For deeper colors, rub longer.

3. Put the colored salt in a cup until you are ready to use it. Keep each color separate.

4. Gently pour 1 layer at a time into the container. Don't jiggle or tip the jar.

5. Make the layers any size you wish. The salt will fall in un-even mounds, especially if you guide the salt as you pour.

6. Fill the jar <u>full</u>. Let it stand overnight, then add more salt.

7. Cover the container tightly.

What to Use

* a glass container with a top
* a box of salt
* colored chalk
* a spoon
* paper towels
* a sheet of paper
* several cups

A great gift idea!

Teriffic Totem

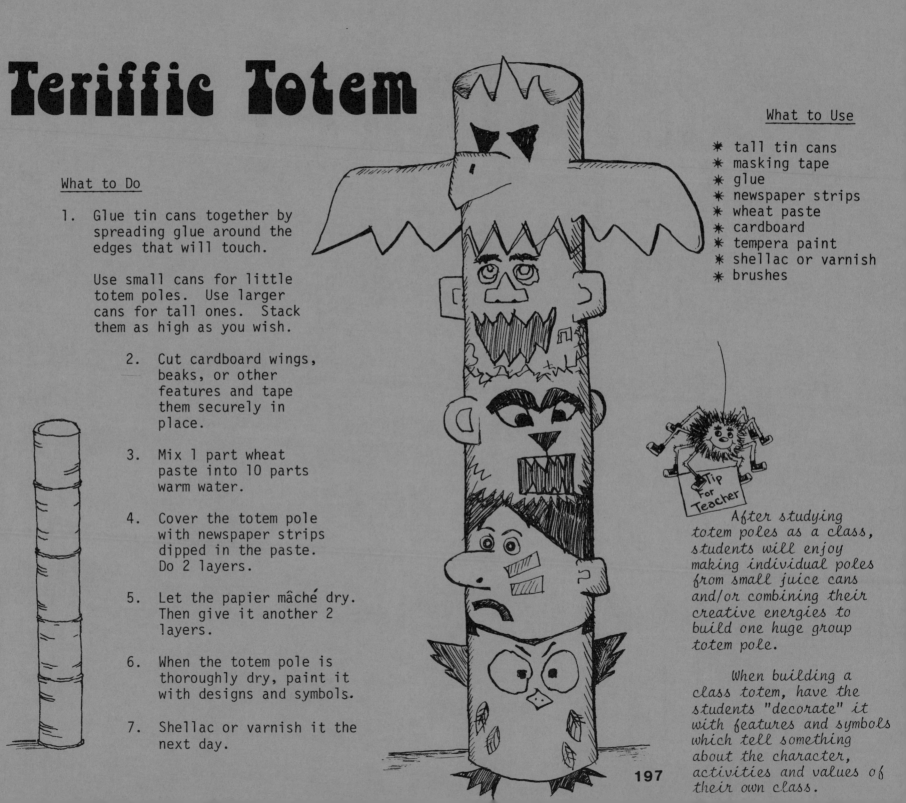

What to Do

1. Glue tin cans together by spreading glue around the edges that will touch.

   Use small cans for little totem poles. Use larger cans for tall ones. Stack them as high as you wish.

2. Cut cardboard wings, beaks, or other features and tape them securely in place.

3. Mix 1 part wheat paste into 10 parts warm water.

4. Cover the totem pole with newspaper strips dipped in the paste. Do 2 layers.

5. Let the papier mâché dry. Then give it another 2 layers.

6. When the totem pole is thoroughly dry, paint it with designs and symbols.

7. Shellac or varnish it the next day.

You can use cereal boxes or oatmeal boxes instead of cans!

What to Use

* tall tin cans
* masking tape
* glue
* newspaper strips
* wheat paste
* cardboard
* tempera paint
* shellac or varnish
* brushes

Tip For Teacher

After studying totem poles as a class, students will enjoy making individual poles from small juice cans and/or combining their creative energies to build one huge group totem pole.

When building a class totem, have the students "decorate" it with features and symbols which tell something about the character, activities and values of their own class.

197

BE A GIANT!

Try it with tin cans.

What to Do

1. Turn the cans upside down.
    Punch a hole in each side of each can.
    (It's easy to do by hammering a nail
    into the side of the can with a rock.)

2. Cut 2 pieces of heavy string.
    (Make each one twice as long as the
    distance from your elbow to your foot.)

3. String one piece through each can.
    Tie a good sized knot in both ends.
    (See the picture).

4. Stand up on the cans, hold onto
    the "handles" tightly and walk.

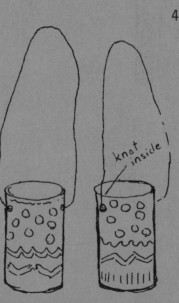

knot inside!

What to Use

* 2 large tin cans with one end removed
* 2 lengths of twine or heavy string
        (each about 6 feet or 2 meters)
* acrylic or enamel paint for decoration

Or, be a giant with tall poles.

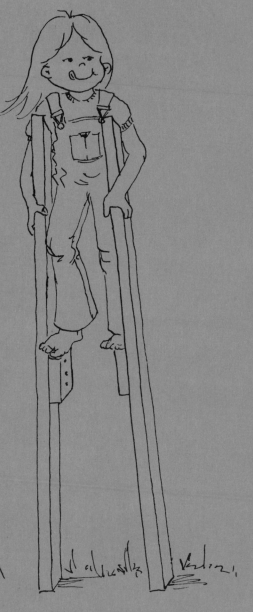

What to Use

* 2 pieces of 1"x2" wood about 6 feet tall
* 2 wood blocks for feet 2"x4"x6"
* glue for wood
* sandpaper
* 6 large wood screws
* hammer or screwdriver

What to Do

1. Glue the foot blocks against the wide side of each tall wood pole. Make sure you place them both at the same height.

   The higher the foot blocks, the taller you'll be! (But it's harder to walk too!)

2. Use 3 screws or nails to fasten each block to the pole.

3. Sandpaper your stilts until they're smooth. That way you won't get any splinters! You can paint them too!

4. Step up onto the foot blocks. Hold the poles under your arms. You'll get a better start if someone helps you when you first begin to walk. Lean on one foot while you pick up the other.

a homemade rainbow

What to Use

* all kinds of scraps of fabric
  in rainbow colors
* scissors   • an old sheet
* pencils   • glue

What to Do

1. Gather some friends together. This
   is a good group project!

2. On an old sheet, draw 6 arcs for a
   rainbow. Trim away any extra sheet
   that isn't a part of the rainbow.

3. Write "red, orange, yellow, green, blue,
   violet" on the stripes with your pencil.
   This will help you remember the colors
   as you work.

4. Cut or tear patches of each color. They
   can be prints, strips, solids, plaids, etc.

5. Glue the red patches on the first stripe.
   Arrange them so that you can mix different
   fabric textures. Overlap the edges.

6. Do the same with the other colors.

7. Hang your rainbow in a window, on a
   bulletin board or from a wire.

8. What do you think of when you look at
   the blue stripe? What people, sounds,
   smells, feelings or experiences come to
   your mind? Try this with all the colors.

The whole class can become involved
in making a rainbow to cover a wall or
fill a bulletin board.
    You might have committees work sep-
arately on individual rainbow "stripes."
    Making a rainbow will be a great
opener for lessons, discussions, or
practice on:

differing textures

measurement
        (measure all those patches.
        Find the perimeter
                    area
                    total rainbow area.)

vocabulary development
        (How many synonyms can you
        find for red?)

writing descriptive phrases
        (a "shimmering emerald pool")

metaphors
        (Orange _is_ a warm friendly
        kitchen _on_ a cold evening.)

Tip
For
Teacher

SILENT FACES

With a mask..........

You can be a wizard..... a jackal..... a queen.....

You can be bold.....or sneaky..... or ferocious..... or timid,

With a mask..........

Start with a paper sack...

You could fill a whole zoo with made-up animals!

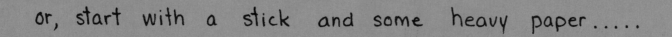

or, start with a stick and some heavy paper.....

You can do a one-person show by playing <u>all</u> the parts!

Papier mâché Masks

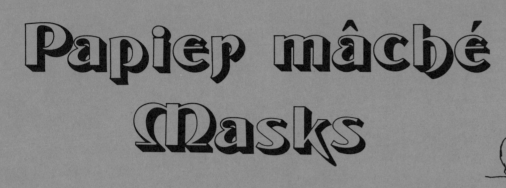

What to Use

* newspaper or paper towels torn into strips
* wheat paste or wallpaper paste
* water
* a bowl and mixing spoon
* paint
* a pie pan, cake tin, or a large round balloon
* petroleum jelly
* cardboard strips

What to Do

1. Carefully mix 1 cup of paste into 10 cups of warm water.
   (For other papier mâché recipes, see the appendix of this book).

2. Turn the pan upside down. Grease the bottom and sides with
   petroleum jelly <u>or</u> blow up your balloon.

3. Now you're ready to dip newspaper strips in the paste and cover your
   pan or half of the balloon with 2 layers.

4. Make eyes, noses, mouths, ears, wrinkles, etc. by gluing on cardboard
   strips, pieces of egg cartons, heavy string, a spool, etc.

5. Cover the mask with 2 more layers of pasted strips.

6. After it's dry, remove the pan or break the balloon and paint the mask with
   tempera paints. You can add hair and other touches now too!

Decorate your mask with paper curls, yarn bits, kinky wire, cardboard, ribbons and bows, buttons, spools, egg carton pieces, macaroni, feathers, toothpicks, Q-tips, tin foil, cotton, paint, or anything else you can find that makes it just the right mask for you!

Personally Puzzled

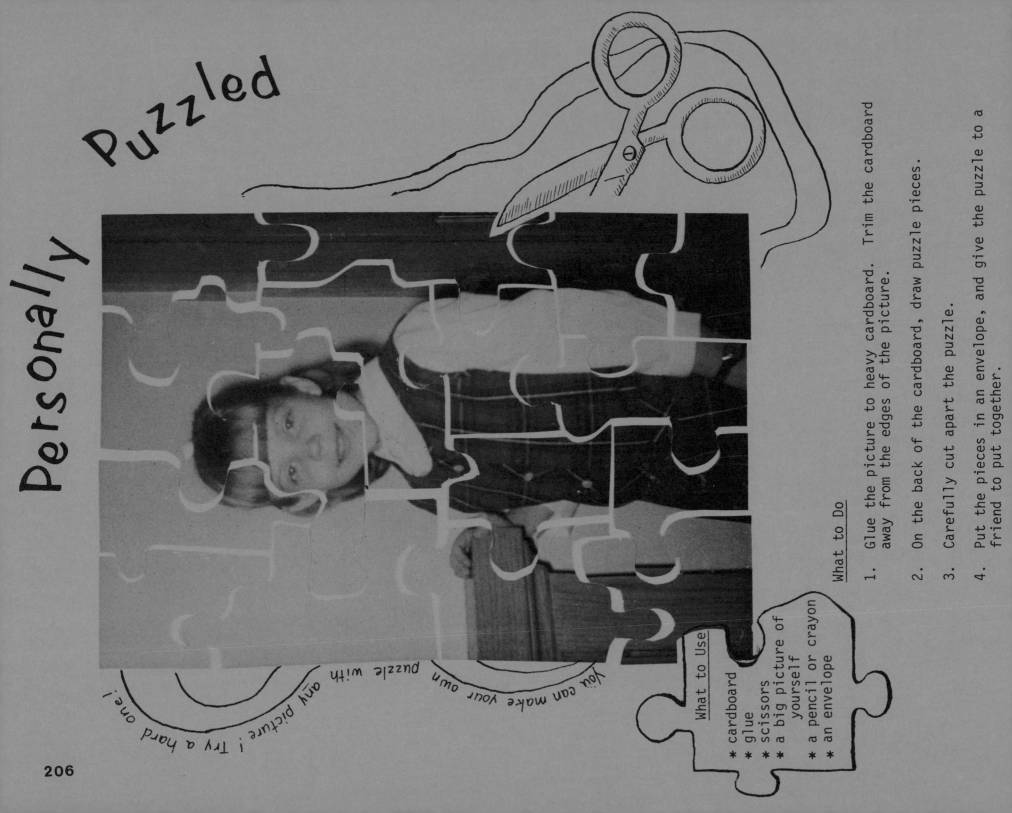

You can make your own puzzle with any picture! Try a hard one!

What to Use

* cardboard
* glue
* scissors
* a big picture of yourself
* a pencil or crayon
* an envelope

What to Do

1. Glue the picture to heavy cardboard. Trim the cardboard away from the edges of the picture.

2. On the back of the cardboard, draw puzzle pieces.

3. Carefully cut apart the puzzle.

4. Put the pieces in an envelope, and give the puzzle to a friend to put together.

Stationery You Can't Buy

Give a personal touch to your letters.

Here are some ideas to start you thinking...

Some Things You Can Use

* note paper or stationery
* white glue
* scissors
* leaves, dry weeds or flowers
* stamp pad or dark tempera paint
* yarn, ric rac or lace
* fabric scraps
* fine paint pen or markers

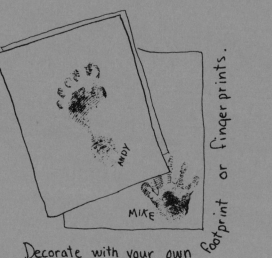

Decorate with your own footprint or finger prints.

Paste on pictures cut out from magazines.

Paste on some leaves or dried flowers.

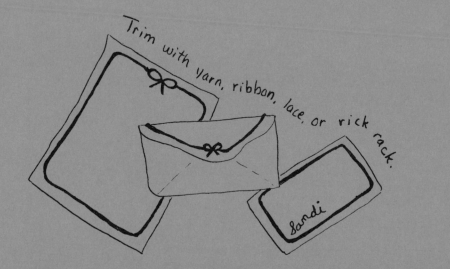

Trim with yarn, ribbon, lace, or rick rack.

Sketch designs or add doodles.

Pinwheels

What to Use

* heavy construction paper or lightweight tagboard
* scissors
* a penny
* a straight pin
* crayons, markers or paint for decorating
* a pencil with an eraser or a stick or a straw

What to Use

1. Cut a piece of paper into a square, or trace the pattern on the next page.

2. Trace around the penny right in the center.

3. Now is a good time to decorate both the front and back of your pinwheel. Try some stripe designs or crazy pictures!

4. Then cut in from each corner to the edge of the circle. Cut on the dotted lines.

5. Mark the corners 1, 2, 3, 4 as you see in this picture.

6. Bend each numbered corner into the center. (Don't fold them).

7. Stick the pin through all four corners into the center.

8. Then put the pin into the eraser of the pencil or into the end of your straw or stick.

9. Now . . . blow on it or run in the wind and watch your pinwheel spin.

208

A DANCING DOLL

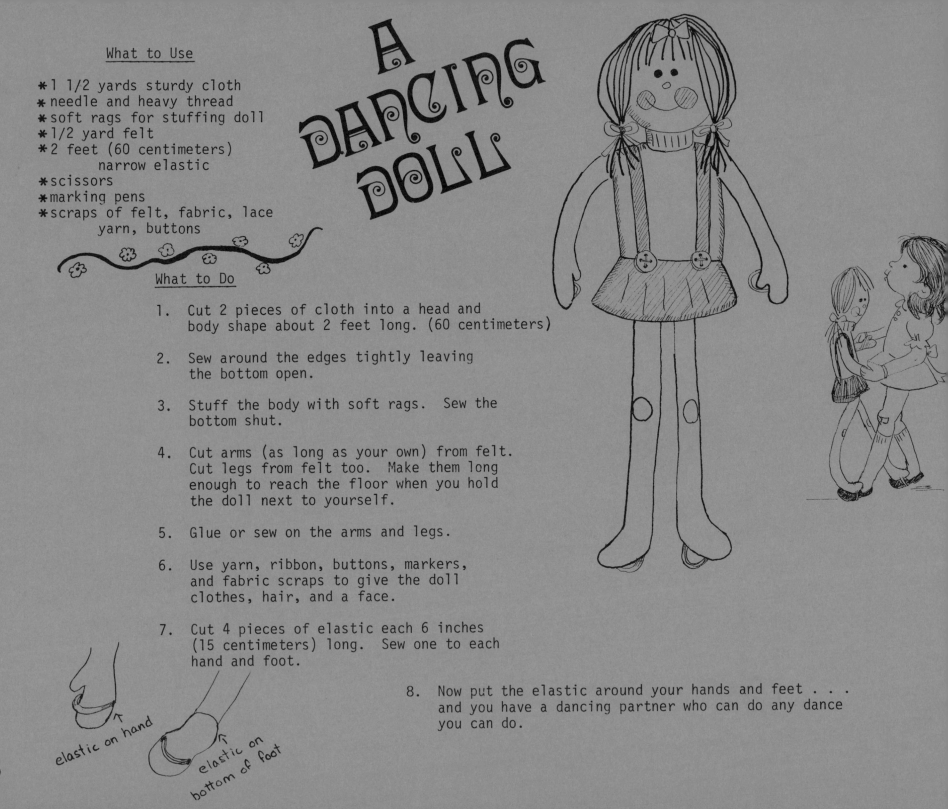

What to Use

* 1 1/2 yards sturdy cloth
* needle and heavy thread
* soft rags for stuffing doll
* 1/2 yard felt
* 2 feet (60 centimeters)
    narrow elastic
* scissors
* marking pens
* scraps of felt, fabric, lace
    yarn, buttons

What to Do

1. Cut 2 pieces of cloth into a head and body shape about 2 feet long. (60 centimeters)

2. Sew around the edges tightly leaving the bottom open.

3. Stuff the body with soft rags. Sew the bottom shut.

4. Cut arms (as long as your own) from felt. Cut legs from felt too. Make them long enough to reach the floor when you hold the doll next to yourself.

5. Glue or sew on the arms and legs.

6. Use yarn, ribbon, buttons, markers, and fabric scraps to give the doll clothes, hair, and a face.

7. Cut 4 pieces of elastic each 6 inches (15 centimeters) long. Sew one to each hand and foot.

8. Now put the elastic around your hands and feet . . . and you have a dancing partner who can do any dance you can do.

elastic on hand

elastic on bottom of foot

210

ME-CUBES

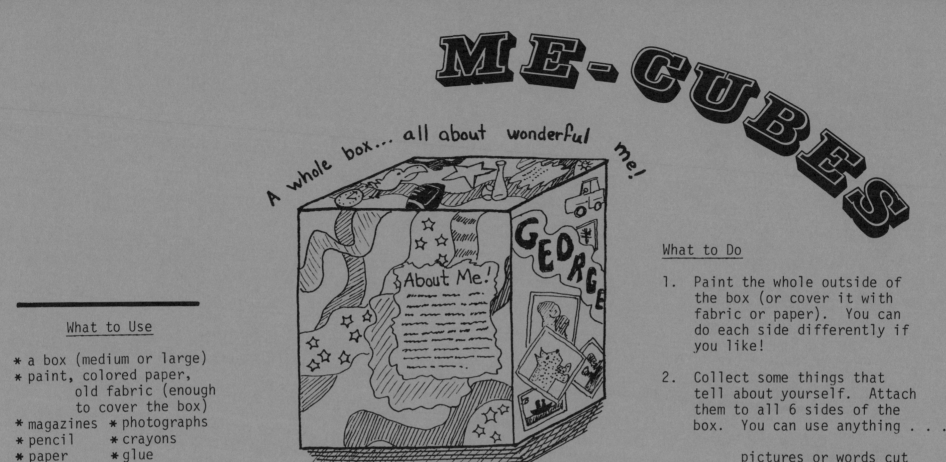

A whole box... all about wonderful me!

About Me!

GEORGE

What to Use

* a box (medium or large)
* paint, colored paper,
    old fabric (enough
    to cover the box)
* magazines   * photographs
* pencil   * crayons
* paper   * glue

What to Do

1. Paint the whole outside of the box (or cover it with fabric or paper). You can do each side differently if you like!

2. Collect some things that tell about yourself. Attach them to all 6 sides of the box. You can use anything . . .

    pictures or words cut
        from magazines
    photographs
    drawings
    stories

You might even want to write an AUTOBIOGRAPHY on one side. (That's a true story about your life.)

Let the cube tell about:

your friends	your family
your likes	your dislikes
your looks	your feelings
your ideas	your dreams
your secrets	your experiences
your plans	your mistakes

and anything else special about you!

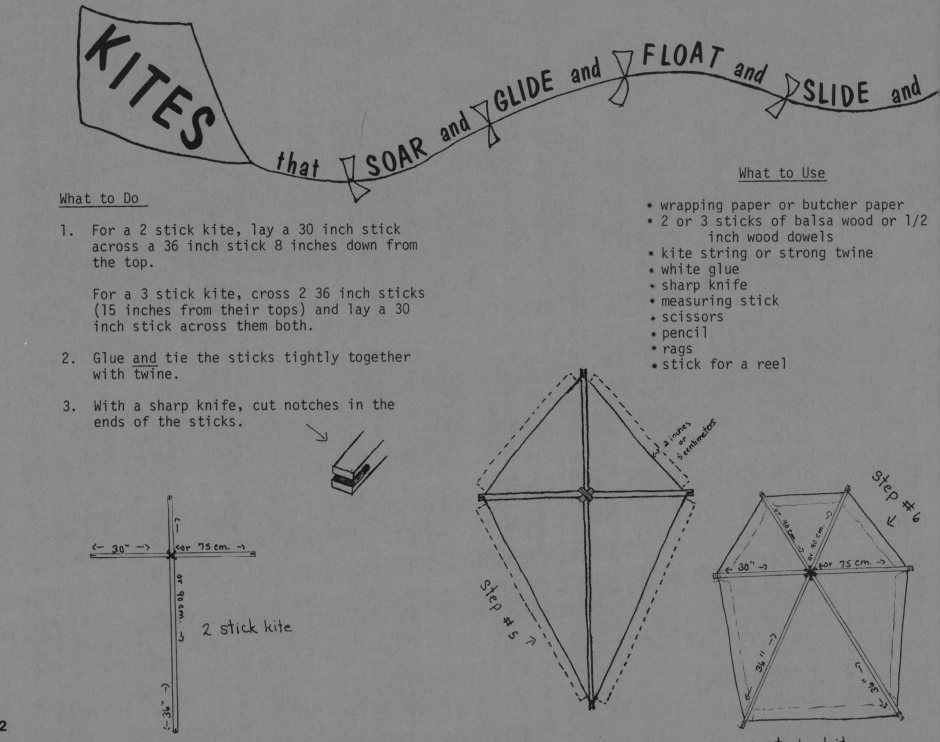

KITES that ✗ SOAR and ✗ GLIDE and ✗ FLOAT and ✗ SLIDE and

What to Do

1. For a 2 stick kite, lay a 30 inch stick across a 36 inch stick 8 inches down from the top.

   For a 3 stick kite, cross 2 36 inch sticks (15 inches from their tops) and lay a 30 inch stick across them both.

2. Glue <u>and</u> tie the sticks tightly together with <u>twine</u>.

3. With a sharp knife, cut notches in the ends of the sticks.

What to Use

* wrapping paper or butcher paper
* 2 or 3 sticks of balsa wood or 1/2 inch wood dowels
* kite string or strong twine
* white glue
* sharp knife
* measuring stick
* scissors
* pencil
* rags
* stick for a reel

2 stick kite

← 30" → ←or 75 cm. →

or 90 cm.

← 36" →

2 inches or 5 centimeters

step #5

step #6

← 30" → ←or 75 cm. →

or 90 cm.

36"

36"

3 stick kite

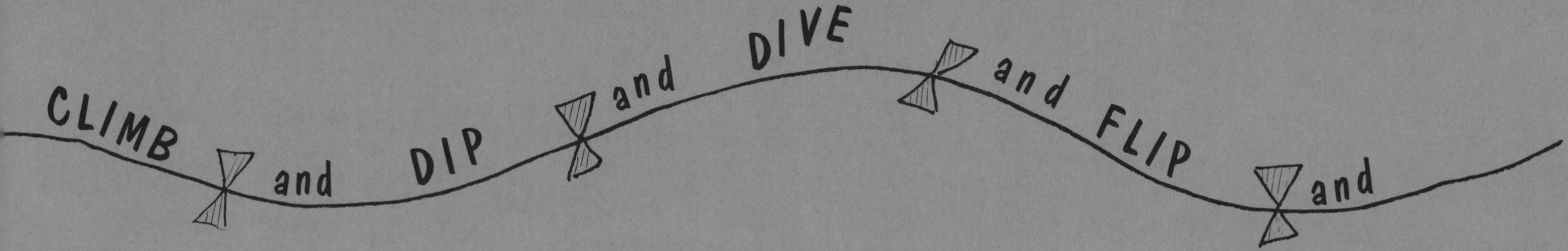

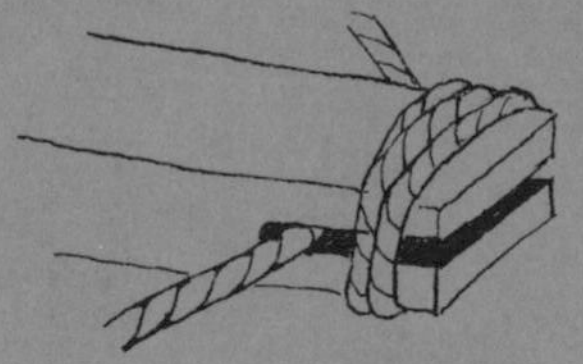

4. Run string all the way around the outside edges of the kite through each notch. Wind it around each end a few times.

5. Lay the kite frame on wrapping paper. Cut the kite covering 2 inches bigger than the frame. Color or paint the front of the kite.

6. Fold the edges of the covering over the string and glue them down.

7. Make a bridle for your kite (on the front side). Tie a piece of string to both ends of each stick. Where they all meet (point X) tie on a flying string.

8. Tie on a tail with some rags.

9. Wrap your flying string around a stick, and go fly a kite!

Point X

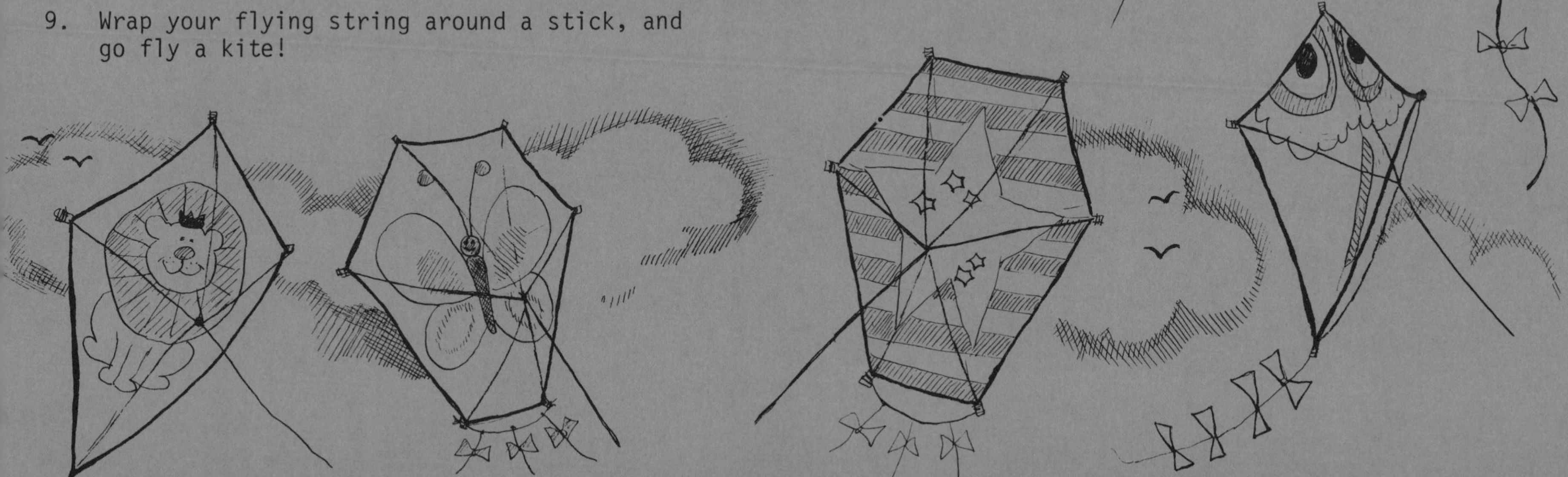

213

What to Use

* a yard of plain wrapping paper
* 2 feet (or 60 cm.) thin wire
* white glue
* crayons or paint
* kite string
* scissors
* stick of wood for a reel
* pencil

a Chinese flying fish kite

What to Do

1. Fold the paper in half and draw a fish about 12 inches wide X 36 inches long (or 30 X 90 cm.).

2. Cut out the fish. Since your paper is doubled, you'll get two!

3. Glue the two pieces together by spreading a light coat of glue along the top and bottom edges of the fish. Do not glue the mouth or the back end together.

4. Paint or color both sides of the kite.

5. Cut a piece of wire a bit longer than the size of the fish's mouth. Bend it into a circle, twisting the ends together.

6. Fold the edges of the fish's mouth over the wire and glue or tape it down on the inside.

7. Tie a short piece of string at 3 places on the wire. Where these 3 join together, tie on a string for flying the fish.

214

Everybody Needs a Stick !

A stick is good for leaning on...
      for scratching your back...
      for taking on a hike...
      for talking to...
  or just for having around !

What to Use

* a stick
* acrylic or enamel paint
* a small brush

What to Do

1. Choose a sturdy stick for yourself. Take your time! Keep looking until you find just the right one!

2. Paint your stick with bright designs. Or paint pictures that fit the markings and textures of the stick. You might want to glue on feathers or buttons or other treasures.

Tip for Teacher

This activity goes well with a unit on Indians. Students will enjoy learning about the use of coup sticks by some Indian tribes.... and they'll want to make their own!

Also, there are dozens of measuring activities and comparisons that can accompany the choosing and decorating of personal sticks.

Important Information for Candle-Makers

1

Be very careful with wax. It is flammable.
This means it can catch fire easily.
So: Never put a wax-filled container right on
     the heat.
     Always heat wax on medium or low heat.
     Always use a double boiler.
     (The picture shows you how to make one.)
     If the wax begins to smoke, remove it from
     the heat.
     Keep hot pads around for handling hot pans
     and cans.
     Get some adult help before you make candles.

2

If hot wax gets on your
skin, run cold water over
it right away. When the
wax is cool, you can peel
it off.

If you get any wax on
your clothing, let it dry.
Scrape off what you can,
then put the cloth between
two layers of newspaper and
press with a hot iron.

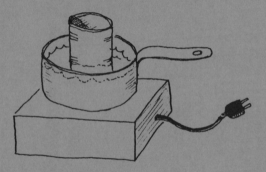

It's a good idea to keep
some sand around when you're
heating wax. If the wax
catches fire, water won't help.
Dump sand on the flames !

3

4

An easy way to color candles is to add
shavings or pieces of crayons to the wax
after it starts to melt.

Here's a hint for putting in wicks:
Tie one end of the wick to a pencil
and hang it over the center of the
candle.

5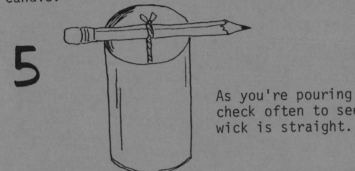

As you're pouring or dipping,
check often to see that your
wick is straight.

When you're dipping candles,
keep a can of ice water handy.
Dip the candlestick in the water
after each time you dip it in the
wax. This will help it cool fast!

6

7

When you're pouring candles into cardboard containers,
sometimes the sides bulge. To keep this from happening,
tie string around the mold before you use it.

On the other hand, you might like the bulgy shape!

Keep lots of newspaper
spread in layers around
your work area.

8

A funnel will help you pour
candles with less spilling.

swiss cheese candles

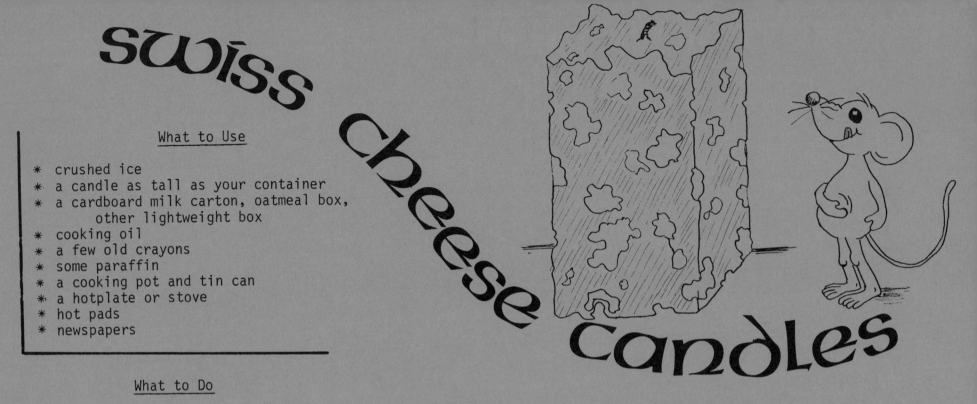

What to Use

* crushed ice
* a candle as tall as your container
* a cardboard milk carton, oatmeal box,
      other lightweight box
* cooking oil
* a few old crayons
* some paraffin
* a cooking pot and tin can
* a hotplate or stove
* hot pads
* newspapers

What to Do

1. Ask for some help from an adult because you'll be melting the paraffin and it burns very easily.

2. Get the mold ready by rubbing the inside with oil (unless it is wax coated) and by cutting it to the size you want.

3. Place the candle in the center. It will stay in place if you pour a little melted paraffin around the bottom of it and hold it for a few minutes.

4. Carefully melt enough paraffin to fill the mold. Use medium heat. You can color your wax by adding a few crayon pieces.

5. Fill the mold ½ full with crushed ice.

6. Pour hot paraffin over the ice.

7. Fill the mold to the top with ice, and then pour paraffin in again.

8. After it cools a while, pour off any water.

9. Let the candle sit overnight.

10. In the morning tear off the cardboard.

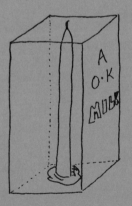

Double-Dip Candles

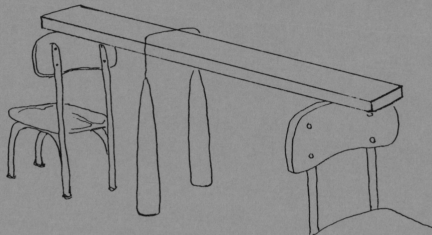

* hot plate or stove
* a tall narrow can
* a cooking pot
* a tall juice can or coffee can
* candle wicks
* small pieces of crayon
* newspaper

What to Do

1. Get an adult to help you, because melted wax can be dangerous.

2. Fill the pot ½ full with water and set the can inside it.

3. Turn the heat on low under the pot, and place paraffin in the can. Melt enough paraffin to fill the can about 3/4 full. Add crayons now if you want color.

4. Remove the tin of wax from the pot. You can place it back into the hot water whenever it needs heating again.

5. Cut about 35 cm. or 14 in. of wick. Bend the wick in the middle and dip both ends into the can. Pull it out and wait a few minutes until the wax hardens some.

6. Dip the candles again and again until they are as fat as you want them to be. Always keep the wick straight as you are dipping.

7. Hang the candles up to harden. Then cut them apart. They're ready to burn....but do it carefully!

Sand-y Candles

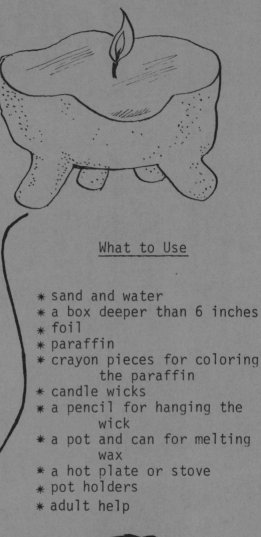

What to Do

1. Wrap the box with foil.

2. Mix enough water with the sand to make it quite damp but not sloppy.

3. Fill the box with the damp sand.

4. Dig or press a hole into the sand that makes a shape you like. You can use your fingers to make legs on the candle. If you do make legs . . . they need to be good and fat.

5. Cut a length of wick and hang it into the center of the opening.

6. Pour melted paraffin into the hole.

7. Allow the candle to cool. Then remove it from the sand.

8. Experiment with some other shapes!

What to Use

* sand and water
* a box deeper than 6 inches
* foil
* paraffin
* crayon pieces for coloring the paraffin
* candle wicks
* a pencil for hanging the wick
* a pot and can for melting wax
* a hot plate or stove
* pot holders
* adult help

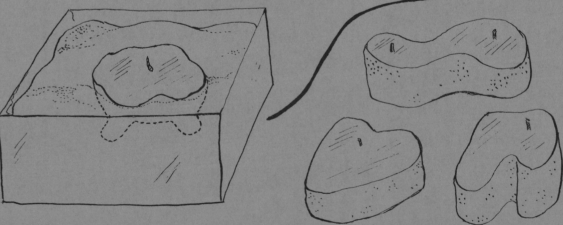

towers to burn

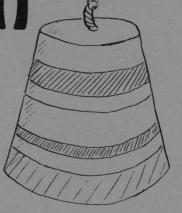

What to Use

* paraffin
* wicks
* crayons for color
* containers for molds
* lots of newspaper

* a cooking pot
* a can for each color wax
* crayons for color
* a hot plate or stove
* hot pads

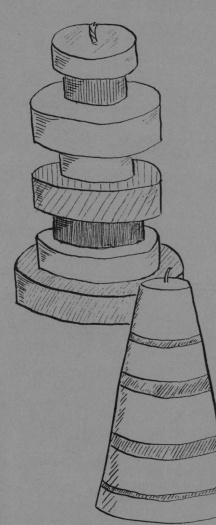

What to Do

1. Get an adult to help you.

2. Choose some waxed paper cups or milk containers for molds.

3. Hang a wick into your mold.

4. Melt the wax for the first layer and pour it as thick as you'd like it to be.

5. Let the wax get quite firm. Then pour the next layer.

6. When all the layers are poured, cut off the wick and let the candle harden overnight. In the morning, tear away the mold.

OR

You can make layers in separate containers. When they're hard, stack the slabs and "glue" them together with a blob of soft wax between each two layers.

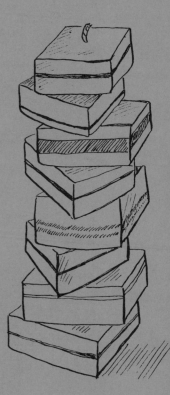

An Un-Piggy Bank

Have you ever had a hippo bank? or a bear bank? or a beaver or walrus bank?

Choose an animal and a balloon..... then make your own <u>un</u>-piggy bank!

What to Use

* torn newspaper strips
* torn paper towel strips
* papier mâché mixture
       (wheat paste and water)
* a balloon the shape you want
* a sharp knife
* string
* cardboard
* tape
* paint
* shellac
* thick yarn
* a cork

What to Do

1. Pour 1 cup of wheat paste
    into 10 cups of water. Mix
    until it's smooth.

2. Put 3 layers of pasted newspaper
    strips around a blown-up balloon.

3. Let the balloon hang or sit
    on a bowl until it's dry.

4. Add features to the animal
    by taping on pieces of cardboard.

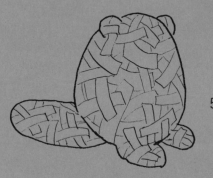

5. Mix more paste and cover all the animal with 3 more layers of paper strips. For the last layer, use plain colored paper towel strips.

6. After the paste dries use a sharp knife to cut a slit in the top for coins. Also cut a hole the size of the cork in the bottom.

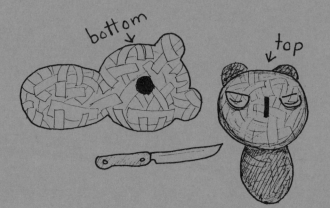

bottom

top

7. Then, paint your bank with tempera paints. Glue on raised lines with heavy yarn.

8. Shellac over the whole bank. When it's dry you can start saving money.

ellac

223

QUICK & EASY BEAN BAGS

Sew or glue on buttons and felt and pictures and yarn and scraps and ribbons.

What to Use

* an old mitten or hot mit
  or
* fabric to cut new shapes
* heavy yarn
* large needle
* felt and yarn scraps
* marking pens
* glue
* dried beans or rice

What to Do

1. Decorate a mitten with felt scraps, yarn, and buttons
   or
   cut and decorate any shape you choose.

2. Fill the mitten with dried beans or rice. Don't pack it too full.

3. Use heavy yarn to tightly stitch shut the open edge.

Add designs with markers too!

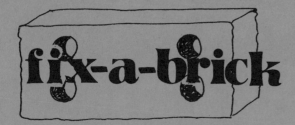

fix-a-brick

Found an old brick or cement block?

Clean it up! It can be........

a holder...
for pencils and supplies

a book end

a door-stop

a knic knac shelf

part of a bookcase

a mail box
for private messages

PRIVATE
TOP SECRET
KEEP OUT

What to Use

* bricks or cement blocks
* enamel paint
* glue
* fabric, felt or paper scraps
* scissors
* odds and ends like buttons,
   feathers, cardboard,
   pipecleaners, beads,
   yarn

225

Fruit & Vegetable Personalities

Turn a fruit or vegetable into a lively person .....
a silly animal ..... a funny face ..... a crazy creature....

What to Use

* Any of these:
pear
peach
apple
carrot
squash
banana
cucumber
celery stalk
orange
lemon
melon
plum
turnip

* and for decoration:
grapes
cherries
nuts
raisins
celery chunks
carrot slices
cheese chunks
marshmallows
cloves
lettuce
toothpicks

Fasten the foods together with toothpicks.

Give it a name!

If you can bear to do it to a new friend, you can eat what you've made!

....but please don't eat the toothpicks......

A Creepy Creature Catcher-Keeper

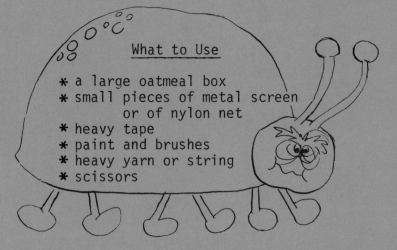

What to Use

* a large oatmeal box
* small pieces of metal screen or of nylon net
* heavy tape
* paint and brushes
* heavy yarn or string
* scissors

What to Do

1. Cut some windows in the oatmeal box.

2. Cut pieces of screen or netting a little larger than the windows.

3. Tape the screen inside the window openings. Make sure you tape securely on all four sides of the windows.

4. Paint and decorate your creature cage.

5. Punch a hole in each side and attach a handle of yarn or string.

COZY QUILTS

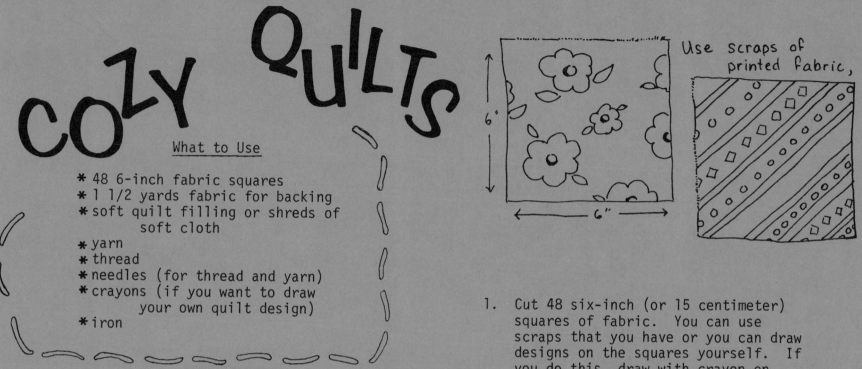

Use scraps of printed fabric,

What to Use

* 48 6-inch fabric squares
* 1 1/2 yards fabric for backing
* soft quilt filling or shreds of soft cloth
* yarn
* thread
* needles (for thread and yarn)
* crayons (if you want to draw your own quilt design)
* iron

1. Cut 48 six-inch (or 15 centimeter) squares of fabric. You can use scraps that you have or you can draw designs on the squares yourself. If you do this, draw with crayon on cotton material. After your drawings are done, cover the squares with waxed paper and another cloth. Then iron them to make the drawings permanent.

2. Use a needle and double thread to stitch the squares to each other. Sew them into rows of 8, then sew the rows together.

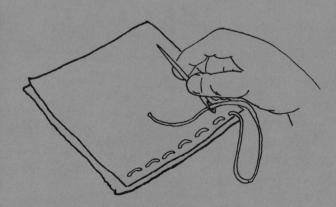

Put two squares with right sides together. Tie a knot in the thread and stitch in and out along one edge.

or use fabric you decorate yourself!

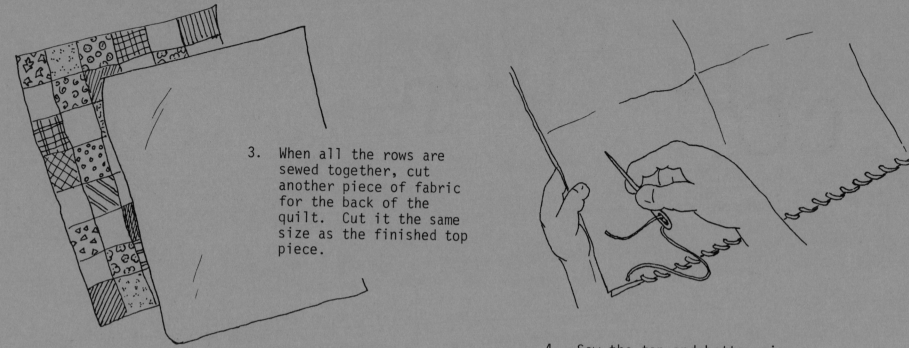

3. When all the rows are sewed together, cut another piece of fabric for the back of the quilt. Cut it the same size as the finished top piece.

4. Sew the top and bottom pieces together with heavy yarn. With each stitch bring the needle over the edge and down through the fabric. Leave one end open.

5. Stuff the quilt with shreds of soft cloth or fluffy quilt filling from a fabric store. Spread it evenly. Stitch the end of the quilt.

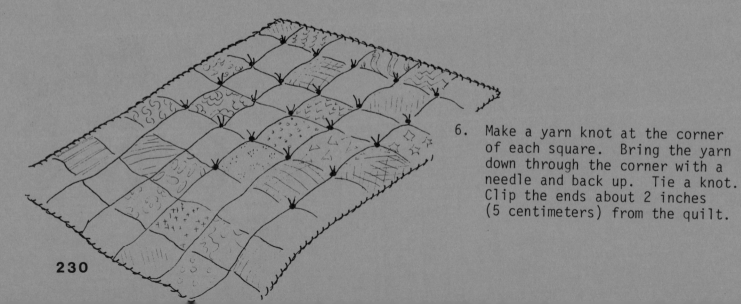

6. Make a yarn knot at the corner of each square. Bring the yarn down through the corner with a needle and back up. Tie a knot. Clip the ends about 2 inches (5 centimeters) from the quilt.

230

A quilting bee is a fun and valuable class experience. You might ask each student to design a square that is uniquely his. Then put small groups to work putting the quilt together.

What to do with it? Display it proudly, then donate it to someone who needs warmth.

Tip For Teacher

231

Touch and Tell Scrapbook

What to Use

* *scrapbook or construction paper
* *glue
* *scissors

_____

What to Do

1. If you don't have an empty scrapbook make one by fastening together several construction paper pages. You can punch holes in the pages and string them together with yarn.

2. Then search around your house, neighborhood, classroom or school grounds to find samples of things with different textures. (That means things that FEEL different when you TOUCH them!)

3. Paste each sample in your scrapbook. Write a word that tells how it feels.

4. Try touching each page with your eyes closed. Can you tell what it is?

Can you find something that feels

bumpy?	silky?
scratchy?	rough?
furry?	slippery?
smooth?	wrinkled?
greasy?	rubbery?
cracked?	prickly?
sticky?	scaly?

Trade scrapbooks with a friend. See if he or she can describe how each of your samples feels.

Tip For Teacher

Use a "Touch and Tell Scrapbook" for tactile discrimination and vocabulary development. Have students make a group scrapbook. Then prepare an envelope of labels for students to match with textures.

scratchy   fuzzy

Whirly Birds!

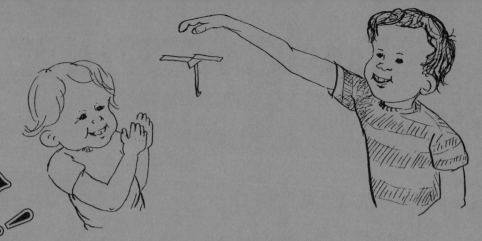

What to Use

* lightweight paper
* crayons or markers
* scissors
* a pencil
* a ruler

What to Do

1. Make a copy of the figure below. You can trace it onto your paper right from this page. Copy it exactly.

2. Then, cut on all the dotted lines.

3. Fold forward along lines 1 and 2.

4. Fold forward along line 3 and backward along line 4.

5. Fold backward along line 5.

6. Hold it up high in the air, and let it drop. It should whirl and twirl.

7. Decorate your whirlybird with lots of colors!

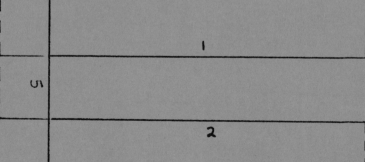

TALL PLACE-FINDERS

To mark the place — so you won't have to look,
Make a tall friend to keep in your book!

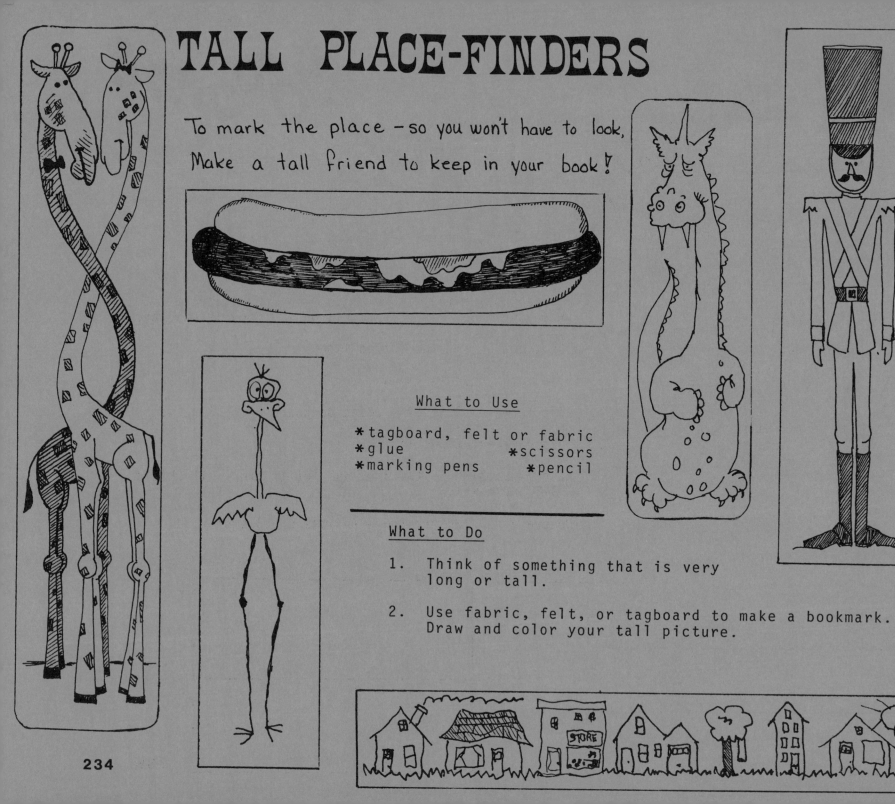

What to Use

* tagboard, felt or fabric
* glue   * scissors
* marking pens   * pencil

What to Do

1. Think of something that is very long or tall.

2. Use fabric, felt, or tagboard to make a bookmark. Draw and color your tall picture.

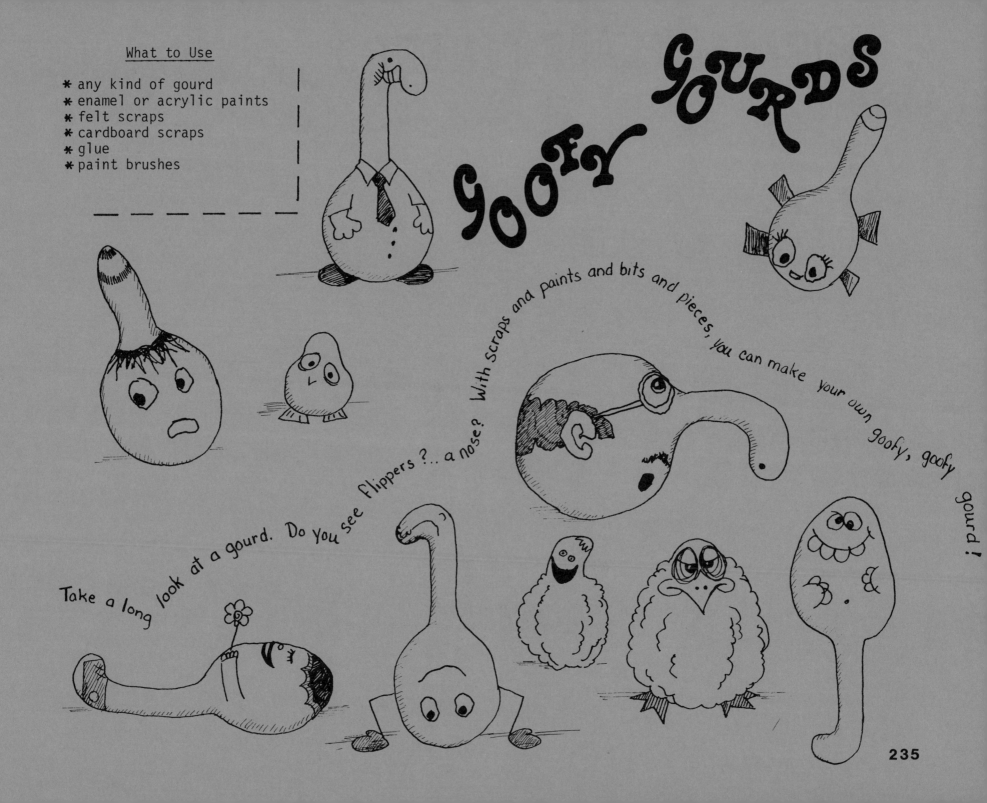

What to Use

* any kind of gourd
* enamel or acrylic paints
* felt scraps
* cardboard scraps
* glue
* paint brushes

GOOFY GOURDS

Take a long look at a gourd. Do you see flippers?... a nose? With scraps and paints and bits and pieces, you can make your own goofy, goofy gourd!

What can you do with a tree?

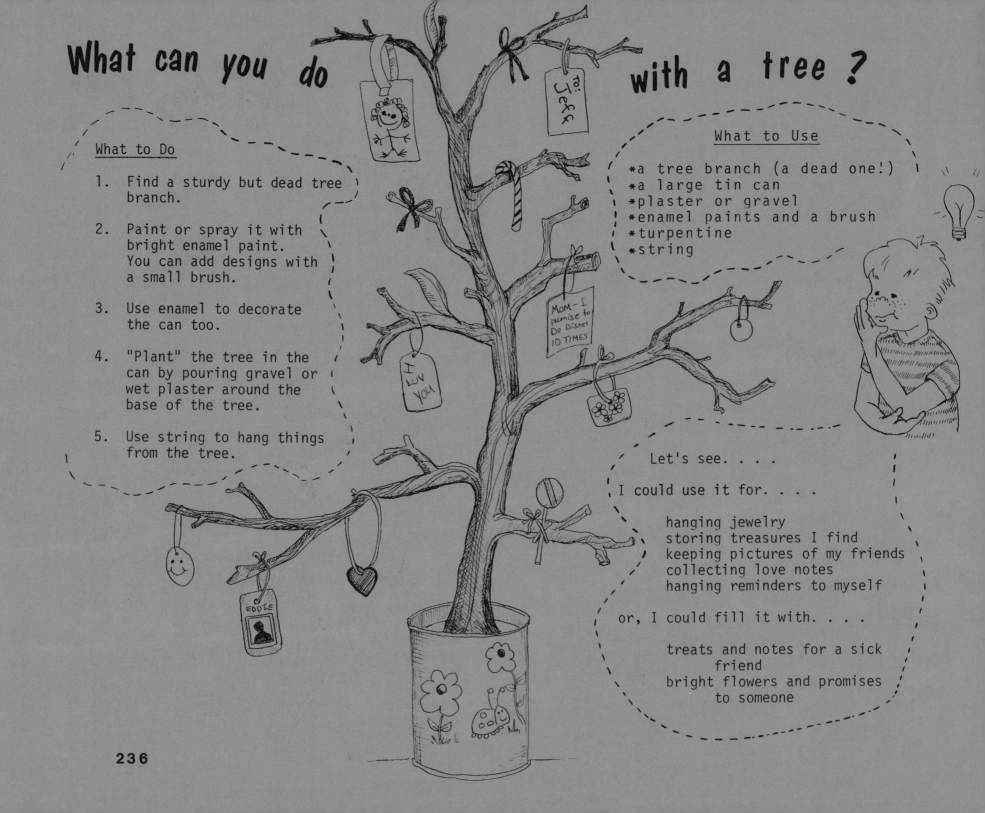

What to Do

1. Find a sturdy but dead tree branch.

2. Paint or spray it with bright enamel paint. You can add designs with a small brush.

3. Use enamel to decorate the can too.

4. "Plant" the tree in the can by pouring gravel or wet plaster around the base of the tree.

5. Use string to hang things from the tree.

What to Use

* a tree branch (a dead one!)
* a large tin can
* plaster or gravel
* enamel paints and a brush
* turpentine
* string

Let's see. . . .

I could use it for. . . .

hanging jewelry
storing treasures I find
keeping pictures of my friends
collecting love notes
hanging reminders to myself

or, I could fill it with. . . .

treats and notes for a sick friend
bright flowers and promises to someone

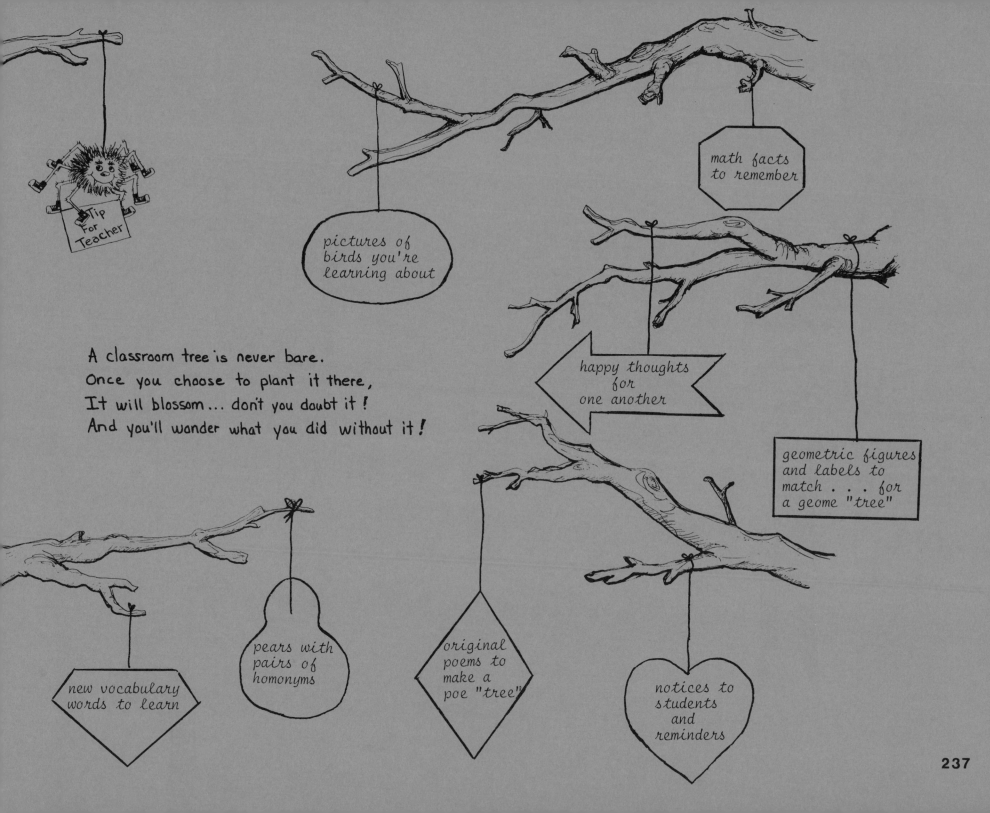

Tip For Teacher

math facts to remember

pictures of birds you're learning about

happy thoughts for one another

geometric figures and labels to match . . . for a geome "tree"

A classroom tree is never bare.
Once you choose to plant it there,
It will blossom... don't you doubt it !
And you'll wonder what you did without it !

new vocabulary words to learn

pears with pairs of homonyms

original poems to make a poe "tree"

notices to students and reminders

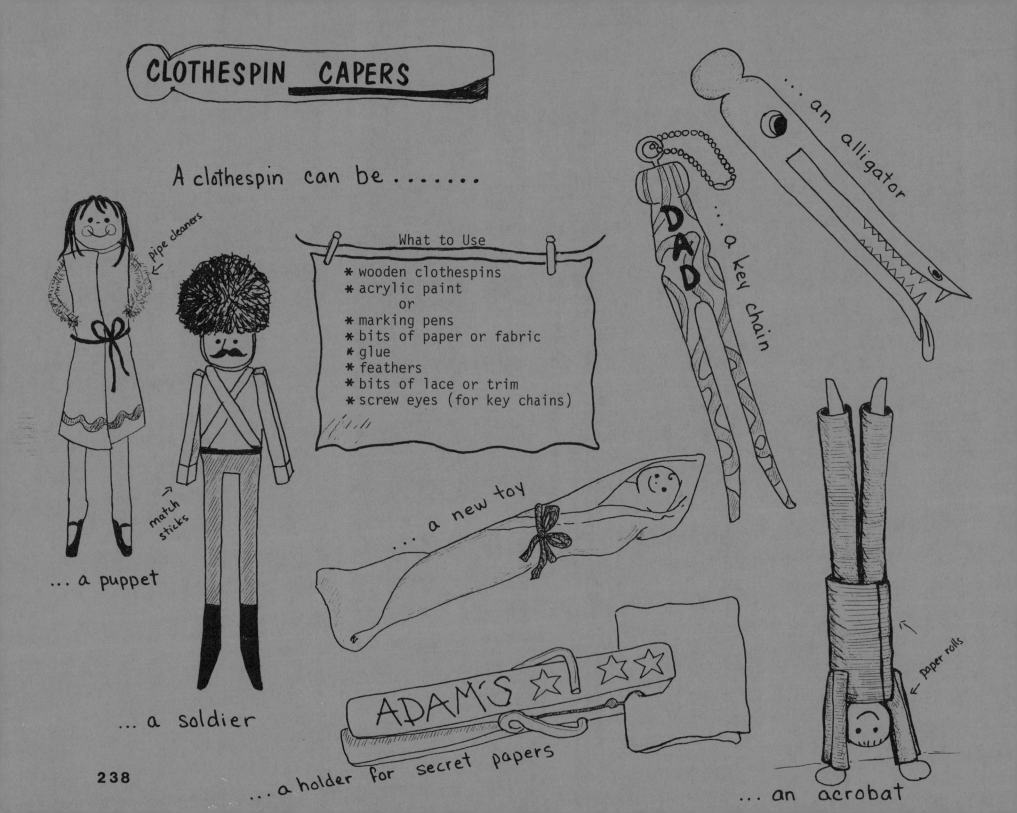

CLOTHESPIN CAPERS

A clothespin can be........

What to Use

* wooden clothespins
* acrylic paint
    or
* marking pens
* bits of paper or fabric
* glue
* feathers
* bits of lace or trim
* screw eyes (for key chains)

pipe cleaners

match sticks

... a puppet

... a soldier

... a new toy

... a holder for secret papers

ADAM'S ☆ ☆ ☆

DAD

... a key chain

... an alligator

... an acrobat

paper rolls

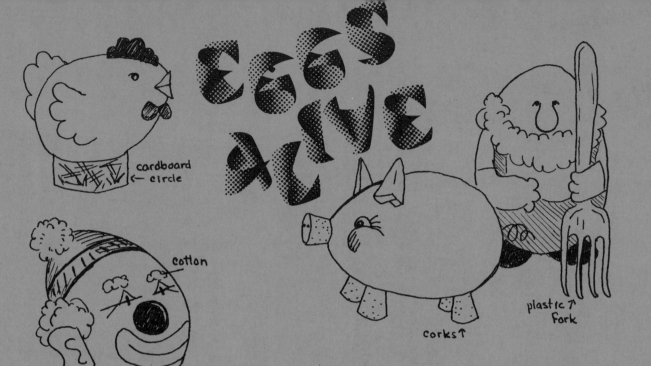

EGGS ALIVE

What to Use

* eggs
* a bowl
* a darning needle
* paint or marking pens
* lightweight cardboard

* trims for eggs:
    lace, rick rack,
    ribbon, felt, fabric,
    cotton balls, glitter,
    felt, yarn, pipe cleaners,
    buttons, toothpicks
* glue
* tweezers

cardboard ← circle

cotton

pipe cleaner →

corks↑

plastic↑ fork

What to Do

1. Let the eggs warm to room temperature.

2. Hold an egg over the bowl. Carefully prick a hole in each end with the needle. Poke the needle <u>way</u> in so that it breaks the yoke. Make one hole a little bigger.

3. Gently blow on the smaller hole until the egg is empty.

4. Wash the egg and let it dry.

5. Cut some cardboard strips and staple them into rings. These make good resting places for the eggs.

6. Turn the egg into a person or an animal by adding decorations. You can put on faces with marking pens or a tiny paintbrush.

←yarn

You can dye the eggs before you start!

239

4-in-1 Hide-away

What to Use

* 5 square yards of felt or heavy fabric
* colored felt scraps
* white glue or rubber cement
* markers
* yarn
* a friend or mother with a sewing machine

What to Do

1. Cut 5 pieces of fabric each about 1 yard or 1 meter square.

2. Ask someone to sew one square to each of the four sides of the fifth square.

   Now you have a special kind of a "tablecloth" that fits over a card-table and encloses a private hideaway under the table.

3. Make each square of the fabric into a different kind of a house or building. Glue or paste on doors, windows, decorations made from cloth and yarn. If the fabric is not felt, you can try drawing on it with marking pens or crayons.

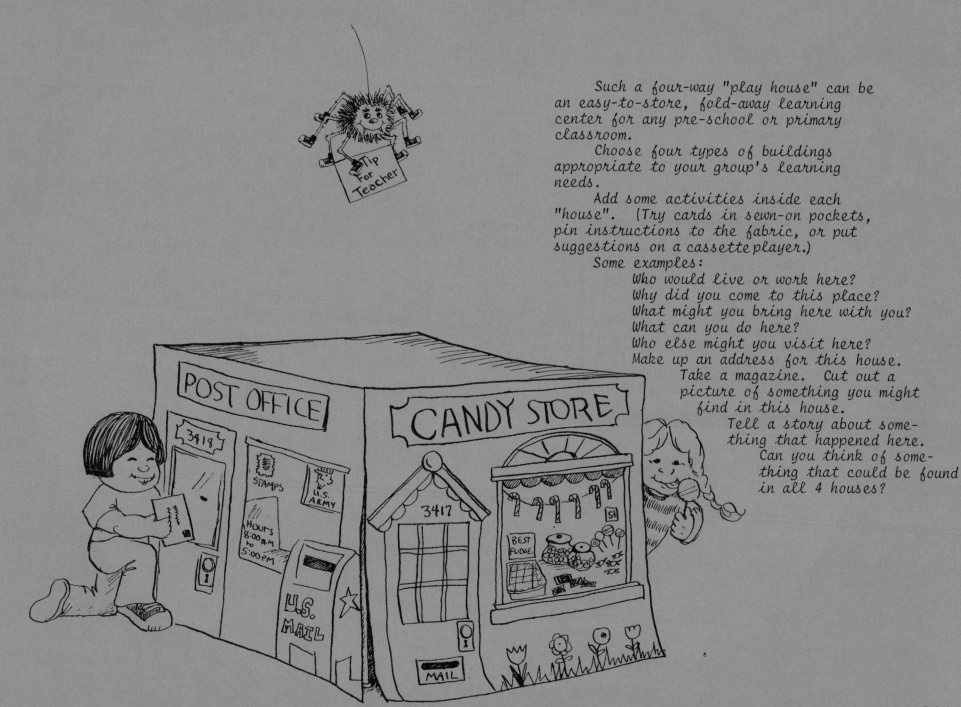

Such a four-way "play house" can be an easy-to-store, fold-away learning center for any pre-school or primary classroom.

Choose four types of buildings appropriate to your group's learning needs.

Add some activities inside each "house". (Try cards in sewn-on pockets, pin instructions to the fabric, or put suggestions on a cassette player.)

Some examples:

Who would live or work here?
Why did you come to this place?
What might you bring here with you?
What can you do here?
Who else might you visit here?
Make up an address for this house.

Take a magazine. Cut out a picture of something you might find in this house.

Tell a story about something that happened here.

Can you think of something that could be found in all 4 houses?

PUMPKIN TOTE

A Halloween tote to make without any tricks.... big enough to hold lots of treats and strong enough to last and last... unless it gets bitten by a werewolf!

What to Use

* a big, round sturdy balloon blown up and tied
* newspapers
* paper towels
* wheat paste
* yarn
* scissors
* orange and black tempera paint
* 2 large brass fasteners

What to Do

1. Mix 1 part wheat paste into 10 parts warm water. Dip newspaper strips in the paste.

2. Cover the balloon with 2 good layers of papier mâché. Don't cover the tied end.

3. Let it dry. Give the balloon 2 more layers. Then cover it with a paper towel that has been soaked in paste.

4. Hang it up to dry.

5. When it's dry, pop the balloon, and trim away the top edges.

6. Paint it with tempera paint. (Shellac it too for a longer lasting paint job.)

7. Poke a brass fastener through each side.

8. Tie a sturdy yarn handle to both fasteners.

Now you're ready to gather treats.

Watch out for werewolves!

HAPPY HALLOWEEN!

A Walkie-Talkie for two Walking Talkers

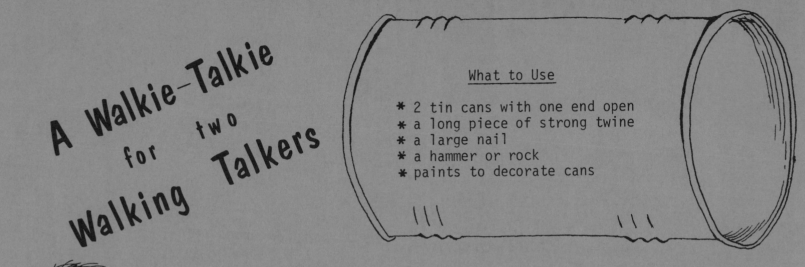

What to Use

* 2 tin cans with one end open
* a long piece of strong twine
* a large nail
* a hammer or rock
* paints to decorate cans

....send special messages....bright ideas.... private plans.... deep, dark secrets....

What to Do

1. Make a hole in the center of each can by hammering the nail part way in with a hammer or a rock.

2. String one end of the twine into each hole. Tie a large knot inside each can.

3. You can decorate the cans with painted designs.

4. You need two people . . . each one holds a can. Pull the line tight between the two of you. Now you're ready to send and receive messages.

CARPET CUT-UPS

Many carpet stores have samples and scraps to give away.

You can tape some scraps together
to make fun, fuzzy rugs
for your bedroom,
playroom,
or schoolroom!

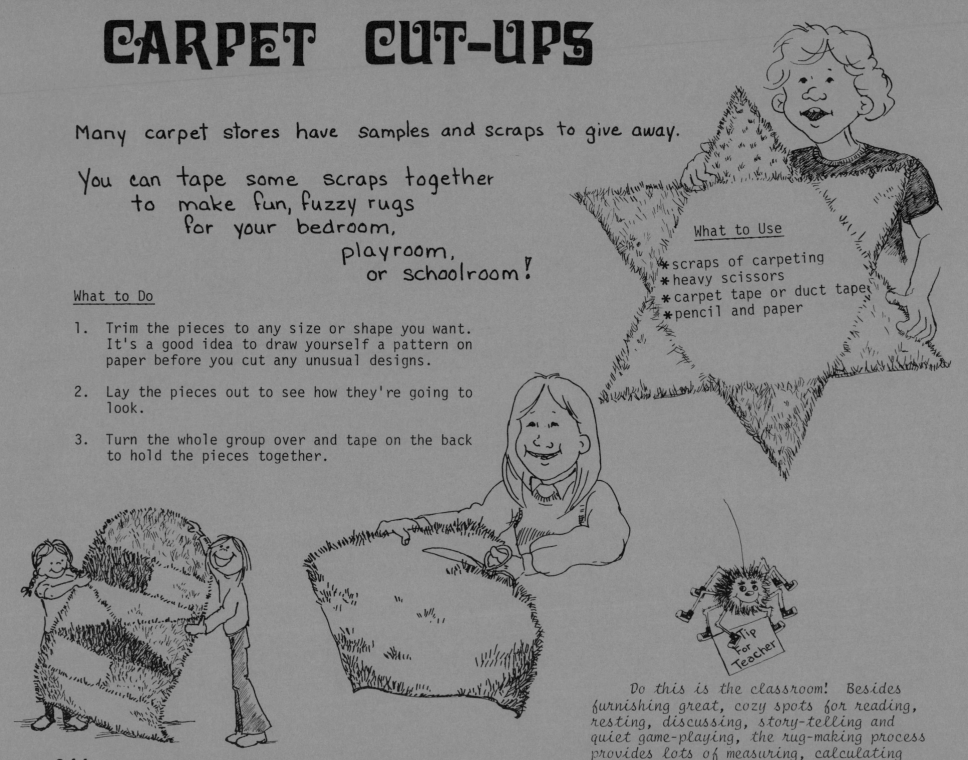

What to Use

* scraps of carpeting
* heavy scissors
* carpet tape or duct tape
* pencil and paper

What to Do

1. Trim the pieces to any size or shape you want. It's a good idea to draw yourself a pattern on paper before you cut any unusual designs.

2. Lay the pieces out to see how they're going to look.

3. Turn the whole group over and tape on the back to hold the pieces together.

Tip For Teacher

Do this is the classroom! Besides furnishing great, cozy spots for reading, resting, discussing, story-telling and quiet game-playing, the rug-making process provides lots of measuring, calculating and problem-solving experiences.

Things to do

Chapter 8

when there's nothing to do

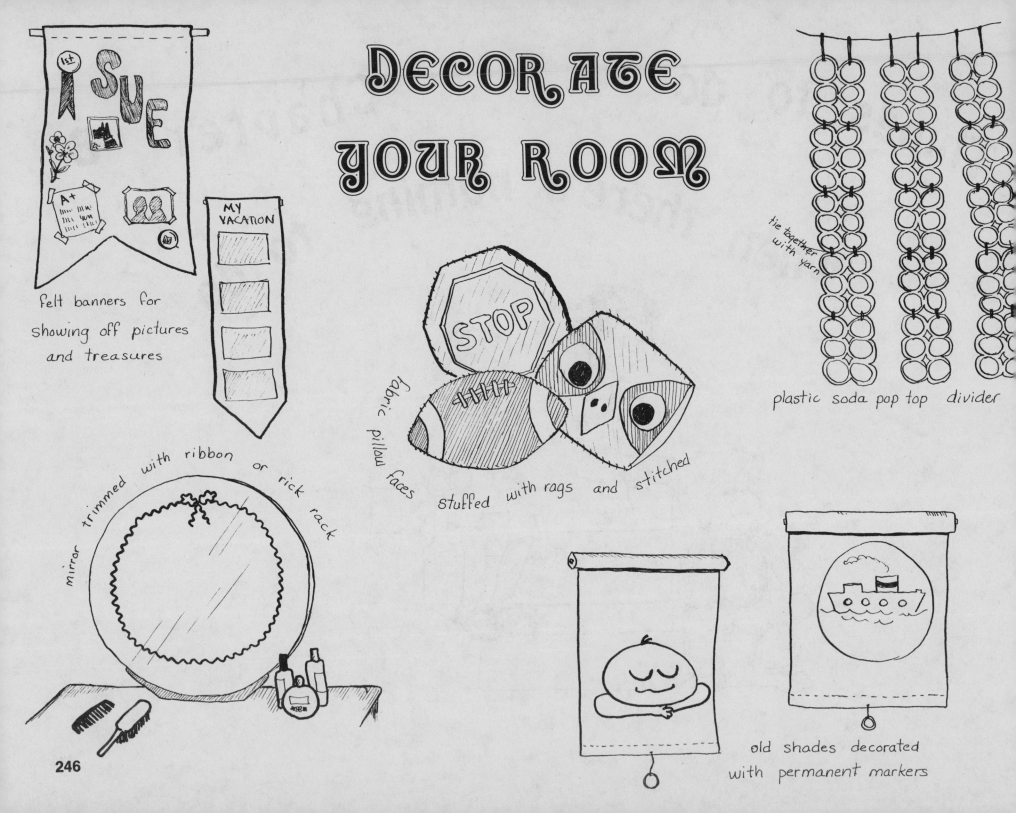

DECORATE YOUR ROOM

felt banners for showing off pictures and treasures

MY VACATION

fabric pillow faces stuffed with rags and stitched

plastic soda pop top divider

tie together with yarn

mirror trimmed with ribbon or rick rack

old shades decorated with permanent markers

246

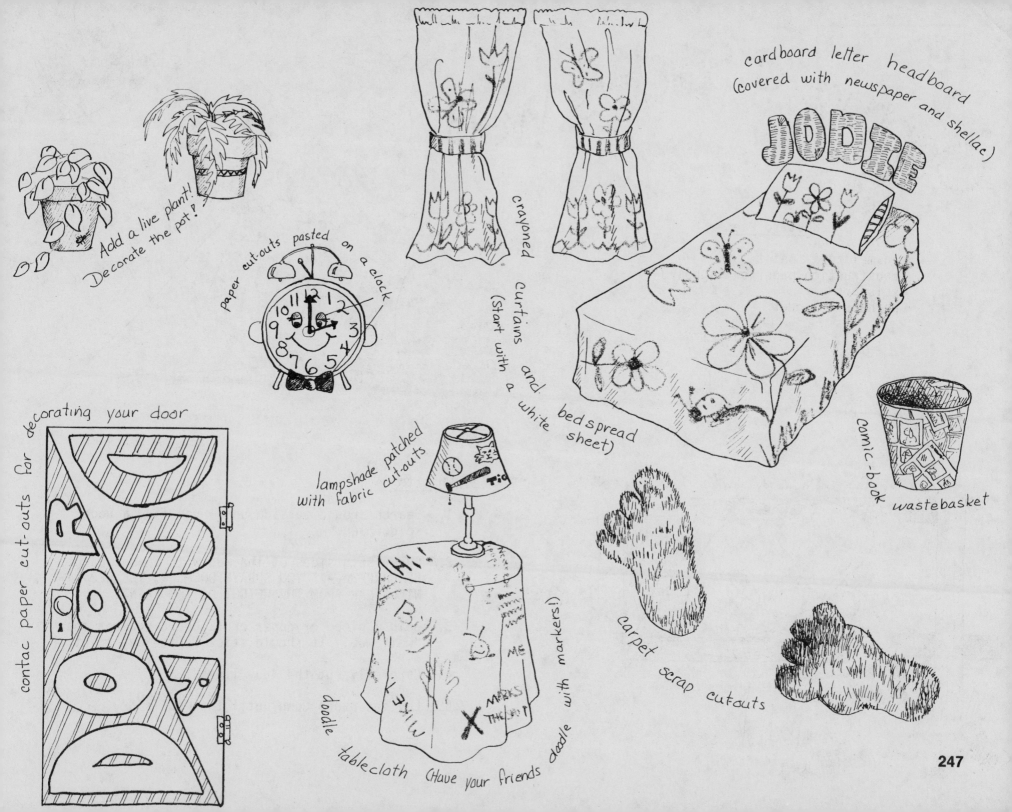

Add a live plant! Decorate the pot!

cardboard letter headboard (covered with newspaper and shellac)

JODIE

paper cut-outs pasted on a clock

crayoned curtains and bedspread (start with a white sheet)

contac paper cut-outs for decorating your door

DOOR

lampshade patched with fabric cut-outs

comic-book wastebasket

carpet scrap cutouts

doodle tablecloth (have your friends doodle with markers!)

Capture a Spider's Web

Did the spider spin a new web?

What to Use

* enamel spray paint
* construction paper or tagboard
* scissors
* perhaps a ladder

Don't try this on a windy day!

guy lines

What to Do

1. Search around outside until you find a good spider web.

2. Spray both sides of the web with enamel paint. BE CAREFUL--IF YOU SPRAY TOO MUCH, THE WEB WILL TEAR FROM THE WEIGHT OF THE PAINT.

3. Hold a piece of paper or tagboard against the "wet" web. It should stick to the wet paint.

4. Carefully cut the "guy lines".

5. Lay the paper down until the web is dry.

GO WATER PAINTING!

When you paint with water
there's no mess.... no fuss.....
You can paint
on anything
that water won't ruin!

All you need is a brush ... and water!

.... on windows

... on brick walls

.... on fences

...on paper

... on sidewalks

Try squeezing water from a bottle too!

play name games

Use the letters of your name to make a story title. Then, write the story.

Don A
Feb 3

Don't Open Now

Patty C
Feb 3

Purple Alligator Traps Two Youths

Here are some special things to do with your own name.

JEN´ NI FER´

Make up a rhythm to go with your name. Beat it out on a drum. Dance to it!

Look up its meaning. Act out its meaning!

Sing your name!

Make up a whole song about you! ♪ ♪

Shana MacKenzie 14
− Cheri Case 9
No fun 5

Add and subtract names.

Write words that equal the answer!

AMY 3
+ SAMUELS 6
ONE GREAT... 9

Spell words using the letters in your name. How many can you spell?

OLIVER
FINOTTI
OIL   LITTER
VOTER FILTER
LOVE   OVER
LIVER OVEN
ROTTEN

Hide your name in a sentence or story.

Andrew Madson

The young man drew his sword as he crept up behind the sleeping dragon. Just as he was about to plunge it into the dragon's side, a voice behind him called, "Are you mad, son?"

Again came the voice, "Look at your dragon!" The young hunter looked and his face grew red.

She fierce dragon was a huge rock, covered with moss.

See if a friend can find it!

251

Feed the Ants....

Find a mound of sand or dirt where ants are living.

Feed them tiny crumbs of bread or bits of chocolate..... and then....

watch !

Where do they go?

How do they carry the food?

What happens?

CATCH A SHADOW

your shadow will show itself near a bright light or in the sunlight.

Have someone trace your shadow on a large piece of paper or on a sidewalk.

Watch your shadow change as the light moves.

Make your shadow take different forms.

Trace other shadows too!

What to Use

* white mural paper
* colored chalk
* scissors
* a friend

253

START A RUBBER BAND CIRCUS

What to Use

* heavy paper or lightweight cardboard
* rubber bands (any sizes and colors)
* white glue
* crayons or marking pens
* pencil

What to Do

1. Place some rubberbands on your paper or cardboard to arrange a design you like. Try pictures of faces or animals or strange creatures or people!

2. Lightly draw around each rubber band with pencil. Then lift the rubber band and squeeze glue along the pencil line. Lay the rubber band on the glue.

3. When the glue is dry, you might wish to color inside the spaces with crayons or marking pens.

HOP A DIFFERENT HOPSCOTCH

* an old shower curtain or a piece of vinyl
* waterproof marking pens
        OR
* sidewalk and some chalk

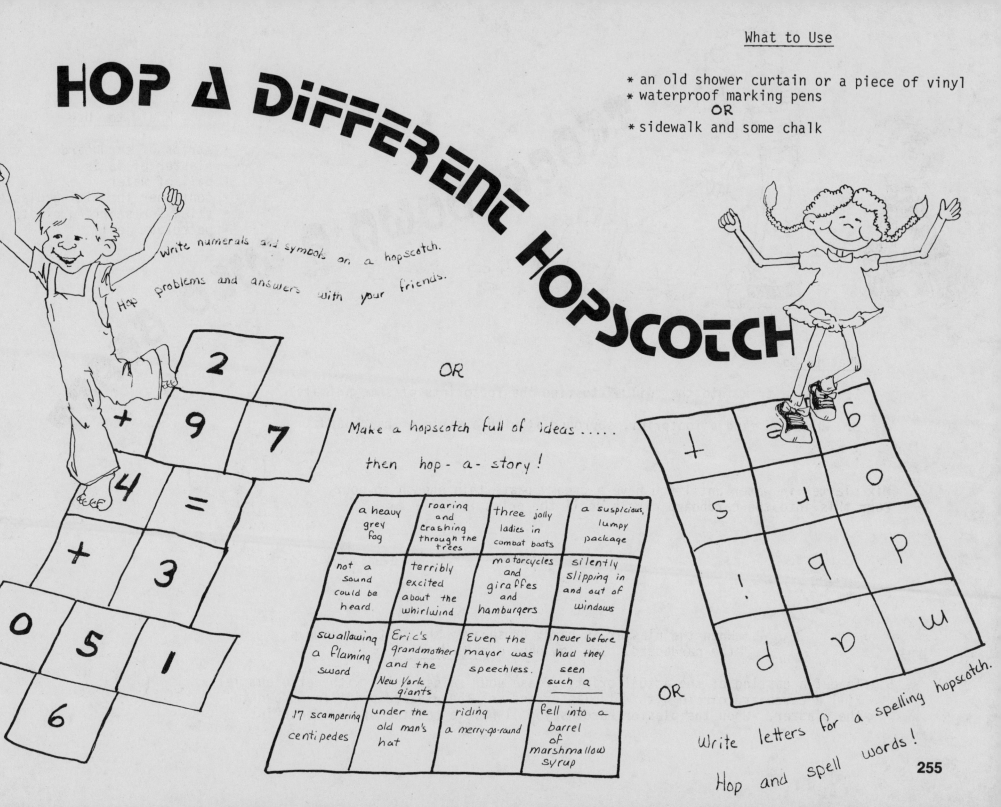

Write numerals and symbols on a hopscotch.

Hop problems and answers with your friends.

OR

Make a hopscotch full of ideas.....

then hop-a-story!

a heavy grey fog	roaring and crashing through the trees	three jolly ladies in combat boots	a suspicious, lumpy package
not a sound could be heard	terribly excited about the whirlwind	motorcycles and giraffes and hamburgers	silently slipping in and out of windows
swallowing a flaming sword	Eric's grandmother and the New York giants	Even the mayor was speechless.	never before had they seen such a ___
17 scampering centipedes	under the old man's hat	riding a merry-go-round	fell into a barrel of marshmallow syrup

OR

Write letters for a spelling hopscotch.

Hop and spell words!

255

TRACK DOWN A WILD BEAST

What to Do

1. Take a trek into the "wilds" to find the footprints of some animals.

2. When you find a footprint, surround it with a strip of cardboard.

3. Mix plaster in water until you have a creamy paste thin enough to pour. Pour this into the cardboard circle until the print is full.

cardboard circle —

4. When the plaster is hard, brush away the dirt and remove the cardboard. You now have a <u>raised print</u>.

5. To get a casting of the actual print, grease your raised print with petroleum jelly. Fill a cardboard circle with wet plaster and set the greased print face down in the plaster. When the plaster hardens you'll have a casting of the footprint!

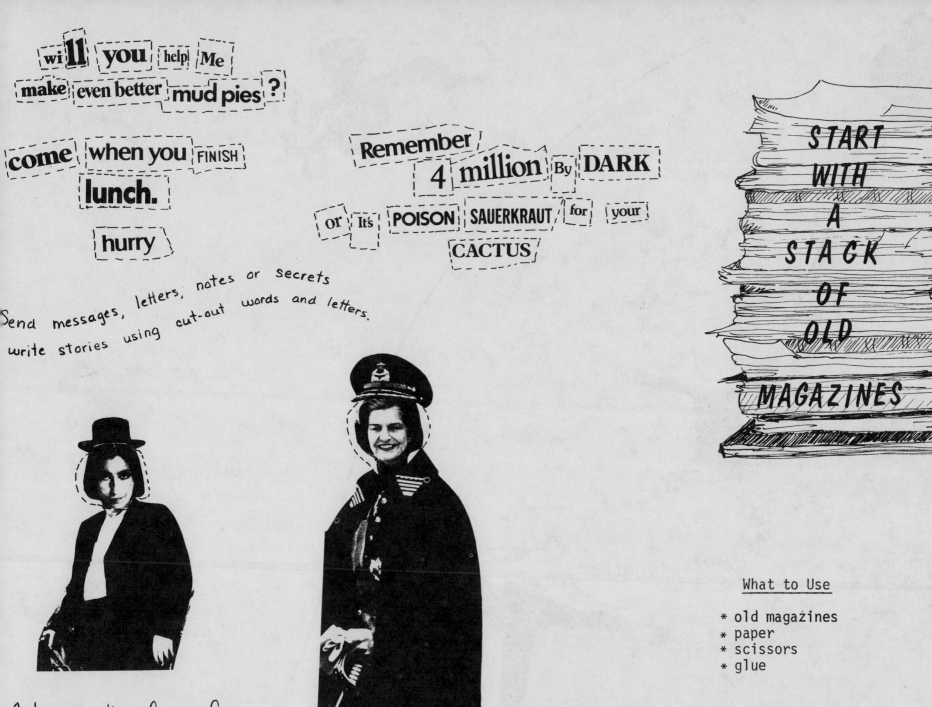

wi**ll** **you** help Me make even better **mud pies** ?

come when you FINISH **lunch.**

hurry

Remember **4 million** By **DARK** or It's **POISON** **SAUERKRAUT** for your **CACTUS**

Send messages, letters, notes or secrets write stories using cut-out words and letters.

START WITH A STACK OF OLD MAGAZINES

What to Use

* old magazines
* paper
* scissors
* glue

Cut away the faces from magazine pictures. In their place glue faces of famous people or friends.

257

Cut out parts of people . . . .

glue the parts together . . . .

to make new people!

an octopup?

a horsish?

Make imaginary animals . . . . .

a chickigator?

by combining halves of animal

dinopuss?

Give a name to the new

258

Find pictures of 3 people.

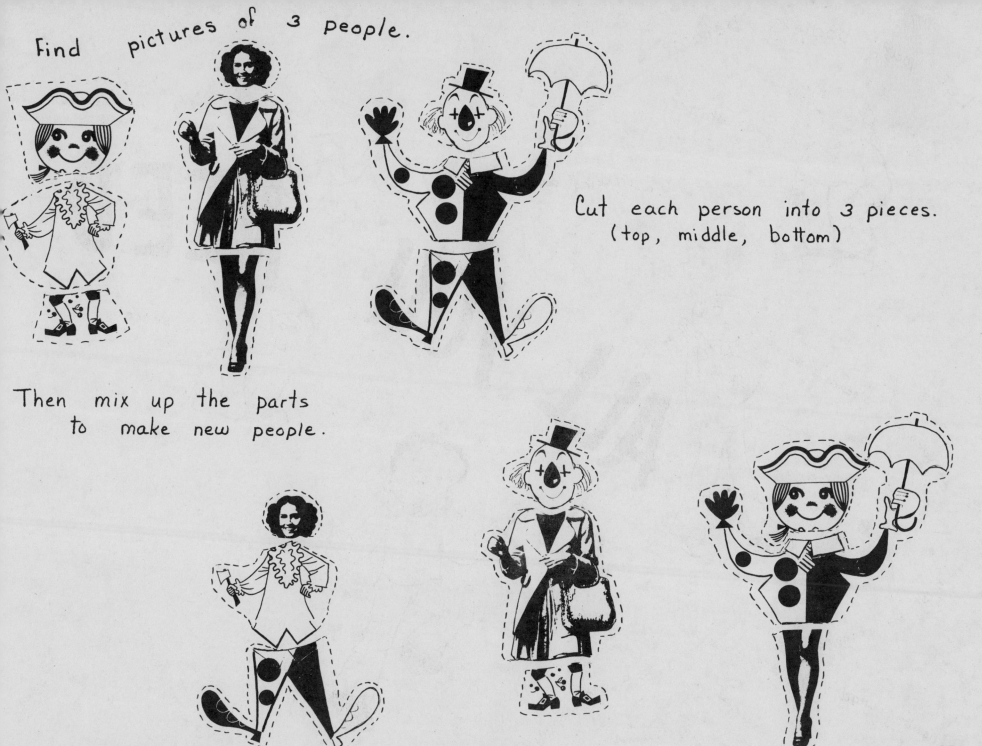

Cut each person into 3 pieces.
(top, middle, bottom)

Then mix up the parts
    to make new people.

Let your body become.....

...a sad whisper

...a creaking door

...a rushing stream

ALL YOU NEED

...a secret

...a yellow daisy sleeping in the sun   zzzzzz

...a hungry, circling gull

...maist fog creeping over the city

...a gentle spring rain

...crashing waves

...a howling wind

260

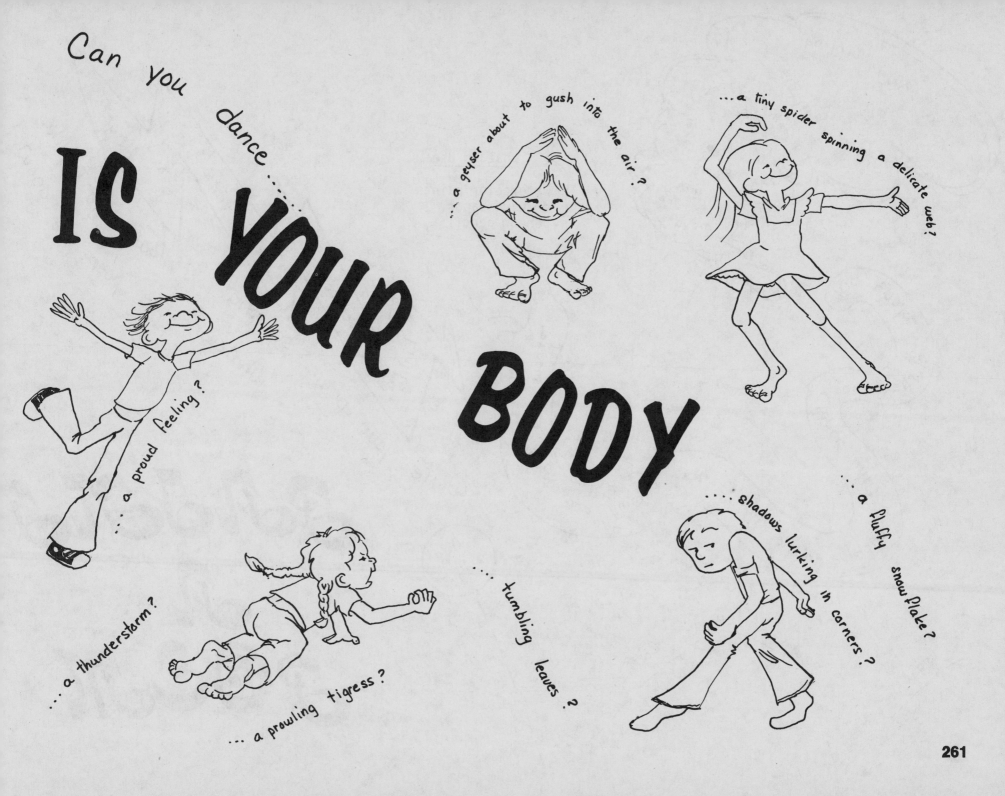

Can you dance ....

IS YOUR BODY

... a geyser about to gush into the air?

... a tiny spider spinning a delicate web?

... a proud feeling?

... a thunderstorm?

... a prowling tigress?

... tumbling leaves?

.... shadows lurking in corners?

... a fluffy snowflake?

261

Twirling, swirling whistling wind like a gigantic pot stirs the world of witches brew.

The snake slithers in silence until a prickly thistle tickles his tummy and makes him sneeze.

Lightening scratches the sky with its forked fingers.

Bounce High Bounce low Bouncing ball Where did you go?

What to Use

* watercolor paints
* drawing paper
* pen or pencil

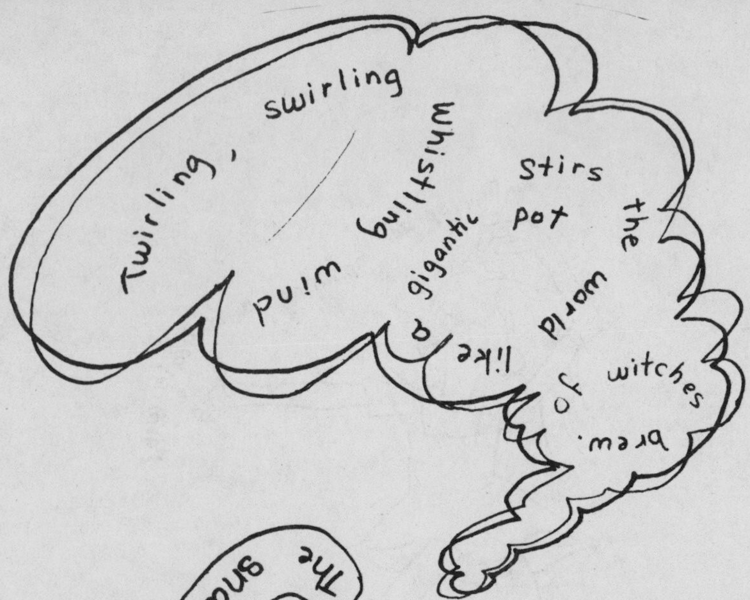

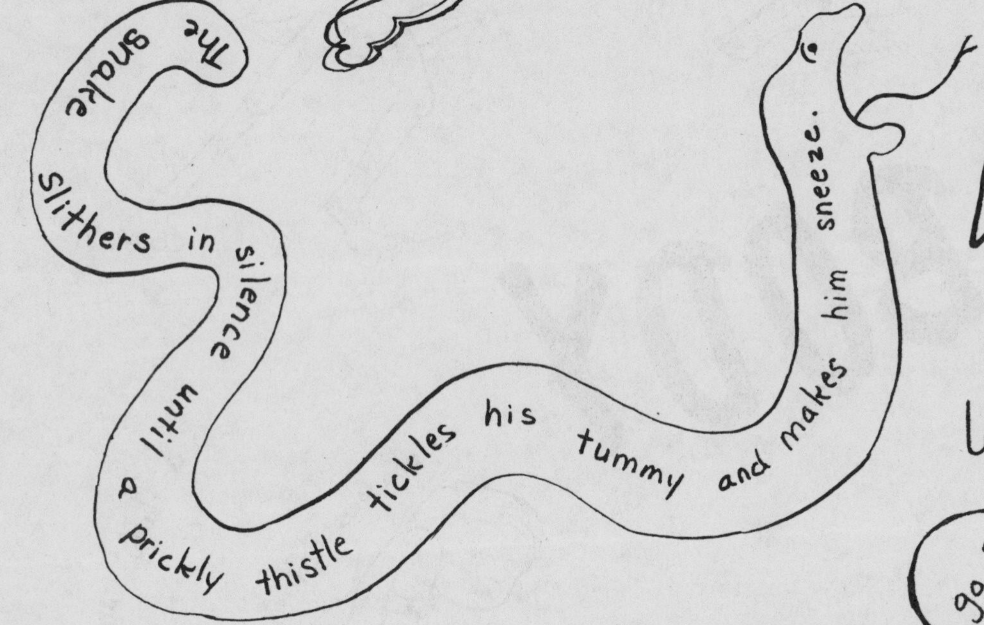

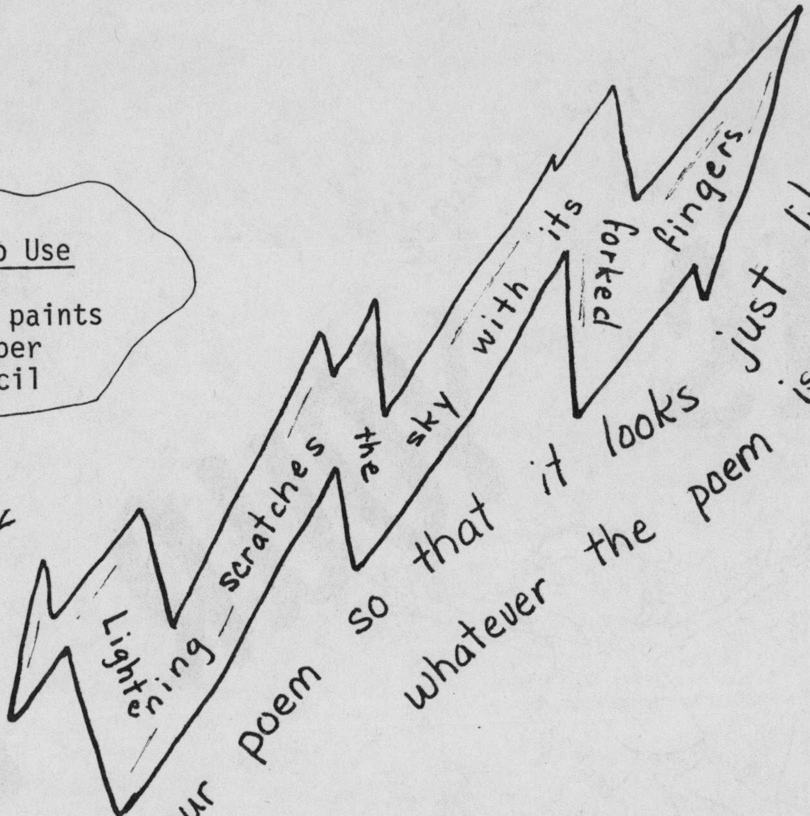

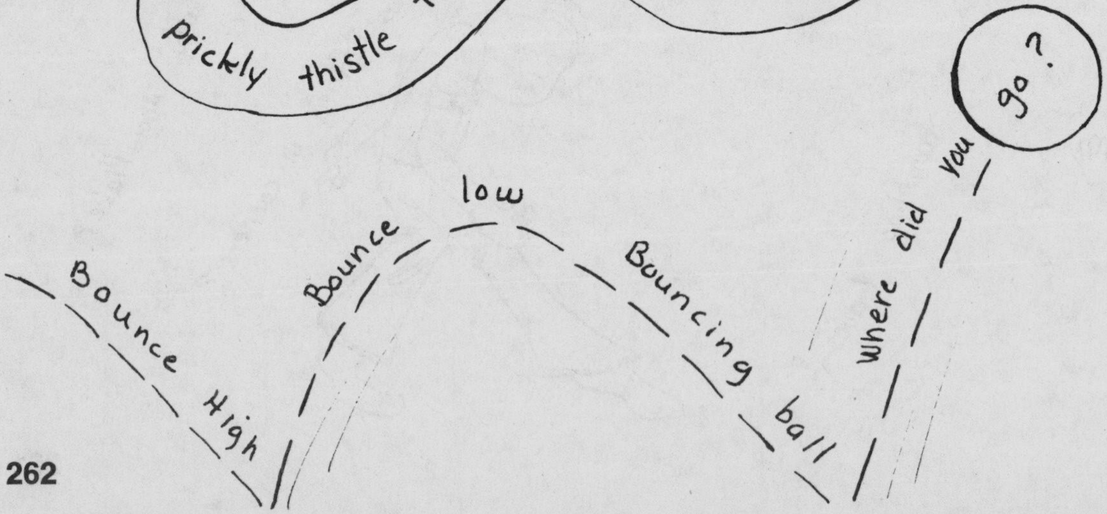

Write your poem so that it looks just like whatever the poem is about!

PAINT A POEM

GO PEOPLE WATCHING

Take a walk around your school, house, or neighborhood.

Stop and <u>watch</u> people.   Watch them   working
playing
thinking
sleeping.

Watch one person at a time carefully.
What is she doing?   What does his face show?
How long does it take?   Does he like what he's doing?

Ask questions.   Take notes. Share your experiences
in people watching by telling someone else.

Invite people into your classroom to do or make something. Let students watch or join as others do activities for fun or for a living!

Tip For Teacher

MAKE A LIVE MURAL

* brown or white mural paper
* crayons, markers
          or
  paints and brush
* scissors
* pencil
* your arms, legs, and head

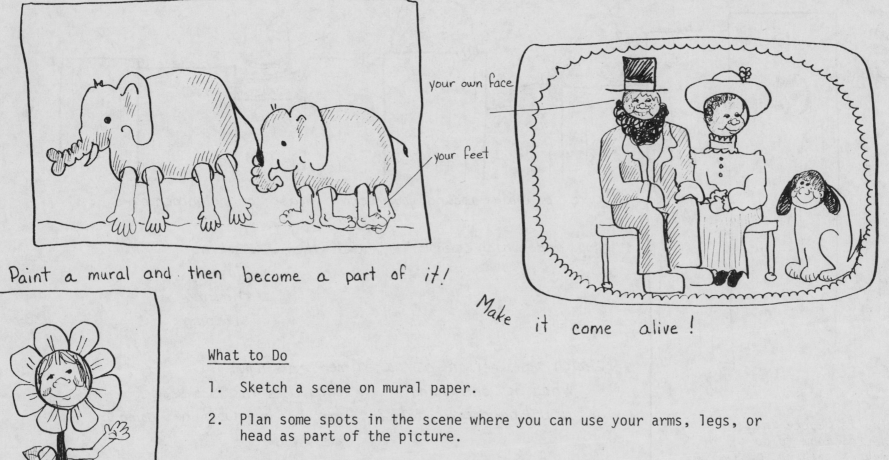

your own face

your feet

Paint a mural and then become a part of it!

Make it come alive!

your face and arms

What to Do

1. Sketch a scene on mural paper.

2. Plan some spots in the scene where you can use your arms, legs, or head as part of the picture.

3. Color or paint the scene.

4. Cut out the holes you've planned.

5. When the paint is dry, get in the mural and share it with someone! You might tell a story to go along with your painting.

PUT ON A CHIN ACT

Tie a towel over your nose, eyes, — hair. —

your chin

What to Use

* large napkin or a towel
* cold cream
* tempera paints and brush
    or
  lipstick and eyebrow pencil
    or
  watercolor marking pens

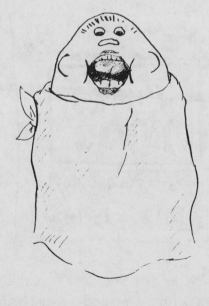

Lie on a table like this.

your chin

What to Do

1. Rub cold cream on your chin.

2. Draw or paint an upside-down face on your chin. You might ask a friend to do this.

3. Lie on a table. Hang your head over the edge. Cover your eyes, nose and hair with a towel....and start talking!

Try: smacking your lips, puffing out your cheeks, sticking out your tongue, etc.

Try a conversation between two people.

go grave rubbing

R.I.P

What to Use

* large sheets of thin paper
* masking tape
* thick black wax or fat black crayons

Go searching for a special tombstone or monument.

Tape on paper and rub the whole surface with black wax.

Try tree stumps, church doors, man-hole covers.

HARVEY DRAK
A DEAR OLD SOUL
1810 - 1894

Available from shoe repair shops:

A good rubbing material is a heavy, black, waxy mixture called heelball.

JONES   R.I.P

MAKE YOUR OWN

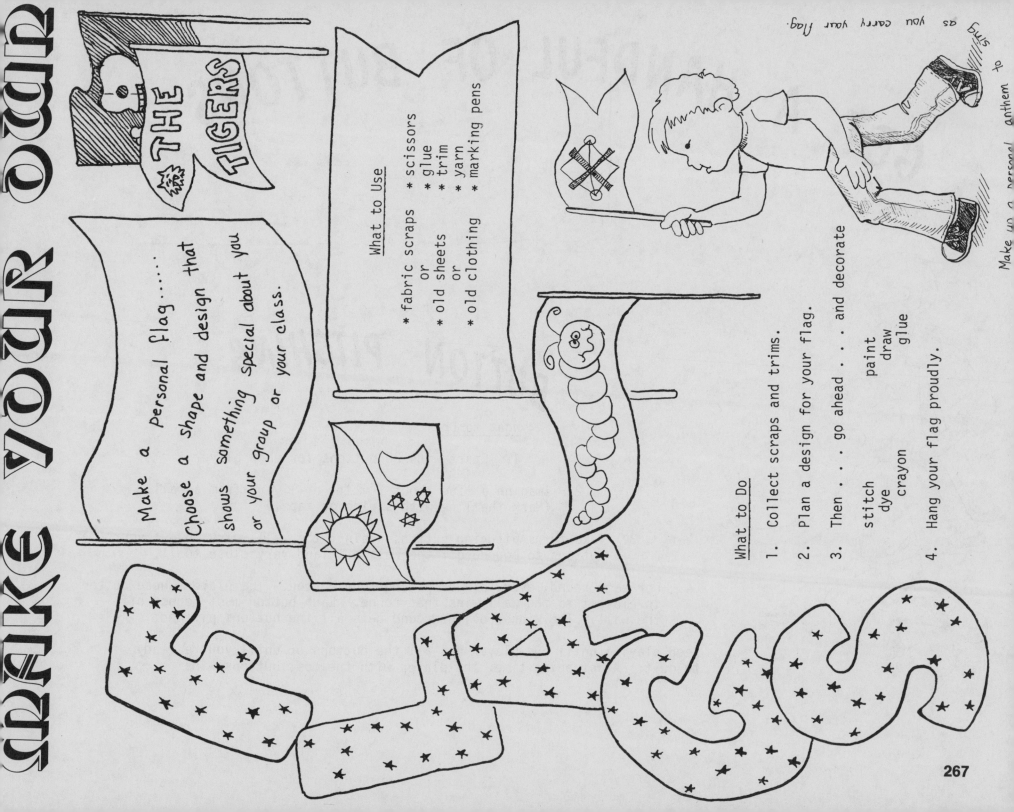

THE TIGERS

Make a Personal Flag.....

Choose a shape and design that shows something special about you or your group or your class.

What to Use

* fabric scraps   * scissors
    or   * glue
* old sheets   * trim
    or   * yarn
* old clothing   * marking pens

What to Do

1. Collect scraps and trims.

2. Plan a design for your flag.

3. Then . . . go ahead . . . and decorate

     stitch   paint
     dye   draw
       crayon   glue

4. Hang your flag proudly.

Make up a personal anthem to sing as you carry your flag.

GET A HANDFUL OF BUTTONS

BUTTON PITCHING

What to Do

1. Start with 20 buttons for each player.

2. Imagine a line about 1 meter or 1 yard from a wall.
   (Mark the line with string or tape.)

3. Take turns pitching buttons against the wall. Try to get your
   buttons to bounce off the wall but land very close to it.

4. For each round, every player pitches one button. The player whose button
   is closest to the wall wins that round. Each button must bounce off
   the wall. The winner of the round gets all the buttons pitched.

5. Keep playing until one player has all the buttons or until you're ready
   to quit. At stopping time, the player with the most buttons wins.

HOW MANY BUTTONS ?

Play with 3-10 people or even more!!

possible total was anywhere from 0-9

What to Do

1. Start with 3 buttons for each player, and all players sitting in a circle.

2. For each round, every player puts 0, 1, 2, or 3 buttons in her hand and closes her fist.

3. Next, every player makes a guess at what the total number of buttons will be when the hands are opened and buttons are counted.

4. Open hands and count buttons. If anyone guesses the exact total, he is out.

5. Keep playing rounds until only one player remains. The object of the game is to try to get out by guessing the correct total, because the last one in is the loser.

This is a super game for practicing addition!

Tip For Teacher

Can you invent some other button games?

269

BURY a TREASURE

Take a valuable possession or a special surprise

and bury ..... or hide it.

Then make a treasure map
and have fun watching
a friend go hunting!

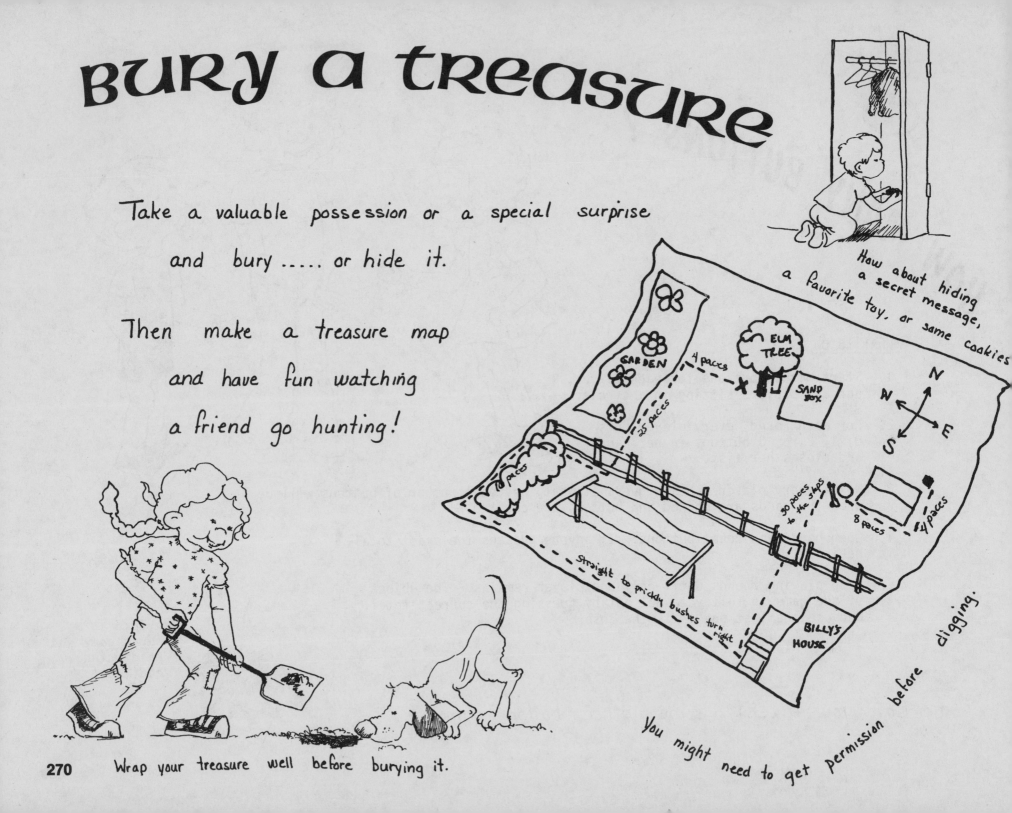

How about hiding a secret message, a favorite toy, or some cookies

GARDEN

4 paces

ELM TREE

SAND BOX

N

25 paces

30 paces to the steps

8 paces

4 paces

Straight to prickly bushes turn right

BILLY'S HOUSE

You might need to get permission before digging.

Wrap your treasure well before burying it.

TELL LIES

Tell about

dangerous escapades

and daring feats

Tell "monster stories"

and "fish stories"

Get together with some friends and....

tell lies.....

exaggerate.....

make up wild stories.....

or share dreams.....

Use "lie-telling" for stretching imaginations.. and for teaching children to discriminate between fantasy and reality!

Tip For Teacher

THINGS TO DO WITH A MIRROR

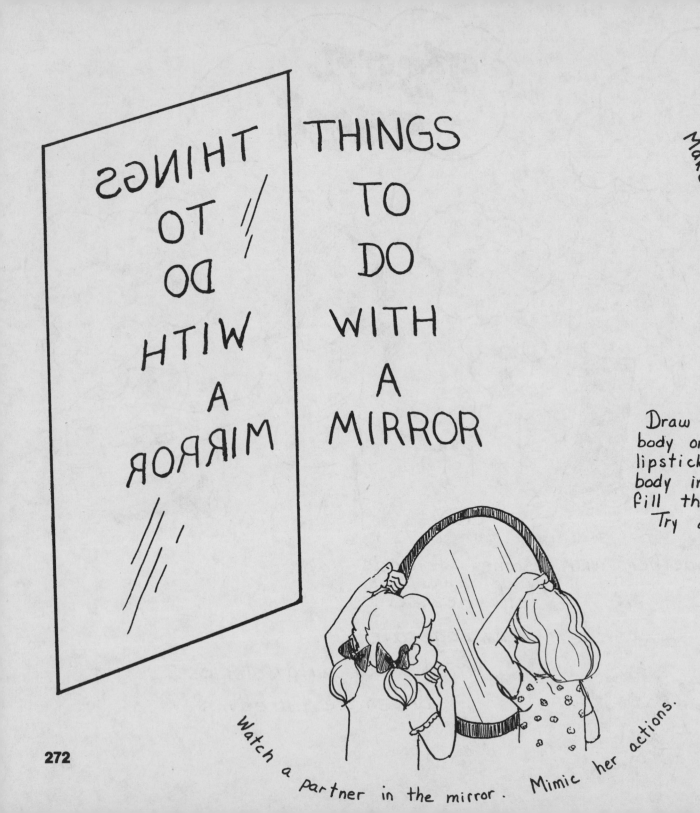

Make faces!

Have a face-making conte[st]

Draw the outline of a body on the mirror with lipstick. Now hold your body in a position to fill the outline.
Try a different one!

Watch a partner in the mirror. Mimic her actions.

TOP SECRET

COME TO THE OLD BRIDGE AT 5:00 (or else)

MR. BIG

BEWARE

Write secret messages backwards. Give them to a friend to read in the mirror.

Try to do something by watching your actions in the mirror as you do it.... peel a banana, wrap a present or thread a needle.

Sit next to a mirror and write a letter only watching in the mirror. Don't look at your hand. Can you do it?

Silently mouth words in front of a mirror. Can your partner tell what you're saying?

Paint or draw the reflection of a picture.

273

doodle a tablecloth

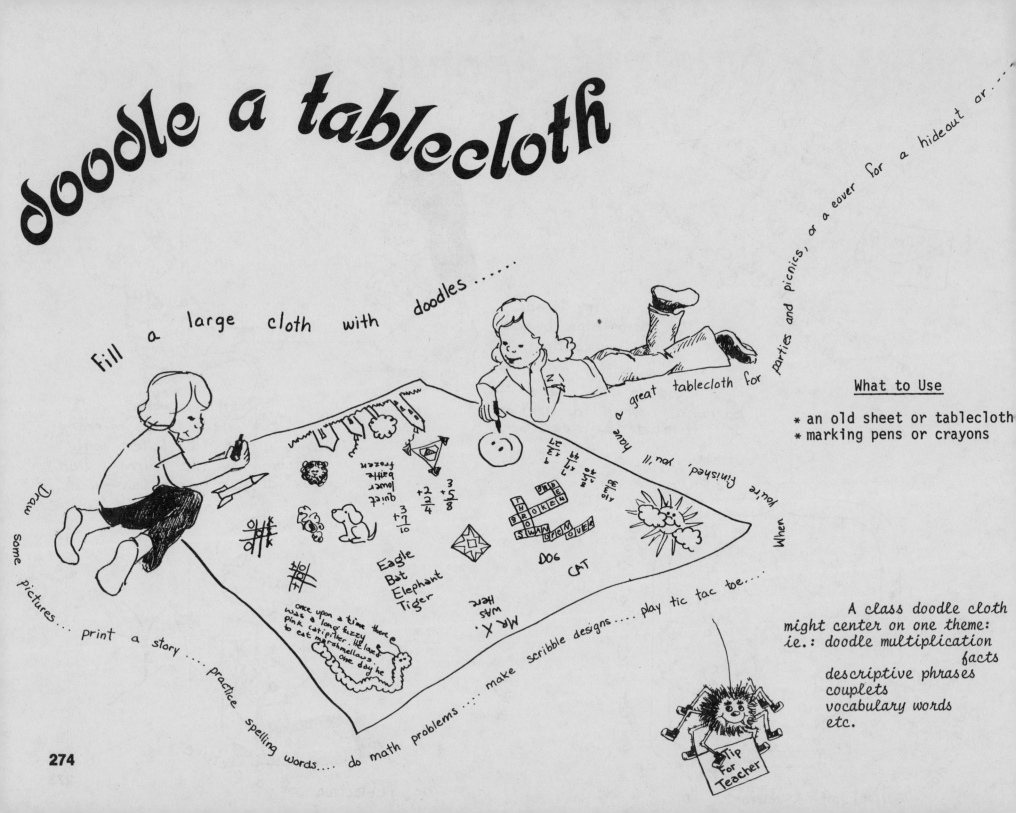

Fill a large cloth with doodles......

a great tablecloth for parties and picnics, or a cover for a hideout or....

When you're finished, you'll have

Draw some pictures... print a story.... practice spelling words.... do math problems.... make scribble designs.... play tic tac toe.....

Eagle
Bat
Elephant
Tiger

DOG CAT

MR X. WAS HERE

once upon a time there was a long fuzzy pink catipiller. He loved to eat marshmellows one day he

quiet flower battle frozen

$3\frac{7}{10}$

$\begin{array}{r} 3\\ +2\frac{2}{4}\\ \hline \end{array}$

$\begin{array}{r} 3\\ +\frac{5}{8}\\ \hline \end{array}$

What to Use

* an old sheet or tablecloth
* marking pens or crayons

A class doodle cloth might center on one theme:
ie.: doodle multiplication
                facts
descriptive phrases
couplets
vocabulary words
etc.

Tip For Teacher

274

GROW A CRYSTAL GARDEN

What to Use

* a pie tin
* some pieces of charcoal
* 1/2 Cup water
* 1/2 Cup salt
* 1/2 Cup liquid blueing
* 1 Cup ammonia
* a few drops of blue, green,
  and yellow food coloring
* a mixing bowl
* a spoon

What to Do

1. Place enough pieces of charcoal in the pie tin to cover the bottom.

2. Mix water, salt, blueing and ammonia. Pour it carefully over the charcoal.
    Make sure all the charcoal gets wet.

3. Squirt a few drops of the food coloring over the charcoal. Do not use red
    food coloring.

4. WAIT. . . . .the garden should grow beautiful crystals by the next day.

FRIENDLY THINGS TO DO

by yourself

How many ways do you know to make or keep a friend? Name some. Then do something special for a friend.

Make a new friend....
Write to:

International Friendship League
40 Mt. Vernon Street
Boston, Massachusetts 02108

For $2.00 you can become a member, and they'll send you the name of a pen pal.

Draw-a-friend...... life on the drawing, write some characteristics of a friend.

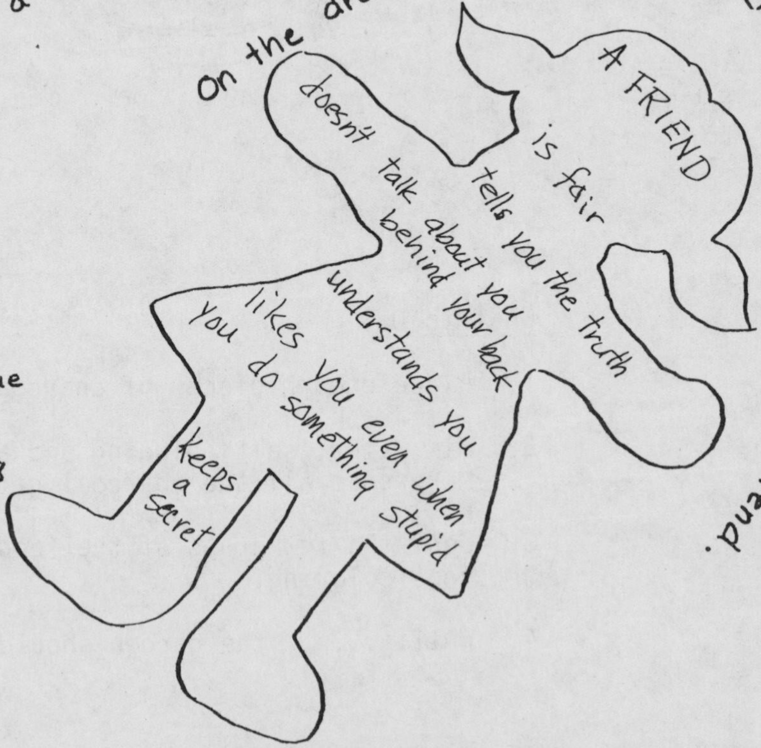

A FRIEND

is fair

tells you the truth

doesn't talk about you behind your back

understands you

likes you even when you do something stupid

keeps a secret

Are you a good friend?

or with a friend

Make up a friendship dance!

Tell your friend three things you like about her.

Read a book together, especially one of these:

My Friend John by Zolotow + Shecter (Harper Row)

Rosie and Michael by Viorst (Atheneum)

ROSIE and MICHAEL

Find someone who needs a friend and, together, do something especially friendly for that person!

Ghost Writer

What to Use

* paper (not hard surface)
* small brush
* invisible ink (see below)
* source of heat (iron, light bulb, toaster)
* adult help

What to Do

1. Paint a message on paper with:

   orange juice   vinegar
   lemon juice   apple juice
   7-Up   milk
   1 teaspoon sugar, salt, or baking soda dissolved in 2 teaspoons water

2. Use a small brush, your finger, or a toothpick to paint a message.

3. Let the paper dry completely.

TO READ THE MESSAGES:

Hold the paper near a toaster, hot light bulb, or the surface of an iron. BE CAREFUL.

The writing will turn brown.

OR

What to Use

* plain writing paper
* watercolor paints
* waxed paper
* water
* brush
* pencil

What to Do

1. Lay waxed paper over plain writing paper.

2. With a pencil, write a message on the waxed paper. Press hard! That's the secret writing.

3. Give the plain writing paper to a friend. That's the secret message with the invisible writing!

TO READ THE MESSAGES:

Brush a "wash" of thin water-color over the paper. The color will not stick to the writing, so you'll be able to read the message.

STRIKE UP A BAND !

A musical instrument is a good thing to have
When you want to sing a happy song,
dance to a swinging rhythm,
march in a parade,
celebrate a special occasion,
or... just make a joyful noise!

Here are some easy-to-do musical instruments. Try one, and go make music!

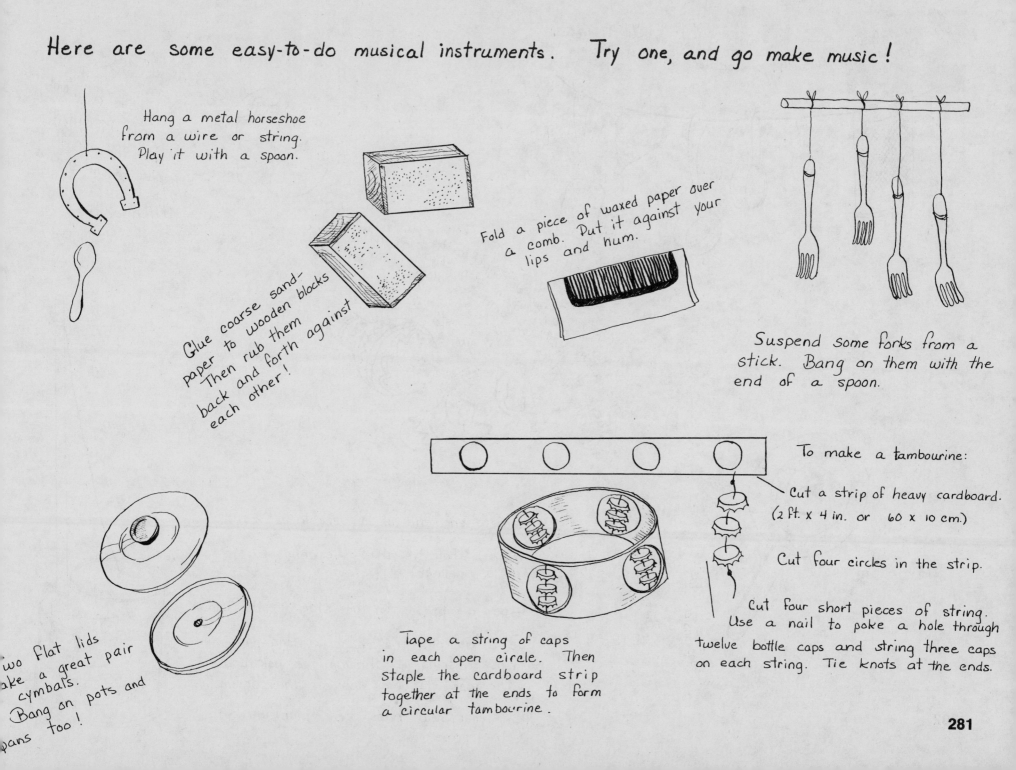

Hang a metal horseshoe from a wire or string. Play it with a spoon.

Glue coarse sandpaper to wooden blocks. Then rub them back and forth against each other!

Fold a piece of waxed paper over a comb. Put it against your lips and hum.

Suspend some forks from a stick. Bang on them with the end of a spoon.

Two flat lids make a great pair of cymbals. Bang on pots and pans too!

Tape a string of caps in each open circle. Then staple the cardboard strip together at the ends to form a circular tambourine.

To make a tambourine:

Cut a strip of heavy cardboard. (2 ft. x 4 in. or 60 x 10 cm.)

Cut four circles in the strip.

Cut four short pieces of string. Use a nail to poke a hole through twelve bottle caps and string three caps on each string. Tie knots at the ends.

281

Hang metal kitchen utensils from a heavy string. Hit against them with a wooden stick or a ruler.

Drop some pebbles or gravel into an empty soda pop can, and tape it shut. Fasten the can to a stick and papier mâché around it or paint.....
then shake!

Papier mâché over two old light bulbs. When they're dry, decorate them with paint. Then bang the bulbs on the floor until the glass breaks.

Now you have a great pair of maracas!

Staple two paper plates together with beans inside. Fasten to a stick!

Remove one end of a very large can.

Pound a hole in the other end. (Use a rock as a hammer)

Tape a broom to the side of the can.

Tie a knot in the end of a long piece of rope. String it through the hole and tie the rope to the top of the broom.

Play your new "bass" by plunking on the rope.

Don't forget to use one very fine instrument.... your voice!

This chapter was written to give you some ideas

for those days and times
when your mind feels like stretching...
and your body is itching for SOMETHING to do...
SOMETHING a little different
or silly
or special.....

Some of the pages will give you more ideas.

That's what this page is for.

your own ideas

Kaleidoscope
of
Ideas

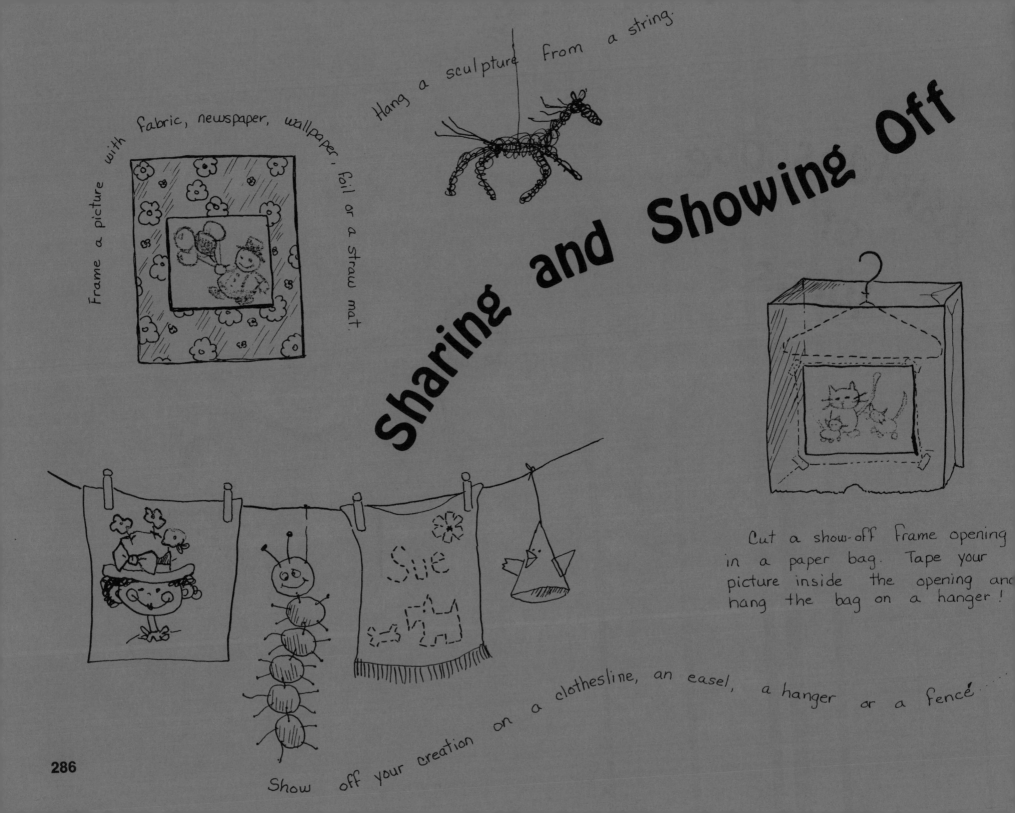

Hang a sculpture from a string.

Frame a picture with fabric, newspaper, wallpaper, foil or a straw mat.

Sharing and Showing Off

Cut a show-off frame opening in a paper bag. Tape your picture inside the opening and hang the bag on a hanger!

Sue

Show off your creation on a clothesline, an easel, a hanger or a fence.

Show off your masterpieces

in an old window frame

a pie tin

a shoebox

a plastic meat tray

a ham can

a picture frame

a box lid

a coffee can lid

Display a sculpture

on a mirror ·······

or set it on a

salt-box pedestal!

Have you tried this?

Mix salt with dry tempera paint. Sprinkle it over an area spread with glue to make salt pictures.

Paint buttermilk on drawing paper. Then draw a picture with chalk.

Paint on a table top with flour paint. Just mix flour, water and food coloring. It spreads beautifully and washes right off the table when you're done creating!

Make use of the snow outside to make winter sculptures. Create snow or ice persons, animals, machines or contraptions.

Paint (or rub with a rag) vegetable oil over the back of drawing paper to make the drawing or painting transparent.

Paint a picture on paper with rubber cement. Spray the paper with water-base spray paint or brush on a thin coat of watercolor. When the paint is dry, rub off the rubber cement.

Coat a bottle or jar with white glue. Then wrap it with yarn, ribbon or rick rack. It'll make a pretty container for a fabric flower, a tissue paper flower or a real one!

Go for a walk with a bottle of glue and a small flat board. Collect natural objects and glue together a collage as you travel along.

Fill a big sturdy balloon with helium. (You can get helium in small cans at some hardware stores.) Tie a postcard and a note (covered with plastic) to the balloon. The postcard should be addressed to yourself, and the note should ask whomever finds the balloon to mail you the postcard and tell where they found it!

Make a super shrink up! Cut out shapes from clear plastic lids. (They come on containers of liver from your meat department) Or you can use broken pieces of plastic glasses too. Color and draw on the plastic with permanent markers. Then - lay the shapes on a cookie sheet and put into a 350° oven for a few minutes They will shrink!

Turn the day around! Do everything backwards. Start off with a bedtime story, an evening snack and end the day with breakfast!

288

Turn an apple, orange, lemon or lime into a good smelling pomander. Stick whole cloves into the fruit, then wrap it with a piece of cheese cloth or nylon netting. Tuck a cinnamon stick in with the fruit and tie the bundle with yarn. Hang the pomander in a closet. The smell gets sweeter as the fruit dries.

Draw tiny pictures and slogans on balloons, using a fine point marking pen. Then blow up the balloons!

Paint or draw a picture that you know will make someone laugh!

Trace around your hand. Use your pattern to cut 30 hands from green paper. Glue the hands, one touching another, into a wreath. Add a big red bow!

Create a new calendar - - Design a calendar like nobody has ever seen. Hang it in your room or give it to someone special.

Make your own campaign buttons . . . to campaign for or promote anything! Cut heavy cardboard circles (3 inch or 8 centimeter diameter). Color slogans on the front and glue a safety pin to the back with white glue.

Print a picture from a magazine or newspaper! Rub a white candle over the picture. (Don't light the candle!) Lay white paper over the wax-y picture, and rub the surface with a spoon. You'll get a backwards print.

Carve personality into a pumpkin (or a watermelon or a squash!) Try faces and shapes different from the usual jack-o-lantern face!

Adopt-a-letter! Choose a letter of the alphabet . . . and show it off!! Draw a fancy design using the letter . . . . Promote the letter . . . . Tell what is great about it . . . Have a beauty contest and enter your letter against other letters.

Go cloud watching! Imagine the clouds are creatures or painted scenes or people or monsters. Lie on your back and watch them move. Make bubble paint (see page 97) and paint some cloud scenes.

Carve notches or dig holes in the side of your crayon, then color with it sideways.

Write or draw holding 2 crayons in one hand.

289

The Recipe File

Play Dough

2 Cups salt
2 Cups flour
1/2 Cup shortening
1/2 Cup water (or more)
food coloring or dry tempera
peppermint oil

- Mix salt, flour, snd shortening with your hands
- Gradually add water and keep mixing until
      the dough is not too sticky
- Work in a few drops of peppermint oil and some
      color
- Use the dough to model - and keep it stored in
      a covered container in the refrigerator

Bubble Paint

Ivory Flakes
water
food coloring or tempera paint

- Mix water with soap flakes until you have
      a thick creamy mixture. Add color.
- Then whip with a mixer until fluffy.
- Paint on shelf paper or waxed paper.
  Use your fingers.

Boiled Paper

It ends up looking like leather!

wrapping paper or shelf paper
water
fabric dye

- Dissolve dye in hot water
- Crumple up paper and place it in the pan of dye
      and water
- Boil for 5 minutes
- Rinse the paper in cold water
- Carefully squeeze out the water, and spread the
      paper to dry

Crepe Paper Clay

1 1/2 Cups torn crepe paper pieces
1 1/2 Cups water
1/2 Cup flour

- Let torn paper soak in water overnight
- Drain off water
- Mix in flour and knead like dough
- Mold the mixture into shapes
              or
- Spread the "clay" over a form made from
      cardboard or wire

Baked Clay

2 Cups salt
2 Cups warm water
5 Cups flour

- Mix salt, flour and water. Add more (or less) water
       as needed to make an easy-to-handle dough.
- Knead the dough until it's smooth.
- Roll out to a 1/2 inch thickness.
- Cut shapes with a knife or cookie cutters.
- Bake at 300 for an hour.
- Paint and shellac.

Soap and Sawdust Clay

1 1/2 Cups Ivory Soap Flakes
1 1/2 Cups sawdust
water

- Mix enough water into soap flakes to make a
       thick creamy mixture.
- Whip soap until it is stiff and fluffy.
- Gently mix in sawdust.
- Mold the mixture into shapes or figures
- Let the figures dry for several days.

Make-Believe-Marble

1 Cup white glue
1/2 Cup water
Plaster of Paris
tempera paint (Liquid)

- Put water in a container.
- Sprinkle plaster on water until you get a
       thick creamy mixture.
- Add glue to plaster mixture.
- Drip some tempera over the plaster and stir
       just until the mixture looks streaked.
- Pour into a mold and harden.

Sawdust Clay

2 Cups sawdust
1 Cup wallpaper paste
water

- Mix dry paste with sawdust.
- Add water slowly until you have a thick dough.
- Model into shapes.
- Let harden overnight.

Fingerpaints You Make Yourself

Try: liquid starch and food coloring or tempera
              or
       instant pudding
              or
       mud
              or
       wheat paste and water and tempera paint
              or
       liquid starch and soap flakes and tempera paint

Cornstarch Dough

1 Cup baking soda
1/2 Cup water
1/2 Cup cornstarch

- Mix soda, water and cornstarch in a saucepan
- Cook over low heat and stir until mixture
      becomes very thick
- Add food coloring if desired
- Cool and knead until it's smooth
- Model into figures or roll out dough and cut
      shapes
- Let dry. Figures can be painted and shellacked
- Store the dough in a plastic bag in the refrigerator

Homemade Papier Mâché Paste

3 Cups water
1 1/2 Cups flour
oil of peppermint

- Stir flour into cold water
- Cook over low heat until the mixture thickens
      to a creamy paste
- Add more water if the paste gets too thick
- Cool
- Add a few drops of peppermint oil
- Use the paste to coat paper strips

How to Make Papier Mâché

You need paper: and paste:
    newspaper   wallpaper paste
    newsprint   wheat paste
    paper towels   liquid starch
    tissues   white glue mixed with an equal
    wallpaper   amount of water
    tissue paper   homemade paste (see recipe)

- Tear paper into strips
- Coat strips with paste
- Mold the strips over a base

Rainbowmakers' Secrets

* To mix smooth plaster, sift plaster slowly into warm water, stirring with your hand as you mix. Try to get a creamy mixture the consistency of thin pudding.

* Don't ever pour plaster down a drain. It will harden. . .and really clog the plumbing!

* Un-bent paper clips inserted into wet plaster make very good hangers for plaster plaques.

* Chicken wire laid in wet plaster will strengthen your plaster casting.

* Add a few drops of liquid soap to tempera paint to make it stick to tin cans or tin foil.

* *CRAYOLA* makes crayons especially for drawing on cloth.

* Spray chalk drawings with evaporated milk. This will preserve the drawing for a long time!

* Add a few drops of perfume, bath oil or oil of peppermint to keep clay mixtures sweet-smelling, and to keep them from spoiling.

* A few tablespoons of vegetable oil added to modeling dough makes it easier to handle.

* Powdered alum will keep homemade doughs and clays from getting moldy. Add a tablespoon or two to your dough.

* Good fabric dyes are available from: Putnam Dyes, Inc.
  Department 24
  Post Office Box 40
  Quincy, Illinois 62301

Pages 'n Pages of Inspiration

GREAT BOOKS FOR KIDS 'N GROWNUPS TO READ

Art Today and Every Day by Romberg and Rutz (Parker)

Beautiful Junk by Madian (Little, Brown)

The Children's Book of Painting by Kampmann (Van Nostrand)

Going for a Walk With a Line by MacAgy (Doubleday)

Look Again by Tana Hoban (MacMillan)

Put Your Mother on the Ceiling: Children's Imagination Games by DeMille (Viking)

Rain Makes Applesauce by Scheer (Holiday House)

Sometimes I Dance Mountains by Byrd Baylor (Charles Scribner's Sons)

Story of Art for Young People by Ruskin (Pantheon)

Thirteen by Charlip (Parents' Magazine Press)

When Clay Sings by Byrd Baylor (Charles Scribner's Sons)

When the Sky is Like Lace by Horwitz (Lippincott)

Whole Kids Catalog by Cardozo (Bantam)

The Young Potter by VanBaker (Frederick Warne)

MORE GOOD IDEA BOOKS

Art Activities for the Very Young by Hoover (Davis Publications)

Art from Found Materials by Stribling (Crown)

Best Rainy Day Book Ever by Scarry (Random House)

Big Bird's Busy Book by Frith and Lerner (Random House)

Charlie Brown's Super Book of Things to Do and Collect (Random House)

Childcraft: The How and Why Library Volume XI: Make and Do (Field)

I Saw a Purple Cow and 100 Other Recipes for Learning by Cole, Haas, Bushnell and Weinberger
        (Little, Brown)

The Kid's Arts and Crafts Book by Petrich and Dalton (Nitty Gritty Productions)

The Little Kids' Craft Book by Vermeer and Lariviere (Taplinger)

Making Things: The Handbook of Creative Discovery by Wiseman (Little, Brown)

100 Ways to Have Fun With An Alligator and 100 Other Involving Art Projects by Mogelon
        (Art Education)

Play Book by Caney (Workman)

Recipes for Art and Craft Material by Sattler (Lothrop)

Snips and Snails and Puppy Dog Tails by Fiarotta (Workman)

Sticks and Stones and Ice Cream Cones by Fiarotta (Workman)

Sunset Crafts for Children (Lane Books)

What Can I Do Today? by Klimo (Pantheon)

BOOKS FOR SPECIAL KINDS OF PROJECTS

<u>Arts and Crafts You can Eat</u> by Cobb (J.B. Lippincott)

<u>Betty Crocker's Cookbook for Boys and Girls</u> (Golden Press)

<u>Collage and Construction</u> by Weiss (Young Scott Books)

<u>Easter Eggs for Everyone</u> by Coskey (Abingdon Press)

<u>Creative Food Experiences for Children</u> by Goodwin and Pollen (Center for Science in the Public Interest)

<u>The Gadget Book</u> by Weiss (Thomas Y. Crowell)

<u>Growing Up Green</u> by Skelsey and Huckaby (Workman)

<u>Kids are Natural Cooks</u> by Parents' Nursery School (Houghton Mifflin)

<u>The Kid's Cookbook</u> by Petrich and Dalton (Nitty Gritty Productions)

<u>Making Puppets Come Alive</u> by Engler and Fijan (Taplinger)

<u>Music Instruments for Children to Make</u> by Hawkinson and Faulhaber (Albert Whitman)

<u>Mobiles</u> by Zarchy (World)

<u>Paint, Brush and Palette</u> by Weiss (Young Scott Books)

<u>Paper: Folded, Cut, Sculpted</u> by Temko (MacMillan)

<u>Papier Mâché</u> (Lane Books)

<u>Peanut Craft</u> by Donna (Lothrop)

<u>Sheet Magic: Games, Toys and Gifts from Old Sheets</u> by Parish (MacMillan)

<u>Tie and Dye Made Easy</u> by Maille (Taplinger)

<u>25 Kites that Fly</u> by Hunt (Dover)

. . . . at the rainbow's end?

Rainbows have no end.

They just fade into mists of cloud,

or pause behind pots of shining golden stuf

only to reappear another time. . . .

. . . . another place. . .

A rainbow is forever. . . . .